Unmaking the Nation

Unmaking the Nation
THE POLITICS OF IDENTITY &
HISTORY IN MODERN SRI LANKA

Edited by
Pradeep Jeganathan & Qadri Ismail

Social Scientists' Association
Sri Lanka

First published in 1995 by the
Social Scientists' Association (SSA)
12 Sulaiman Terrace,
Colombo 00500
Sri Lanka.
www.ssalanka.org

The global distribution rights to this book, are held by South
Focus Press, and it is distributed by the Ingram Book Company
and Baker & Taylor in the US and Ingram International
throughout the rest of the world. This book may be ordered
from any bookstore in those countries, and is also available from
amazon.com. International wholesale orders from booksellers
anywhere may be placed with www.ipage.ingrambook.com

ISBN: 0-9748839-7-2 &
ISBN-13: 978-0-9748839-7-7

Printed and bound in the United States
on acid free paper.

Contents

Preface to the Second Edition

It is a pleasure to write briefly to mark the second edition of *Unmaking the Nation*, which was first published in Colombo in 1995, and was subsequently re-printed several times in Sri Lanka. The project began while I, a very young scholar, was enjoying immense stimulation from engagements with a variety of colleagues both at the Social Scientists' Association and the International Centre for Ethnic Studies, where I was engaged in several over lapping projects. While we were all concerned to contribute our very best scholarship to the Sri Lankan intellectual tradition, we did not expect this little collection to attract the attention it has, and much less deserve a second edition. On the one hand, several articles, including Maunaguru's "Gendering Tamil Nationalism" and Ismail's polemical "Unmooring Identity" have gone on to be scholarly classics, while the arguments of the introduction have, most recently, inspired Catharine Brun and Tariq Jazeel's volume *Spatialising Politics: Culture and Geography in Postcolonial Sri Lanka* (2009). I take heart at such engagements. On the other hand, the perhaps provocative title of the book, and several other essays, particularly my own, has drawn the ire of an extremist fringe. Criticism of any sort is welcome, but arguments that advance scholarship in astute and constructive ways, are more valuable than entertaining broadsides.

While this collection has been read and well received by scholars outside Sri Lanka, having made its way to a number of libraries, and several class rooms in the United States, the absence of a global edition has hampered colleagues abroad who wish to teach it, or have students refer to it. The advent of flexible, sophisticated printing technologies has allowed us to surmount this barrier; this edition will be available globally, through our publishing partners in the United States, under the imprint, SSA Sri Lanka.

A special thank you is owed to Gananath Obeyesekere and Arjun Appadurai for their generous comments on the first edition, which still grace the back cover of the second, and to Dennis McGilvray, for being so kind as to write an early, comprehensive review in *The Journal of Asian Studies*, in 1997. Finally, I thank again, everyone at the SSA, who has helped with the book over the years, its reprinting and its distribution and advertising, especially Kumari Jayawardena and her associates, and of course, the printers of the first edition Karunaratne & Sons, for doing much to make this second global edition a reality.

Pradeep Jeganathan
Colombo
October 2008

Introduction:
Unmaking the Nation

Pradeep Jeganathan &
Qadri Ismail

"Each generation must," declared Frantz Fanon in *The Wretched of the Earth*, "discover its mission, fulfil it, or betray it."[1] Appearing at the beginning of the chapter "On National Culture," these words are addressed to the intellectuals of newly decolonized countries, charged with the mission of unifying the nation, of virtually creating it from scratch. The Martinican psychiatrist turned Algerian revolutionary, the Ur-theorist of post-colonial nationalism, wrote thirty years—a generation—ago. His generation of third world intellectuals at decolonization, whether the forties South Asian or sixties African, never doubted what they had to do: make the nation. We—the contributors to this book, who share a generation—do not live in such certain times. Our project is different. We suspect the nation.

"When one speaks... of a nation... as a homogeneous political entity" Rosa Luxemburg warned us, not only does one "elide the class conflicts simmering beneath," but one also assumes that "people homogeneously inhabit any given piece of territory." But they do not. "Those who speak thus of the nation, beg the question, who is that "nation" and who has the authority and the "right" to speak for the "nation" and express its will? How can we find out what the "nation" actually wants?"[2] We, the contributors to this volume share these questions and concerns; we are not enamored by the possibilities of the nation and nationalism, rather we are deeply suspicious of its claims and consequences. Not simply because the nation has failed—a viable claim in the Sri Lankan context; but because the "powerfully homogenizing... constrain[ing], oppress[ive] and eviscerat[ing]"[3] manner of its constitution makes it untenable both as an idea and as a form of social organization; because the nation—to be precise, those with the power to act in its name—has always suppressed its women, its non–bourgeois classes, and its minorities. The contributors to this book come together in the belief that the inclusive pretences of the nation must be exposed, that not just its inadequacies but its very superfluousness must be called into question; it is in this spirit, that we join the on going debate on the nation.

Locally, for us, the inauguration of this debate is marked by the publication of the influential and therefore controversial *Ethnicity and Social Change*.[4] Its editors hoped that its arguments:

> ...will at least force some of the exponents of Sinhala and Tamil nationalism to look more closely at the myths, misinterpretations and misunderstandings that have nourished their ideologies.

Ethnicity and Social Change, provided an important new direction to debates on the Sri Lankan nation; by suggesting that received narratives of ethnicity and the nation needed to be rethought, the volume also argued, that the nationalist project was also a political project that was inevitably implicated in a history of power. The "facts" of ancient and modem Sri Lankan history, long thought to have been resolved and fixed by conservative, nationalist historiographic practice were now open to the very questions that could be posed to conservatism and nationalism: a new intellectual space constituted within new political narratives emerged.

The late Serena Tennekoon utilized this new space in her thoughtful paper, "Symbolic Refractions of the Ethnic Crisis: The *Divaina* debates on Sinhala Identity (1984-1985)" which was published in *Facets of Ethnicity in Sri Lanka*, the sequel to the first volume.[5] Here Tennekoon took a long analytical look at the fierce discussion on *Ethnicity and Social Change* that had taken place in the Sinhala nationalist press, and asked a new question about the consequences of an intellectual intervention from within the space of the Sri Lankan nation:

> Barthes' reconceptualisation of myth and history raises a question relevant to the continuing discourse on Sinhala identity to which my article contributes: Is it possible to "demystify" mythic

discourse, or, to continue Barthes' sanguine metaphor, arrest the haemorrhage of reality with a massive transfusion of historical and social scientific analysis?[6]

Tennekoon answered her own question by noting that the "answer is evident in the *Divaina* debates, which demonstrates that attempts to "demystify" Sinhala cultural identity provoked "remystification." Her response to this "remystification" to call for yet more "demystification," echoes Barthes' call to "speak *excessively* about reality."

These questions are still with us, even as the Sri Lankan debate over identity and history in the space of the nation has expanded to include new voices and points of view. David Scott's essay in our collection provides a provocative and already controversial answer to Tennekoon's question of 1987. Scott examines the consequences of R.A.L.H. Gunawardana's brilliant 'The People of the Lion,' published in *Ethnicity and Social Change*; an essay that, as he puts it, "more than any other enables us to gain the threshold of a rational historiography of the Sinhala past;" an essay that, "if it gets its history right," would destroy the basis of the Sinhala nationalist claim. But, as Scott argues, the terrain on which to fight and "win" this debate can be subject to appropriation: a Sinhala nationalist — K.N.O. Dharmadasa, in this case — can always respond on that very terrain by disputing Gunawardana's facts. "Remystification," as Tennekoon observed is the response to "demystification."

Hence, Scott argues that the debate has reached an impasse. For the debate to move forward there must be a shifting of the turf, of the bases of the debate itself; Scott's move is to propose the "dehistoricising of history." Challenging the presupposition that "history has always already begun, and therefore it always merely continues," Scott argues that history "ought to be taken as what shall be thought." History in the current Sri Lankan space then, must not belong "primarily to time, nor to succession, nor to causality, but to community; or to being-in-common."

Scott's paper exemplifies what the contributions to this book seek to do: "refuse to be governed by the questions of one's adversaries... to *risk* changing the problematic in which those questions have appeared to us natural, legitimate or even imperative." The other contributors to this collection take up this challenge in different ways. Jonathan Walters, looks anew at religion — and therefore identities based on appropriations of religion — ...in Sri Lanka, as an "interpretive category," a way of seeing and being – in the world, not as a system of belief or a natural relation between people. He suggests "multireligion" as an alternative to "syncretism" in discussions of encounters between different faiths, or interpretive categories. Multireligion, or multireligious fields, he argues, function by Othering. And he illustrates this process ethnographically, with readings of religious encounters on Sri Lankan public buses. Exposing the constructed nature of this process, as Walters does, constructed in the course of a complex psychological, social and political interaction, enables us to get around the dilemma of seeing our Others as natural, historical, and eternal enemies. It enables a questioning not only of this process of Othering, but also of how the religion–based self, a dangerous collective creature in the Sri Lankan context, is constructed.

Qadri Ismail's efforts are to "unmoor identity." He argues that "whenever an ethnic identity is being projected one can... always read in that projection class, gender and other interests that the identitarian would seek to elide." His task is to expose that process of elision. And if identity is not what it claims to be, Moor identity becomes an exemplary site for the demonstration of these general inherent instabilities. What could not be a more taken-for-granted "identity" in the Sri Lankan social formation? But as it becomes clear when text after text, produced by heterogenous agents, are analyzed by Ismail the Sri Lankan Muslims can not be defined by any one of the easy essences of "race," "ethnicity," "religion" that seemed so self-evident at first pass. Rather what is concluded is that "identity is about hegemony not about community;" Moor identity, like all other identities is inseparable from a history of power.

Pradeep Jeganathan takes another look at that vexed subject the power of history— that Scott has already problematized. Instead of merely producing more knowledge about the past, or its relation to the present, Jeganathan asks new questions about the history of such knowledges of the past. Authoritative colonial interventions, he argues, are central to the production of these new fields of knowledge, from the mid-nineteenth century onwards. The argument of this essay is not only that colonialism produces an "invention of tradition," but rather its efforts are to focus the discussion on the epistemological fields within which these "inventions" take place. These theoretical arguments, then, translate into simple, but startling revelations: that Anuradhapura was "made" in the mid–nineteenth century, following the translation of the *Mahavamsa*, that Anuradhapura became the centre of ancient Sinhala civilization through the transformation of the *Mahavamsa* into an authoritative, positivist, historical text. By the end of that century, "unjungled, measured, marked, sanitized and aesthetisized," Anuradhapura was commodified and made ready for tourism — by colonials and natives. Ready, also, for Sinhala nationalists like the Anagarika Dharmapala and his disciple Walisinha Harischandra, to make Anuradhapura the ancient, continuous, centre of Sinhala civilization. What Jeganathan contests, therefore, is this "very self–evidentness of Anuradhapura today." He also illustrates the important collusion at the "moment of departure" of nationalist thought, between the colonial authority and the nationalist, that Partha Chatterjee has eloquently theorized.[7] Collusions that must be drawn attention to as part of the project of unmaking the nation.

Malathi de Alwis' contribution to this unmaking draws critically on Chatterjee's more recent text on nationalist practice.[8] The elegant binarism of Chatterjee's argument about gendered nationalism, suggests that the public sphere created by the nationalist resolution of the woman question, enabled women to imbue themselves with "spiritual" qualities and thereby operate within that sphere without endangering their femininity. Yet as de Alwis examines in detail the historical and contemporary contours of the gendered Sri Lankan public sphere, marking the movement of women from the private to the public, she challenges Chatterjee's argument. Making a categorical shift from gendered spirituality to gendered respectability, de Alwis provides us with histories of women who were "missionaries of the respectable" and "house-wives of the public." Simultaneously, however, she demonstrates quite concretely how these interventions of women in the public sphere, were and continue to be destabilized by their "sexualization," or the unmaking of their respectability.

Sitralega Maunaguru also stresses the importance of gender in the unmaking of the nation, pointing out that such arguments "must be remade until it can be assumed." Taking as her historical terrain the struggles of latter day Tamil nationalists, Maunaguru shows us how the multiple, shifting subject positions of women available in these movements are in themselves oppressive and constricting. She also examines attempts by autonomous women's groups to challenge the violence of the

Sri Lankan and Indian armed forces, and also the brutalities of the Tamil militant groups. Patriarchal structures in Tamil society, in turn, focus on these resisting women, attempting to reassert control over their bodies and sexuality. P.L. de Silva addresses the other side of the gender question in relation to Tamil nationalism, that of violent masculinity. He looks at the question of militarism in relation to the Liberation Tigers of Tamil Eelam (LTTE): its fetishization of death, its frantic efforts to impose order upon its world, its manipulation of the emotions of its cadre and concludes, if some-what optimistically, that the "combat mode" the LTTE has chosen to operate in is "doomed to failure in the long term."

Thangarajah's essay in this volume, while being a work still in progress, nevertheless makes important points about the logic of nationalism. His ethnographic object, the Veddas of the east coast, are a minority within a minority. Yet, they have been positioned by Tamil nationalism, in much the same way as majority Sinhala nationalism has positioned the Tamils. That is, demands of assimilating into an exclusively mono-cultural Tamil Hindu community have been made of these Vedda groups, in much the same way as Sinhala nationalism has demanded assimilation of Tamils and Muslims. And also in the same way, the effort to construct a unified notion of "Tamil speaking people" has backfired: in the final analysis, the Veddas, the victims of a powerful and long–standing process of Othering, have chosen to reconstitute an exclusive, nostalgic identity, seeking refuge in an "ideology of victimhood."

The problems of the nation are not, then, problems of "Sinhalaness," "Tamilness" or "Moorness" *per se*. The problem rather is in the making of diverse peoples into "Tamils," "Sinhalas," or "Moors;" and then in turn of making those peoples into Sri Lankans. Or put another way, there is a fundamental contradiction, a continuous oscillation between possible heterogeneity and implied homogeneity in the project of nationalism. The nation has many histories, but it claims one as its own; its people have many identities but they must inhabit one; the nation has many political coalitions within it but they are to be suppressed in the aid of one mission: nationalism. And the pursuit of this single minded, monolithic object has brought nothing but violence, terror, and destruction to us all.

Acknowledgements

If this volume has any worth at all, it is the efforts of our contributors that have made it what it is. Their own contributions apart, Malathi de Alwis, David Scott and Jon Walters took the time to read several of the essays, and made thoughtful and insightful comments. Krisantha Sri Bhaggiyadatta, Mangalika de Silva, Colin Fernando, and Farzana Haniffa did a great deal of copy editing, proof reading and typing; Selvy Thiruchandran and the staff at the Women's Education and Research Center provided us with proof printing facilities. Their assistance was invaluable.

But our greatest debt lies elsewhere. For if this volume has drawn together a group of young scholars who share a generation, they will all acknowledge another, of an earlier generation, who has in a myriad different ways listened to, argued with and influenced their ideas; who has enriched their work at every turn. Kumari Jayawardena has been with us at every stage of this project: her erudite comments, given gently and generously have taught us a great deal. In as much as we have not learnt enough from our interactions with her and thought through the complexities of political interventions as she has, her work lies before us, and we are her predecessors.

Notes

1. New York: Grove Weidendfeld, 1991 (1963).

2. Rosa Luxemburg, "The Right of Nations to Self—Determination," in *The National Question: Selected Writing by Rosa Luxemburg*, (New York, Monthly Review Press, 1976), pp. 135,141. See Kumari Jayawardena's essay, "The National Question and the Left Movement in Sri Lanka," in *Facets of Ethnicity in Sri Lanka*, Charles Abeysekera and Newton Gunasinghe (eds.) (Colombo: SSA, 1987), for an important reading of the Lenin-Luxemburg debate.

3. "Introduction," in *Nationalisms and Sexualities*, Andrew Parker, Mary Russo, Doris Sommer and Patricia Yaeger (eds.) (New York: Routledge, 1991), p.3.

4. Colombo: SSA, 1984.

5. Charles Abeysekera and Newton Gunasinghe (eds.) (Colombo: SSA, 1987).

6. Tennekoon, p.38. Her references are to *Mythologies*, (London: Jonathan Cape, 1974), pp. 109-159.

7. *Nationalist Thought and the Colonial World: A Derivative Discourse?* (London:

Zed Books, 1986).

8   *The Nation and its Fragments: Colonial and Postcolonial Histories,* (Delhi: Oxford University Press, 1994).

Dehistoricising History

David Scott

[H]istory — if we can remove this word from its metaphysical,
and therefore historical, determination — does not belong primarily to time, nor to succession, nor to causality, but to community, or to being–in–common.

Jean–Luc Nancy[1]

To think this provocation — to dehistoricise history — on the
intellectual terrain of contemporary discourse about "community" and
"history" in Sri Lanka, I begin with a somewhat perverse question: What
if, at the end of "The People of the Lion,"[2] the end, that is, of that meti-
culously exhaustive exercise in historical reconstruction in which, stage
by carefully elucidated stage, the author takes us through the various
forms of collective identity in Sri Lanka — from those most obscure beginnings when "Sinhala" ("the people of the lion") is but the name of the
circumscribed royal kin–group to the more recent past when "Sinhala" is
reconstituted as the name of a "race" of people—what if after all of this
the author had written — as though tossing it all aside, or in our face —
"But so what? What does this history really prove?" A laughter might
have rippled through the sluice–gate of that gesture, the low, derisive
laughter of a profound and carefully laid hoax, of a scandalous almost
malicious irony. How could he, we would have asked ourselves incredu-
lously, how could this esteemed professor of ancient and medieval Sri
Lankan history, an historian so well known for his commitment to the
craft, to the technologies of its muse, to its forms of narrative, to its or-

ders of evidence, how could he, in so singular and intemperate a gesture, heap such thoughtless ridicule upon this distinguished practice of Truth?

But of course the author, R.A.L.H. Gunawardana, did not append this Nietzschean question. Unlike Nietzsche, Gunawardana perhaps believes too much in history, in History.[3] Yet it may well be that the question was in a way *unspeakable* to him, and this not on account of his personal style (his judicious and always reason-able sentences), or his scrupulous attention to his discipline (the unassailable seriousness with which he treats —and *trusts*— the past and its essential representability). It may have been, in fact, *unthinkable* within the discursive space at hand, and this in virtue of the configuration of a political (or anyway, a *politicized*) debate in which a "past" was being mobilised and deployed as the guarantee of claims about community in the present. So, in any case, I will read it, that is, as framed by the horizon of its own politico–discursive present. And yet each time that I return to this already classic text — return to it now from *within* the new horizon of discursive space that by its formidable labour of criticism it has made available to us to (re)think the relation between "history" and "community" in Sri Lanka — I imagine him asking it — *But so what?* — I imagine him *risking* it. I imagine it because history (or History) appears to us today in Sri Lanka (but also I think more generally in this transnational Age of Culture) as the Natural and Sovereign horizon of adjudication for rival claims about community. And the question that I want to urge upon myself (and upon those *with* whom I think) is how to so change this thought, *our* thought, about history, to so radically alter the presuppositions by which we can endeavour to think the possibility of community in history, the possibility of the past's authority in the present, that we have to confront our own thought as alterity, as opacity. And this effort of thinking *against ourselves* has perhaps to take the form of an imposition upon ourselves of the task of relieving ourselves of the reassuring burden of the past as that fixed and resolute presence by which our politics of community is guaranteed; an imposition upon ourselves of the task (as political as it is epistemological) of standing *where we are* with nothing beneath us or behind us but the *project* of the unrepeatable *now*: the project, in short (to paraphrase Stuart Hall), of community without guarantee.[4]

"'The People of the Lion'" has been our first threshold in the at-tempt to formulate critically the relation between history and communi-ty in Sri Lanka. But this very distinction, I submit, and the commanding place it occupies (as that text which, ever *before* us, has always to be ac-knowledged, negotiated, passed *through*), ought to urge us to *read* it and to not merely be read by it. For my purposes, I shall read "The People of the Lion'" as participating in a certain conception of the past's relation to the present, a conception that Jean–Luc Nancy has characterised as "his-toricism." Historicism, Nancy writes,

> is in general the way of thinking that presupposes that history
> has always already begun, and that therefore it always merely
> continues. Historicism presupposes history, instead of taking it
> as what shall be thought.[5]

This in fact will be the central thrust of my argument here, that history ought to be taken as *what shall be thought*. And I shall understand the "unthinkableness" of the question — *But so what?* — as a product of the historicism of "The People of the Lion," as a product of its not taking history as *what shall be thought*, but as a self–evident, causally self–successive flow, the proper elucidation of which can offer to the present assurance and guidance.

However, this will not entail on my part a reading of this re-markable essay that merely criticises it for something like "epistemologi-cal naivete," or error — we can well appreciate these anti-essentialist/anti–foundationalist days the theory–presumption, the theory–conceit of readings of that sort. Rather, I am concerned with another practice (and politics) of reading, namely, one that seeks to make visible the productive space of the text's questions — that seeks to make visible the text's "problem–space," so to put it. The primary concern of this practice of reading is to enable us to gauge not merely whether the text's answers are adequate to the questions at hand, but whether these questions themselves *continue* to be questions worth responding to at all. In other words, the reading which I wish to undertake is concerned less with the substantive details of the text's preoccupation (with what, to put it crudely, it is *about*) than with the critical formulation of the target to be aimed at. This is because what interests me more generally is the problem of strategy in its relation to the intervention of criticism. What I want to understand about criticism is not so much the adequacy of its internal cognitive apparatus, but more what its activity produces, enables, in terms of opening up new discursive space. In this it will be understood that for me our critical concepts are really no more than artisanal implements. "A theory is exactly like a box of tools," as Gilles Deleuze has said — by means of which we attempt to move "obstacles," "block-ages," and to lever open discursive space for political/intellectual work.[6] What is central to my reading of Gunawardana's essay, therefore, is less the history it so masterfully accomplishes than the historiographical strategy that informs it. So the question I want to put to it is whether there is still discursive room left within its historicist problematic for the critical work of thinking community in history in Sri Lanka, or whether what appears possible within it is, while topically interesting, no more than academic. Or to put it another way, even if there is no *a priori* way of ruling out the critical usefulness of the kind of history that "'The People of the Lion'" so eloquently exemplifies, there is nevertheless, the necessity of always asking, at any given conjuncture (by which I have in mind rather more the discursive conjuncture — the conjuncture of a theoretical argument — than that of a sociologically identifiable context), whether this kind of history performs the critical labour that our present demands. I shall want to suggest that in order to carry forward the political project of "'The People of the Lion'" in the wake of the recent criticism of it, it is at least worth raising the question whether what our Sri Lankan present demands isn't a dehistoricised history.

"'The People of the Lion'" is an intervention: it more or less explicitly announces itself as such in its opening passages. But what is the problem–field into which it seeks to insert itself, whose assumptions it wishes to disrupt, to undo? This is important to make explicit, as I have suggested, in order to read the theoretical unconscious of the historiographical strategy that it employs. In the text itself this problem–field is defined in relation to the popular discursive apparatus of Sinhala ideology. I should like to argue that the propositional structure of this discursive apparatus operates at two intersecting but analytically distinguishable levels. The first is that level at which a certain *kind* of story about what the–past–of–Sinhala–as–a–community–really–was is constructed. The fundamental view here of course is that Sinhala consciousness, that is, the collective awareness of a singular "identity" or "community," is immemorial and continuous. This continuity, as we know, is constructed through those foundational narratives (of Vijaya's inauguration of an authentic community; of the Buddha's bestowal upon it of a permanent benediction; of the rise of Anuradhapura as the site of civilization; of Dutugamunu's heroism against a Tamil King, and so on) that mark out the epic of a community which in a certain sense comes before history, and that enters it, when it does, under constant threat and through cycles of loss and restoration.

The second level of the propositional structure of this apparatus is that at which a certain notion of the *relation* between that history of Sinhala as a community and the present as an opening of political options for the construction (or, if you like, the invention) of community is articulated. It is central to the apparatus of Sinhala ideology, it seems to me, that continuity of an inaugural and authentic community informs and indeed serves to guarantee the legitimacy of political claims in the present. The point here is the obvious one (though, I think, one not sufficiently attended to) that the ideological construction of the past is not an academic exercise on the part of Sinhala nationalists, but is a structure of representations inserted into a political project. That is to say, it is *in virtue* of that past, its identifiability, its representability, its age, its beleaguredness, that the privileged claim to priority in the institutional apparatus of the nation–state, is to be judged not only plausible and creditable, but *persuasive*.

My argument shall be that the historiographical strategy of "'The People of the Lion'" consists in formulating as its target the first of these levels of proposition, *but not the second*. And I shall argue, moreover, that by so doing (by not, in effect, explicitly *uncoupling* the historical problem of what the past was from the political problem of the legitimacy of present claims about community) it leaves itself vulnerable to both historicist criticism and academic recuperation.

It is in relation to this formidable discursive Structure of Sinhala ideology that the urgent labour of historical critique — or of history *deployed as a mode of ideology–critique* — was mobilised by concerned Sri Lankan scholars in the 1970s. The immediate political–intellectual problem was to demystify the Sinhala past, to intervene in such a way as to win the terrain of the reconstruction of that past away from ideologues and chauvinists, and to establish the terms for a rational–historical discourse based on the professional examination of the relevant evidence. It was a concern to call into being, as it were, what Habermas might call a sphere of rational–critical debate that would inform public opinion and perhaps even the political process itself.[7] This project for a rational historiography, for a public and secular intellectual discourse guided by the reasoned assessment of the "facts" rather than by "myths," was central to the task undertaken by the newly formed Social Scientists' Association (a forum for broadly Left intellectual discussion) in the seminar they organised in December 1979 around the theme: "Nationality Problems in Sri Lanka." (The formulation is itself perhaps suggestive of a crisis in *thought*, of theory grappling with its own inadequacy, endeavouring to reinvent itself in a vocabulary with which to think the new destabilising object of "ethnicity.") The cogency of the dilemma — to gain a threshold of critical historical reason in a time of unreason — was poignantly captured by the editors of the volume of essays, *Ethnicity and Social Change*, that eventually (in 1984) brought the contributions together:

> Discussion of ethnic or nationality problems in Sri Lanka, particularly the relationship between the Sinhala and Tamil communities has always been charged more with fervour than with intellectual analysis. Emotional bias has been more in evidence than a correct interpretation and analysis of the problem. It was against this background that the SSA organised this seminar. It was significant and indeed path breaking in that it was the first occasion on which Sinhala and Tamil intellectuals had gathered together to discuss and analyse some aspects of the social, economic and ideological roots of the continuing ethnic conflict.

Moreover, in the wake of the violence in July 1983, the editors went on to say:

> We have now seen that the ideological and economic forces behind ethnic conflict can lead to savagery that puts in question the very civilizations we call ourselves heirs to. It is our hope that the papers in this volume will at least force some of the exponents of Sinhala and Tamil nationalism to look more closely

at the myths, misinterpretations and misunderstandings that have nourished their ideologies.[8]

A certain conception — and *expectation* — of history emerges from these remarks, as indeed from the essays that followed. However, if the discourse of Sinhala nationalism turns on the notion of an immemorial identity, a continuous authentic identity, then "'The People of the Lion'" (which was republished in *Ethnicity and Social Change*) is the most timely and formidable of possible interventions. This is because of the extraordinary comprehensiveness of its historical critique. Taking the entire historical record of Sri Lanka as the object of its inquiry, it sets out to be no less than a thoroughly exhaustive response to the claim to a continuous Sinhala identity. The target at which it aims therefore is the actual core of the Sinhala chauvinist argument. And as we know, what the essay persuasively demonstrates, through the patient reconstruction it undertakes, is precisely that Sinhala history, like all history perhaps, moves not by continuities but by a play of breaks and discontinuities, and that the forms of collective identity that emerge within any moment of its movement are not natural but constructed. What Gunawardana effectively demonstrates, in short, is that Sinhala is always–already the proper name of a signifying category and therefore always–already within quotation marks.

It is easy to see the theoretical purchase that Gunawardana's brilliantly conceived essay enables for those of us who would argue *against* the view that Sinhala identity is primordial, and *for* the modernity, in fact the *colonial* modernity, of Sinhala nationalism. It is this essay more than any other that enables us to gain the threshold of a rational historiography of the Sinhala past. Gunawardana, here as ever the historian's historian, relieves us of our anxiety about the past of "Sinhala." Not only is that past rationally reconstructible within the ordered prose of professional history but the evidence assembled pointedly demonstrates that history is, as it were, on our side. Indeed, "'The People of the Lion'" completely refigures the terrain of possible intellectual debate about history and community in Sri Lanka. Henceforth, everything else has to be written, so to say, in its wake, in (or at least in *relation to*) the critical discursive space it has levered open. "'The People of the Lion'" can now operate more or less implicitly as the master–text, its absent presence merely signalled from time to time to indicate the general coordinates of our own perhaps differently engaged but nevertheless affiliated critical moves.

This theoretical purchase however, like *every* theoretical purchase I would argue, is bought at a price. But it seems to me hardly one to despair about because if we openly embrace — as I believe we should the discursive and therefore always *positioned* character of historical narrative, of writing (if we agree with Foucault in effect that truth is but a thing of this world),[9] then we should simply give up the consoling idea that there is really an intervention which can be thought of as putting into place once and for all a guaranteeable strategy. "The People of the Lion" eventually pays the price of the historicism that undergirds its strategy, the very historicism that had been its enabling conceptual handle in displacing the misrepresentations of Sinhala ideology.

The text's strategy entails the assumption that if its reconstruction is correct, if it gets its history right, the nationalist claim is destroyed, for that claim stands or falls (or so the discourse of rational historiography assumes) on the validity of its representation of the past. This is its wager, and so far an eminently productive one. However, performed as it is on the terrain of a notion of history in which what is at stake is a correct representation of a succession of social facts, it invited precisely the kind of criticism recently levelled against it by K.N.O. Dharmadasa, that essentially he, Gunawardana, has gotten *his* history wrong.[10] Suddenly, the productive, that is, *politico – critical* use of "The People of the Lion" is cast into doubt. Suddenly a fresh set of daunting questions seem to present themselves, questions about adequate data, sound scholarship, sources of evidence, strategies of reading, etc. Suddenly we seem on the verge of collapsing into an academic argument about which of the two has actually gotten the Sinhala past right, and even of whether or not there isn't some room for reconciliation between them. Politically speaking, of course, these are bad omens. It seems to me that what Dharmadasa's response unwittingly achieves — achieves, that is, through no foresight of his own — is to change the terrain on which the "past" can be mobilised as critique, and with it the critical yield of "'The People of the Lion.'"[11] Now history, a rational, representable succession, is not confronted with its Other as it were — legend, myth, superstition — but merely with a different, indeed rival, position within its own discursive field of historicist history. It is useful to recall here another remark of Nancy's:

> ... as Nietzsche already knew, the more history becomes a broad and rich knowledge, the less we know what "history" means, even if historical knowledge is also an excellent critical and political tool in the fight against ideological representations and their power. It does not, however, at the same time allow for the possibility of a radical questioning of the representation — and/or the presentation — of history as such. And, therefore, this word runs the risk either of silently keeping a kind of Para—or post—Hegelian meaning or slowly returning to the Greek meaning of historia: the collection of of data.[12]

In my view, with Dharmadasa's intervention, we are at another crucial juncture in the discussion of history and community in Sri Lanka. And for a political criticism of Sinhala nationalism the stakes are of some moment. This is because what becomes important at this point in addressing the strategic question of formulating an adequate response to Dharmadasa, is whether to proceed along the already marked out historicist path, or to pursue some other, as yet undelineated one.

The paradox of proceeding along the historicist path and of trying to reconcile at this juncture the objective of an anti–nationalist critique with the kind of history "'The People of the Lion'" employs, becomes evident, I think, if I ask another question, one even more perverse perhaps than that with which I started: What if Gunawardana had now to concede to Dharmadasa or to someone else for that matter, on the rational terrain of the "facts" themselves that constitute the agreed upon site of dispute, on the basis of newly discovered inscriptions, say, that provided irrefutable evidence of a continuous Sinhala identity from the dawn of historical time to the present? What then? Inasmuch as on the approved notion of history the past is a "storage closet where all the costumes are kept" (in Nietzsche's well–known image in *Beyond Good and Evil*) that merely provides the fitted suits that guarantee the present, then of course it would mean granting the claims of Sinhala ideology. Such, it seems to me, is the logic of rational historiography. Needless to say, Gunawardana would strongly renounce any such reading. But my point is that what we can now more clearly discern in virtue of the altered conditions of reading produced by Dharmadasa's intervention is that rather than disclaiming the game itself, and with it its rules of formation and validity claims, Gunawardana's move is played out within the same language—game of history — or historicism — as that of his intellectual adversaries. Because what it grants — implicitly, of course—is that there is, *in principle*, a *natural* or any way *legitimate* link between past identities and present political claims. It grants *in principle* that consciousness can have an "age," reiterable or changeable across the self – succession of time. It grants in *principle* that a politics of the present can be wagered on a reconstruction of what community might have been in the past. Gunawardana's effort in this wager is not to refute the nationalists on the ground of their assumptions about what it is history is supposed to guarantee politically, but only to say that the nationalists have gotten *their* history wrong, and *therefore* that their political claims are untenable. In effect then, for Gunawardana no less than for his adversaries, history is a constant flow from the past, from before, heading somewhere: it has always—already begun. And therefore, history is such that one can gauge the direction of this flow, measure its pace, its intensity, its volume, history is something about which one could calculate, or, disastrously, *miscalculate* as though one could thereby be confirmed in one's community or else be betrayed in it, by history.

But perhaps Gunawardana is not alone in this. Perhaps we have all been playing the same game of "historicism," repeating with it the modernist dream, so naturalised since Hegel, so politically correct since Marx, that history can somehow redeem us, save us from ourselves.[13] And perhaps it is now time to give up this dream altogether and with it those consoling stories that endlessly evoke for us the absent stages of the coming – into – being of our presence.

It ought to be unambiguously clear that my argument is *not* that historicist conceptions of history are *always* irrelevant to the strategic problem of disarming nationalist discourse. My argument has rather to do with the question how to gauge what kind of historiographical strategy will be most adequate to the target to be addressed. The brilliance of Gunawardana's essay lies precisely in its untimely timeliness, in its precise assessment of the immediate task of intervention, of the object to be unmasked. And the point is that Dharmadasa's criticism only has force if we continue within the discursive field of historicist questions: the what–is–the–real–truth–of–Sinhala–history sort of questions. On my view there is little or no "cash–value" (as Richard Rorty might cynically have put it) in seeking to decide who is right and who isn't in this dispute. And therefore on the sort of view I wish to commend, a "response" to Dharmadasa ought to take the form of changing — not the answer to a question already presupposed in which what *history is* is self–evident — but rather of changing the question itself and with it the problematic in which *what history can* be in a discourse about community in Sri Lanka's present can itself be re–thought. Because what is signalled by the availability of Dharmadasa's response, it seems to me, is, if nothing else, that there is very little if any discursive room left within the historicist problematic at the present juncture for a labour of anti–chauvinist critique.

It should be evident now that what I have been trying to suggest is that had Gunawardana, at the end of "'The People of the Lion,'" said to the nationalists, in effect, "*But so what?*" What it would have signalled is not merely that the accurate reconstruction of the past of Sinhala identity is perhaps really not the crucial point after all, but more importantly *it would have disconnected the story of the past from the politics of the present* and thus made itself invulnerable to historicist criticism. Moreover by so doing, it would have served to indicate that the political task of theoretical intervention is to refuse to be governed by the questions of one's adversaries, that the task in fact is to will, perhaps even to *risk* changing the problematic in which those questions have appeared to us natural, legitimate or even imperative. For this might have made it possible to refuse History its subjectivity, its constancy, its eternity; to think it otherwise than as the past's hold over the present, to interrupt its seemingly irrepressible succession, causality, its sovereign claim to determinacy. For in this thought a different possibility of community might have been made visible — community as a *project*. Community, to quote Nancy one last time, "is not historical as if it were a permanently changing subject within… a permanently flowing time… But history is community, that is, the happening of a certain space of time — as a certain spacing of time, which is the spacing of a 'we.'[14] Here, perhaps, is a provocation that would be useful to think, to think *with* — and not as the penultimate gesture in an overcoming, a getting beyond, so much as the initial move in what needs to be an extended elaboration. What the configuration of that discourse of community might be (and no doubt it will have to be one in which the political forms of being–in–common–of obligation, of friendship, of citizenship — will have to be reformulated) has to be the subject of another set of reflections; all I have sought to sketch here is the thought through which "The People of the Lion" has brought us to the point at which we cannot refuse its urgency.[15]

Notes

1. "Finite History," in *The States of "Theory": History, Art, and Critical Discourse*, David Carroll (ed.) (New York: Columbia University Press, 1990), p. 149.

2. R.A.L.H. Gunawardana's "'The People of the Lion'" has already had an astonishing career, one indeed itself worth inquiring upon. First published as "'The People of the Lion'": the Sinhala Identity and Ideology in History and Historiography," in *Sri Lanka Journal of the Hmnanities* 5 (1979), pp.1–36; it was subsequently published as "'The People of the Lion'": Sinhala Consciousness in History and Historiography" in *Ethnicity and Social Change* (Colombo: Social Scientists' Association, 1984); and most recently with its original title in Jonathan Spencer (ed.) *Sri Lanka: History and the Roots of Conflict* (New York: Routledge, 1990).

3. I am thinking, of course, of the Friedrich Nietzsche of *The Use and Abuse of History* published in 1873.

4. See his "The Problem of Ideology: Marxism Without Guarantees," in *Journal of Communication Inquiry* 10(2)(1986), pp.29—45. For one very thoughtful attempt to disrupt the naturalization of community by a theoretical labour of "supplementarity," see William Corlett, *Community Without Unity: A Politics of Derridean Extravagance* (Durham: Duke University Press, 1989).

5. "Finite," p. 152.

6. It is easy to see here the influence not only of Gilles Deleuze and Michel Foucault, but also of Richard Rorty for all of whom theory is not the name of a General Hermeneutic, a Panoptic uncovering General Truths, but an ensemble of devices for opening up discursive space. For Deleuze and Foucault, see, "Intellectuals and Power: A Conversation between Michel Foucault and Gilles Deleuze," in Michel Foucault, *Language, Counter—Memory, Practice: Selected Essays and Interviews*, Donald F. Bouchard (ed. and trans.) (Ithaca: Cornell University Press, 1977). For some of Rorty's remarks on theory see most recently, "Feminism and Pragmatism," in *Michigan Quarterly Review* 30(2)(1991), pp.231—258. See too Nancy Fraser's very

pointed response to some of the implications of Rorty's argument in "From Irony to Prophecy to Politics: A Response to Richard Rorty," in *Michigan Quarterly Review* 30(2)(1991), pp.259—266.

7.   For an account of the rise and decline of such a sphere in European history see, Jurgen Habermas, *The Structural Transformation of the Public Sphere*, Timothy Burger (trans.) (Cambridge, Mass: MIT Press, 1989).

8.   The quotations are from the unpaginated introdution to *Ethnicity and Social Change* (Colombo: Social Scientists' Association, 1984). The volume's task was perhaps most pointedly carried out in (besides Gunawardana, to whom I turn in a moment) Bandaranayake's concern to "disestablish" the "cultural structures of communalism" and to erect in their place a "modern scientific consciousness in matters of history and ethnicity;" in Siriweera's endeavour to show that the "Mahavamsa—Pujavali tradition" has to be understood in relation to the historical contexts in which these texts were written; in Jayawardena's argument that communalism's "ethnic" autobiography has to be read, as it were, symptomatically, that is against the grain of its own elision of class; and in Abeysekere's demonstration that certain Sinhala claims — such as that minority ethnic groups are disproportionately represented in the higher stale services — are empirically unfounded.

9   "The important thing here, I believe, is that truth isn't outside power, or lacking in power: contrary to a myth whose history and functions would repay further study, truth isn't the reward of free spirits, the child of protracted solitude, nor the privilege of those who have succeeded in liberating themselves. Truth is a thing of this world: it is produced only by virtue of multiple forms of constraint. And it induces regular effects of power. Each society has its regimes of truth, its 'general politics' of truth: that is, the types of discourse which it accepts and makes function as true; the mechanisms and instances which enable one to distinguish true and false statements, the means by which each is sanctioned; the techniques and procedures accorded value in the acquisition of truth; the status of those who are charged with saying what counts as true." Michel Foucault, "Truth and Power," in *Power/Knowledge: Selected Interviews and Other Writings, 1972—1977.* Colin Gordon (ed.) (New York: Pantheon, 1980), p. 131.

10   K.N.O. Dharmadasa, "'The People of the Lion'": Ethnic Identity, Ideology and Historical Revisionism in Contemporary Sri Lanka," in *Ethnic Studies Report* 10(1)(1992), pp.37–59, and in *Sri Lanka Journal of the Humanities* 15(1&2X 1992), pp.1–35.

11   Its belatedness notwithstanding. It comes more than a decade after the first publication of the text it criticises. For an account of the reasons for this see Dharmadasa's note in "Ethnic Identity…," Ethnic Studies Report, p. 56.

12.   "Finite," pp. 152–53.

13   I am reminded here of Hayden White's fine reading of Frederic Jameson's *The Politi-*

cal Unconscious, itself a seminal work in Marxist cultural theory, and whose memorable opening sentence is the imperative: "Always historicist!" See White's "Getting out of History: Jameson's Redemption of Narrative," in his *The Content of the Form* (Baltimore: Johns Hopkins University Press, 1987).

14   "Finite," pp. 161–62.

15   This essay was read at the International Centre for Ethnic Studies, Colombo, in January 1994 while I had the pleasure of being a Visiting Fellow there. I am indebted for the many critical comments offered on that occasion. Its formulation and writing owe much to discussions with many people, in particular to Pradeep Jeganathan and Malathi de Alwis. Its principal debt however is to two people: Regi Siriwardena who sounded the disquiet that got it going, and of course, R.A.L.H. Gunawardana, whose brilliant essay is the occasion for its reflections.

Multireligion on the Bus: Beyond 'Influence' and 'Syncretism' in the Study of Religious Meetings

Jonathan S. Walters

This paper is about how humans meet their "Others," the product of thought about my own experiences as an American who spends as much time as possible living and studying in Sri Lanka and about the historical situations which constitute the foci of my studies. As an historian of religions, my primary interest is in meetings of humans with "Others" who are so designated on the basis of specifically religious differences, and this paper reflects that interest. But of course "religion" is merely an interpretive category — as recent and Western and vague and oftentimes misleading as any number of similar categories scholars employ such as "culture" or "ethnicity" or "ideology" (with which, it is almost a truism to state, "religion" greatly overlaps)—and I believe that the methodological approach which I advance, however cursorily, in this paper, is equally useful in thinking about the meetings of "Others" so designated on the basis of specifically cultural differences or specifically ethnic differences or specifically ideological differences: Our interpretive categories dissolve into each other when we push at their edges, but we are still left with situations — here and now or in the centuries past that live in the minds of historians — in which some humans designate some other humans "Others" as part of the very process of meeting with them.

I begin this paper on a bus in Sri Lanka not only because it allows me to introduce a specific moment in the history of the meeting of religious "Others" from which I can launch a theoretical discussion, but also because Sri Lankan buses remain for me, after more than a decade, still rather "Other." Part of this is due to the fact that Sri Lankan conductors pack buses like sardine tins, squeezing an extra person or two into each seat then filling the aisles, the footboard, the steps. It is common to see several men hanging on window frames or other passengers while travelling outside the bus itself. A minibus designed for 26 will transport more than fifty people; a forty–seat bus one hundred. This is not a source for outrage (as I learned on repeated occasions when, incredulous that the conductor had signalled the driver to stop for additional passengers, I would try to rile sentiments) even though it makes the crowding on a bus or subway train in New York or Chicago at rush hour appear almost paltry in comparison. More striking to me is the culture of etiquette on Sri Lankan buses, within which resignation to the exigencies of public transportation seems for the most part to produce neither the feigned self–absorption nor the barely controlled hostility that in my experience typifies the culture of crowded buses and trains in the United States. I have been struck in Sri Lanka by the intimacy generated in the crowded space of public transportation. Strangers meet, share food and stories and *vistara* ("personal details" about family, home, employment, assets, purpose for travel), sleep on each others' shoulders, take each others' newspapers, all as a matter of course; they cooperate to deal with the inevitable crises like car–sick children, pickpockets, and the enormous parcels that people transport by bus; they often join together in raucous group sing–alongs (*bajaw danawa*). Learning to ride the bus in Sri Lanka – overcoming my American–bred presuppositions about how one rides buses (and my deeply–rooted fear even to make eye contact with strangers on buses and subways in American cities) –has required of me nearly as much cultural training and initiation as has conducting field–work in rural Sri Lankan villages or residing in urban Buddhist monasteries.

Ironically, my obvious "Otherness" on Sri Lankan buses magnifies the very cultural practices that most conflict with my own, for as a foreigner I inevitably stand out as an object for speculation, curiosity and/or stereotyping, especially when I am travelling in remote parts of the Island outside the ordinary tourist loop. Naturally enough - from their perspective - people who know English strike up a conversation with me about my *vistara*. Of course it comes out that I am in Sri Lanka because I study Pali, Sinhala and Buddhist history, and most of the time these details delight my interrogators because a large majority of the country are Sinhala-speaking and Buddhist. My interest in their lan-

guage and religion is clearly a source of pride to Sinhala Buddhists (partly because I, as a white Westerner, still command a certain status due
merely to the lingering belief that white is right and West is best, ham-
mered in by centuries of colonialism; partly because I seem to fulfil certain modern expectations about Buddhism as a missionary religion;
partly because so few non-Sri Lankans resident in Sri Lanka ever bother
to learn Sinhala, let alone Pali or Buddhist history; partly because this
allows me to transcend the "Otherness" of tourists as a partial "insider"
with whom serious religious discussion *could* proceed, in Sinhala rather
than English) and I've grown rather accustomed to such conversations
resulting in heartfelt, sometimes lengthy, expositions of belief or doubt
(followed by dinner invitations or at least an exchange of addresses). After the conversation switches to Sinhala, people several seats away-
perhaps speakers of Sinhala only, to whom I seem both a marvellous
spectacle and a rare opportunity - will turn, sometimes to speak, sometimes merely to gawk.

The disclosure of my partial "insiderness" has not always, however, been received happily. The next question from Tamil speakers is often
(whether in Sinhala or English), "don't you know Tamil?" I have a clever
response (in a mixture of Sinhala and Tamil I reply, "I don't know a single
word." *Mata konjam vat baehae*; that produces chuckles rather than hostility. But one time, rather bizarrely, a conversation of this sort turned
hostile indeed. It was a "full moon" (*poya*) day and I was staying with
friends at a Buddhist temple in the Colombo suburbs, but had agreed to
meet one of my Sinhala teachers across town for dinner. It was pouring
with rain (during the *maha* Monsoon); I got a bus from the temple to
Colombo's main strip, the Galle Road, but discovered to my dismay that
that road was temporarily blocked for a government–sponsored motor
race. I stood in the rain with a large crowd for a long time until finally a
minibus came along. We piled into the van, and not surprisingly the
cramming was worse than usual. I ended up near the back, standing
humped over a seated elderly gentleman with a young Sinhala man likewise humped over me. The young man initiated the usual conversation,
but when I disclosed my *vistara* he exclaimed angrily, in English, "Look at
you: born in the land of the Cross and the Gospel, forsaking your Chris-

tian heritage for the study of heathens. Don't you know that Jesus is coming again, soon? What are *you* doing to prepare for Him?"

The bus fell silent. As the elderly gentleman looked up at me I replied, in Sinhala, "And look at you: born in the Island of Dharma yet forsaking Buddhist tradition for the god of the whites. Don't you know that the Bodhisattva Maitreya will soon become Buddha in the world? What merit will *you* have accumulated to be born at that time?" My outburst pleased the majority of our fellow passengers, who applauded and laughed. But the young man, still wedged against me from head to toe, said nothing more.

I have enjoyed telling that story in Sri Lanka as well as the United States. Friends who hear it realize that *something happened* on that bus. It is more than the sumptuous juxtaposition — this American preaching Buddhist millenarianism in Sinhala to an English—speaking Sri Lankan fundamentalist Christian; however inverted, a real meeting of religions took place in that moment.

My thought about that experience, over more than a decade now, has gone in two directions. On one hand, I have become increasingly dissatisfied with the ideas of "influence" and "syncretism" — the most common analytic/heuristic tools available in the Social Sciences and Humanities for thinking about how religions come together in history — because they seem simply ludicrous when applied to my experience. Who influenced whom? Even if we assume that he was under the "influence" of fundamentalist Christianity, and I of millenarian Buddhism, neither of us infused the other with his stated religious outlook. Likewise, however syncretic his and my views may (or may not) be, certainly no syncretism occurred on that bus. Yet something happened, something that cannot be dismissed as some sort of pluralistic co—existence: there was an encounter, full of challenges, power plays, markings, decisions. The first section of this essay represents my own attempt at articulating the reasons I find the concepts "influence" and "syncretism" inadequate when thinking about the coming together of religious traditions that I have observed while living in Sri Lanka and studying Sri Lankan history.

On the other hand, there was nothing theoretical about my experience on that bus at the time I was having it. I was uncomfortably packed into a tiny van, soaking wet and late for dinner. The other passengers, including Mr. Christianity, were in similar straights. I'm sure the furthest thing from any of our minds was that Buddhism and Christianity were about to meet, however unlikely their champions, in some sort of essential confrontation of which my co–passenger and I were mere embodiments. The view I expressed was as absent of sophistication about Buddhism — judged by intellectualist standards, anyway —as was the apparently dogmatic faith of my co–passenger absent of sophistication about Christianity. We were just two guys on the bus, and that happened. But we were, afterall, on a *bus*, in a public space complete with an audience. As I have thought about this experience, usually while riding buses and trains around Sri Lanka, I have come to see that the location of this encounter was not mere coincidence. The public space of the bus is charged in religious ways; it is what I call a "multireligious field." That will be the focus of this essay's second section.

Religious Meetings in Sri Lankan History

Sri Lanka has long been designated "multireligious." The adjective is descriptive: Sri Lanka is home to four "world religions" (Buddhism, Hinduism, Islam and Christianity) that share the space in urban as well as rural settings. Throughout the country participants in each of the traditions face each other day after day whether in schools and offices, marketplaces and agricultural fields, or on the bus. There is moreover every reason to believe that throughout the country's long and varied history such a "multireligious" society has existed.

Because "multireligious" is descriptive, it has tended to suppress investigation of the kind of "meeting" of religious actors that I am interested in understanding, the kind of meeting that occurs on buses in Sri Lanka. "Multireligious" connotes the disengaged co–existence of separate and separable entities, "Buddhism," "Hinduism," "Islam" and "Christianity." In the main, scholars of Sri Lankan history and religion have focused upon these "entities" in cultural vacuums: individual traditions are studied as though the others were not present and active in the constitution of their individual histories. Thus, many aspects of this historical "coming together" or "meeting" of participants in the various Sri Lankan religions have received virtually no attention. For example, it is little known or thought about that Christians already had a presence in *ancient* Sri

Lanka,[1] long before Roman Catholic then Dutch Reformed then Anglican imperialists initiated the "Christian influence" on "traditional Buddhism" (or "Buddhist–Christian syncretism" a.k.a. "Protestant
Buddhism") that many scholars have, on the contrary, noted. But these
scholars, who do at least recognize a "coming together" of Buddhism and
Christianity since the Colonial Period,[2] have taken a necessary first step
towards a study of what I call "Sri Lankan multireligion" (defined as religious phenomena produced in the "coming together" of participants in
two or more religious traditions). For in Sri Lankan history as well as
modern Sri Lanka, it is evident that the participants in the various religious traditions have not merely kept to their separate corners; their
"coming together" has been long and complex. My thought about "multireligion" represents an attempt at understanding the designation "multireligious" analytically rather than merely descriptively.

Another example of multireligion that scholars of Sri Lankan
history and religion have often noted is the undeniable presence of "Hindu" deities in Sri Lankan Buddhist temples, texts and rituals. This "coming together" of Buddhism and Hinduism is, like the colonial era
"meeting" of Buddhism and Christianity, described either as "Hindu—
Buddhist syncretism" or "Hindu influence on traditional Buddhism."
Taking these two — colonial Christian "influence" and "Hindu–
Buddhist syncretism" — as examples, I want to sketch out some of the
shortcomings in the two models as I see them.

I have been putting quotation marks around "coming together"
and "meeting" because I see a need for alternatives to the term "interaction," which would have been more natural in the contexts where "coming
together" and "meeting" are employed above. In its root meaning, "inter—
action" or "action among" is precisely what I mean by "multireligion." But
the term "interaction" has been employed in the Social Sciences and
Humanities as the necessary counterpart of an unnecessary epistemological peculiarity, namely the linguistic and theoretical treatment of "religions" as "entities"[3] "Interact" is what these "religions" do with each other
in the fantasy world of social scientific discourse where "Buddhism" (or
"Christianity") is also empowered to act, think, need, demand or posit.
My use of "coming together" or "meeting" is intended to restore agency to
the human actors who actually constitute each religious tradition, and
whose doing, thinking, needing, demanding or positing — whose coming

together — is displaced onto reified interpretive categories by phrases like "Christianity's interaction with Buddhism." Neither Christianity nor Buddhism is agentive in history; history is made by Christians and Buddhists.

Closely related to the problematic displacement of human agency in studies of "interactionism" (studies of one reified category's intercourse with another) is their authors' implicit presupposition that these "religions" are *separate* and *separable* entities, or that individual religions represent neat, mutually—exclusive categories. If we can discuss, say, "Buddhism's response to Christianity" then we can, *a priori*, determine what "Buddhism" is (and is not) as well as what "Christianity" is (and is not). Yet in practice this is seldom if ever possible: "Buddhism" and "Christianity" describe wide ranges of often–opposing thoughts, practices, institutions and civilizations. The problem is only deferred by delimiting such statements to read, say, "nineteenth century Theravada Buddhism's response to Anglican Christianity in Colombo," because different nineteenth century Theravada Buddhists responded in different ways to the differing actions and statements of differing Anglican Christians in Colombo. The world of 19th century Colombo was one in which varieties of Buddhism and varieties of Christianity co–existed, and in which the wide spectrum of overlapping meetings of Buddhists and Christians (and, it is seldom added, Hindus and Muslims) belies any treatment of "Buddhism" and "Christianity" as distinct, mutually—exclusive categories.[4] It is precisely this spectrum (in Collingwoodian philosophy, a "scale of forms")[5] that "interactionism" obscures; it is within this "scale of forms," however, that I want to locate the "multireligion" of nineteenth century Colombo.

"Influence" and "syncretism" are aspects of "interactionism" which sham these two defects (the displacement of human agency onto unreal entities and an erroneous presupposition that religions represent mutually—exclusive categories).

"Influence" refers to a transfer of substance from one entity to another. The term literally means "flowing in," and originally referred to the transfer of malefic substances from astrological to human bodies; the Sinhala term that best approximates its original meaning is *grahadoshaya*.[6] It is used in both active and passive senses, depending upon the context: "Hinduism influenced Buddhism" or "Buddhism was influenced by Hinduism." Whether describing a Hindu "infusion" in Buddhism or a Buddhist "borrowing" from Hinduism, "influence" occurs magically. It presupposes invisible entities that can alter each other without the intervention of human agency. Even when one or both of the entities are people ("Col. Olcott influenced Anagarika Dharmapala"), the term still refers to a transfer of some "substance" through "insensible or invisible means, without the employment of material force, or the exercise of formal authority,"[7] that is, magically. The use of "influence" moreover assumes that the "substance" transferred from one entity to another is unchanged in the process: "Hindu" deities in "Buddhist" temples remain Hindu; the temples remain Buddhist.

"Syncretism" originally referred to a rallying together of opposed forces against a common enemy, said to be characteristic of ancient Cretan military practice.[8] Until the mid–nineteenth century it carried distinctly negative connotations.[9] "Later on, the word came to be used mostly without negative overtones, but it continued to be applied in all sorts of ways."[10] Since the 1970's, however, "syncretism" has received considerably more scholarly attention than "influence," thanks to a series of conferences on the topic held in Europe and the United States in the 1960's and 1970's. A useful review of this scholarship which "attempts.... to advance the consensus" reached by scholars at those conferences has been provided by Carston Colpe.[11] Colpe notes that

> when the concept of syncretism is used in describing phenomena, the application of the term is still not the result of an analysis; rather it serves as a disparaging judgement on certain manifestations, a judgement assumed to be obvious. The adjective *syncretic*, used in this way, occurs in countless treatises on religions, where it designates both simple and complex phenomena; its definition is taken for granted and various inferences are drawn from it.[12]

In social scientific discourse on Sri Lanka, at least, "syncretism" is certainly applied as a descriptive rather than analytic concept. Little attention is paid to why or how or who; the term simply describes the presence of alien substances within a religion, i.e., the product of "influence" (which in between the lines always implies simple–minded or crafty actors, usually monks and Brahmins, with some [negative] motivation to corrupt their religion/s in this manner). For this reason, in usage, "syncretism" and "influence" are closely synonymous. As with influence, calling the presence of Hindu deities in Buddhist temples "syncretic" portrays an "infusion" or "borrowing" of something alien (which paradoxically remains alien) within a religion (which paradoxically remains itself). And as with "influence," in usage "syncretism" is usually predicated upon unreal entities that alter each other magically, in the absence of human agency.

The consensus mentioned above represents an attempt to limit usage of "syncretism" to a very specific type of religious meeting. Colpe distinguishes genuinely syncretic forms from overlapping meetings of religions like synthesis (which unlike syncretism is indissoluable), evolution (which unlike syncretism involves only one religion), and harmonization (which unlike syncretism erases differences between the two religions involved). A truly syncretic relationship obtains when two separate systems come together in such a way that a union between them is effected. Like "influence," syncretism in Colpe's analysis leaves alien substances alien within traditions that remain the same; because difference is not erased, a syncretic system can always be dissolved into its component parts. It is "always a transitional phase" because its syncretic character is not passed on to subsequent generations: the alien substances are either harmonized or discarded.

This "consensus" fails to address the problems of agency and essentialism that underlie the unrefined usage of "syncretism," although it does proceed in the right direction by attempting to focus the discussion of syncretism on a limited type of religious meeting. We can further develop the usefulness of "syncretism" by insisting upon a formulation that sees this type of meeting as the result of human agency. The active verbal usage "syncretize" can be an activity, not of unreal entities transferring substances magically but of conscious human agents (like the ancient Cretans) recognizing and attempting to mitigate difference among themselves, for some particular reason, by bringing different things together in a shared space. It describes an attempt at reconciling or joining together opposing beliefs or practices, which presupposes human actors.

Specification of the limits of "syncretism" creates a certain gap in our analytic vocabulary. If "syncretism" no longer refers to all those non–

syncretic meetings — including harmonization, evolution, and synthesis (all conceived on a human scale) — what does? We can agree with Colpe that in its unrefined usage "syncretism" (and the same could be said of "influence") serves as "a useful heuristic tool for tracking down otherwise hidden antecedents of historical facts." Precisely its character as a generalization allows "syncretism" (or "influence") to serve as our marker of those places in history where religious meetings have occurred, where we need to start asking: who met whom? what happened between them? If "syncretism" is to be limited, and "influence" abandoned as meaningless, what can designate those junctures in history that witness a meeting of participants in different religions? My coining of "multireligion" is designed to meet this need. I coin "multireligion" to mean simply what "syncretism" and "influence" are misused for: a situation in *which* adherents to different religious traditions, occupying a shared space, come together in some way. "Syncretism" is one possible result of such a meeting.

In the unrefined sense mentioned above, discourse on "influence" and "syncretism" in Sri Lankan religious history has been useful[13] It has pointed to certain junctures — late nineteenth century urban meetings of Buddhism and Christianity, premodern meetings of Buddhism and Hinduism —that deserve the special attention of scholars. I would hope that looking for "multireligion" would preserve this heuristic function even after the abandonment of "influence" and the severe limitation of "syncretism." Yet this discourse on "influence" and "syncretism" in Sri Lankan religious history has simultaneously fallen into the traps that are hidden within those concepts. Scholars have characterized "religions," rather than religious people, as the actors in history; they have tended toward "interactionism," covering up with the pretense of mutually-exclusive analytical categories the spectrum of meetings that shades off at either end into a (merely hypothetical) "pure Buddhism" and "pure Christianity" (or Hinduism or Islam); they have conveyed disparaging judgements by passing them off as value–free descriptions. I would hope that looking for "multireligion" — with its emphasis on human agency and the overlap of classes — would avoid these pitfalls.

Thus an analysis of "multireligion" in nineteenth century Colombo allows me to see that Buddhism changed because of its meeting with Christianity, as do analyses of this change labelled "Christian influence on Buddhism" or "Buddhist–Christian syncretism." But that is as far as the similarity goes. In my work on this period[14] I have been able to demonstrate that this meeting of Buddhism and Christianity (i.e. Buddhists and Christians) was not a matter of "influence" for it involved agents consciously refuting, rather than infusing, each other. Nor was it "syncretic," because however much Buddhism seems to have adopted Christian forms, the Buddhists who consciously constituted the change under scrutiny were protesting *against* certain views and practices of Christians rather than adopting them. But those Christian views and practices were transformed in the meeting: they became Buddhist views and practices before they were incorporated into Buddhism. This "Buddhicization" was effected through a variety of "meetings" with Christians, including missionaries (who were largely considered opponents by those effecting the change) and their overlapping contemporaries and successors, historians of religions and Buddhologists (who were largely considered allies). These "meetings" constituted considerable change in Christianity as well as Buddhism (among other things, Christian meetings with Buddhists became a major cause of the abandonment of evangelical missions by the mainstream Anglo–American Protestant churches between the World Wars). In other words, the nineteenth century meeting of Buddhism and Christianity in Sri Lanka was constitutive of change among adherents to both religions. It generated all sorts of "meetings" — Christians converted to Buddhism, Buddhists converted to Christianity, Christianized Buddhists, Buddhicized Christians. The meeting itself forced Buddhists and Christians alike to define each other and, consequently, to redefine themselves; neither the "Buddhism" nor the "Christianity" that entered this meeting came out unchanged.

Likewise, "syncretism" and "influence" only go so far in helping us to understand the meeting of Buddhism and Hinduism in Sri Lankan history — pointing to the juncture — before they begin hindering analysis. "Hinduism" is a notorious example of the ahistoricity of discoursing on "religions" rather than the people who constitute them, because "Hinduism" defines so extensive a range of ideas and practices, over such a long period of time, that it is all but meaningless and often counterproductive analytically. The "Hindu deities" found in Buddhist temples in Sri Lanka span this entire range of "Hindu" forms, from the late–medieval killer goddess Kali to Vedic deities like Indra; Vishnu as well as Shiva, and diminutive Vishnus and Shivas like Krishna and Aiyyanar.

Each of these deities has its own history in Sri Lanka: the meeting of "Hinduism" and "Buddhism" has not been singular. Discussions of "Hindu influence" or Hindu—Buddhist syncretism" have kept scholars from seeing how dynamic these many meetings have been.

Take Vishnu, for example. Vishnu stands at the feet of the reclining Buddha in temples throughout the Island. But we cannot call him an "influence" because Buddhists themselves have constructed these temples, and they worship a Buddhist Vishnu. Here "Buddhist Vishnu" does not mean only that Vishnu in Sri Lanka is a Buddhist version of the Vaishnava Godhead (he is called "Sri Vishnu *Devarajanan vahanse*" in Sinhala, a remodelled Indra/ Sakra or king of the divine pantheon conceived within a Buddhist cosmology more than a Cosmic Creator/Sustainer/Fulfiller); this deity is considered a practicing Buddhist Himself. In fact, according to Sri Lankan Buddhists, God becomes God only as a result of His good (i.e. Buddhist) karma.[15] In this way He is decidedly not the Vishnu worshipped by Vaishnavas, of whom (since about the Gupta Period) Buddha was considered a mere *avatara*. And yet the iconography leaves no doubt that we are discussing a single deity. The point is that the Buddhist Vishnu (like the Vaishnava Buddha) encodes a "meeting" that did not result in syncretism (if it were syncretism, Sri Lanka's Vishnu would have to still be the Vaishnava Vishnu, India's Buddha the Buddhist Buddha) and, because of the obviously conscious subordination of Vishnu to the Buddha (or the Buddha to Vishnu), it cannot be understood as passive "influence."

Moreover, there is not a single "Vishnu in Sri Lankan Buddhism" but numerous Vishnus, encoding the different directions this "meeting" took among different people and at different periods in history. The Vishnu in modem Buddhist temples is *worshipped*, an exalted co—participant in Buddhist practice. The roots of the modern conception apparently date back to the tenth—thirteenth centuries[16] a time when Sri Lankans periodically were allied with North Indian (Vaishnava) rulers against the South Indian (Shaiva) Cholas. Vishnu, formerly the chosen deity (*ishtadevata*) of various paramount overlords of India, was rapidly being displaced by Shiva as the Chola imperial victories mounted. Bringing Vishnu into the Buddhist temple at this time signalled a "meeting" of Hinduism and Buddhism in which certain "Hindus" were constituted as allies while others were simultaneously constituted as outsiders (throughout history more Shaivas than Vaishnavas have shared the space with Buddhists in Sri Lanka, but Shiva is usually not present in Buddhist temples and never with the prominence accorded Vishnu). Although it subordinated Vaishnavism to Buddhism, the creation of this "Buddhist Vishnu" was inclusivist. Before about the tenth century, however, when Vishnu was still the chosen deity of Sri Lanka's imperial overlords, He did not enter the Buddhist temple. The appropriation of Vishnu by Buddhists prior to the tenth century was exclusivist. A fine example is the Buddha image at Aukana, in the North Central Province: carved during the Gupta ascendancy, when Vishnu ruled supreme in India, this colossal monolithic stone Buddha image stood on top of Vishnu and several other deities whose images were buried beneath its pedestal.[17]

Saman/Natha, the other "Hindu deity" who in modern temples joins Vishnu at the feet of the Buddha, is not "Hindu" at all; as John Holt has recently shown, he is a Mahayana Bodhisattva who has undergone a long and complex process of acculturation within the Theravadin milieu.[18] Even if we agree with Holt that in this instance syncretism can be verified, it is certainly not Hindu–Buddhist syncretism, and "Hindu influence" certainly falls short as an explanation. Another "Hindu" deity in Buddhist temples, Vibhishana, belongs to the Indic *Ramayana* legends but we cannot see him, either, as the result of "influence" or "syncretism" because he is not deified anywhere outside Sri Lanka; he is what we would have to deem (just to point out how silly interactionism can get) "an indigenously Buddhist Hindu deity." In other work I have demonstrated that the cult of Vibhishana did indeed participate in a complex meeting of Buddhists and Hindus during the Gampola/Vijayanagar Period (about 1344 A.D.) even though there is nothing "Hindu" about him; but this understanding becomes possible only when Hindus and Buddhists, rather than Hinduism and Buddhism, are seen as history's agents.[19]

It is of course possible that genuine syncretism resulted from some of the meetings of Buddhists and Hindus which left "Hindu" deities in Buddhist temples as relics of their occurrence; it would be no more prudent to assume that syncretism did not occur than it would to assume the opposite. The question for historical study is: in what multireligious circumstances did the different deities come into Buddhist temples (and hearts), and why?

Like my own meeting with that Sinhala fundamentalist Christian on the bus in Colombo, meetings among adherents to different traditions throughout Sri Lankan history — large–scale as well as small–scale — are not much illuminated by the analytical/heuristic tools "influence" and "syncretism." While I want to emphasize, with my notion of "multireligion," that these meetings are important areas for scholarly study (they help us to develop an historical perspective on South Asian religions taken together, rather than separately; because these meetings were so often constitutive of change, we must also study them in order to understand the history of those separate South Asian religions), I have suggested that study must proceed with an emphasis on precisely the human agency and overlap of classes that "syncretism" and "influence," as aspects of "interactionism," render opaque, and have sketched out an idea of "multireligion" that stresses those elements.

Understanding religious meetings in Sri Lankan history requires, in short, that we proceed historically. The conditions on that bus in Colombo and a long history of interaction between Buddhists and Christians in Sri Lanka that my confronter/evangel and (I both in our own ways) embody, came into play in that moment. The meeting was not only produced by those pre–existing conditions; it was also productive of them. It constituted the condition on that bus, it constituted my views (I am not a millenarian Buddhist; in fact I think that sort of "Buddhism" could exist *only* in a meeting with an evangelical Christian) and it presumably constituted my opponent's (I have often wondered, does he evangelize like that all the time or did I represent a category mistake which in some way forced him to an extreme perspective? Did his confrontation with me ennoble or detract from his Christian millenarianism?). In different circumstances different responses would emerge (when I snap back at evangelical Christians in the United States I arm myself with Christianity rather than Buddhism; my fellow passenger could never have evangelized the native Sri Lankans on that bus with the same logic he tried on me); different responses would have created different circumstances (imagine if I had shouted "Halleluia, I see the light brother!" – the encounter would have had considerably different effects on me, Mr. Christianity, and our audience in that sardine tin). Who, where,why, what, how – all the texture is in the specific details.

The Bus as a Multireligious Field

I am clearer about why I want an alternative to "syncretism" and "influence" than I am about just what "multireligion" entails. That does not worry me, for I am already accustomed to studying something I cannot define (i.e, "religion"). Indeed, with Collingwood[20] I consider definition to be the *goal* of historical inquiry rather than a transparent basis for it. As an historian of religions I make it my business to learn more about the definition of "religion" by learning more about what religious people have done, for the complete definition of "religion" is precisely the complete history of religions (neither of which will ever exist); if I could truly define religion then there would be no more problems to work on, and I would surely find something more interesting to do with my mind. Likewise, to attempt a definition of multireligion would presume knowledge of what the history of multireligion has been, which is knowledge that I at least lack. So I put forth the idea of "multireligion" as an idea in need of definition, an historical problem which, thanks largely to "influence" and "syncretism," has hardly been addressed. What is multireligion? In other words, how have the adherents to differing religious traditions in differing times and places shared the space they inhabit?

The analogy of "religion" and "multireligion" extends beyond the problem of definition. Like "religion," "multireligion" defines an enormous field. Colpe reviews scholarship which suggests that "syncretism" has occurred throughout most of the history of religions. He proceeds to establish criteria for verifying "syncretism" which render most of this scholarship incorrect. But then we are left asking, if throughout the history of religions adherents to different traditions have been meeting, and if most of those meetings were not syncretic, what were they? My answer, of course, is "multireligion." And indeed, when we think about the various sorts of meetings of adherents to different religions that we all know from personal experience — evangelization, arguing, imitating, watching, pluralistic *laissez–faire*, inter–religious dialogue, universalization — we are left asking, when were individual religions *not* simultaneously involved in multireligions? Are there any religions, at any period/s of history, whose adherents were not participants in multireligious situations?

But we would not move beyond "syncretism" and "influence" if we merely recognized the presence of multireligion and left it at that. Instead, once we see that multireligion has been present in a certain situation we need to start asking questions about that situation, not in order to discover some essence of multireligion but in order to understand historically the complexity and dynamism of that particular instance of it.

Multireligion as I conceive of it is not some sort of omnipresent condition; it is located only in specific conditions. In a multireligious society like Sri Lanka's it is always potentially present whenever and wherever adherents to different traditions meet, but it is not necessarily present. People do not spend all their time confronting other religions any more than they spend all their time practicing their own religions. Instead, they make certain situations, certain fields, their foci for multireligious activity. Just as studies of particular religions must isolate the specific arenas in which they are active, so studies of particular multireligions will have to isolate the specific fields in which religious people meet.

The bus in contemporary Sri Lanka is such a "multireligious field." In a number of ways that I shall elaborate presently, Sri Lankans of all religions make their vehicles (cars, lorries, boats buses, even motorcycles and carts) foci for certain kinds of multireligious activity. The forms that these activities take are remarkably similar despite considerable difference in content; the shared forms constitute the bus as an arena in which adherents to different religions can "come together" or "meet." For convenience, I will refer to these "forms" as belonging to two categories—"religious marking" and "rituals of travel."

"Religious marking" refers to the practice of ornamenting vehicles with religious kitsch. This usually includes pictures of one or more religious subject affixed to the panel over the windshield inside the vehicle and phrases of religious import painted in fancy script on that same panel and/or the area just above the back bumper (outside the bus). The most common pictures are glossy prints or reflecting stickers. Buddhists commonly portray the Buddha, the Buddhist flag, certain Buddhist structures and/or the monk Sivali. Hindus portray a variety of deities including Ganesha, Vishnu, Skanda and Shiva. Christians portray Jesus, the Virgin Mary and/or certain chosen saints. Muslims, prohibited by Islamic law from iconographic representation, portray the Ka'bah at Mecca or the name of Allah in Arabic script. The phrases are sometimes general wishes for a good journey ("Pleasant trip"[*subha gamana*]), sometimes more tradition—specific benedictions (Refuge in the Triple Gem" [*tunuruwan saranayi*]; "Jesus Saves").

"Rituals of travel" refers to a wide range of religious practices enacted during the journey. It is very common for drivers of all traditions to touch the steering wheel then bring their hands together as though praying three times before commencing the journey, at which time they will often also light incense, place flowers or electric lamps, and/or chant, vow or pray before the pictures that are situated above their windshields. Along the country's major routes, and on many smaller routes as well, there are special shrines at which the bus (or car, or cart, or lorry) will come to a screeching halt.[21] The conductor (or owner) will get a few coins, fold his hands and bow his head before the shrine, then dedicate the coins to the deity represented by the shrine. On buses, certain people will stand as the bus passes certain such shrines; certain people will add coins to the donation (or at least participate directly by touching the conductor's coins). Other people will not participate at all. This practice at these shrines takes place both going and returning. The shrines that certain buses stop at or certain people stand for are, like "religious markings," tradition—specific: Buddhists will stop at (stand at) Buddhist temples and reliquaries; Christians at churches and roadside images; Hindus at kovils; Muslims at mosques.

At the very least, it is clear that the bus in Sri Lanka is a forum in which adherents to different religions, far from remaining invisible to each other, constitute their own presence. If the journey is long enough, one can usually determine who is Buddhist, who is Hindu, who is Muslim and who is Christian; as for the owner of the bus and/or the driver and conductor, this is evident from the very beginning. But the religious markings, like the rituals of travel, are not as static as they may at first seem. They constitute languages in which a variety of statements can be made. As a result, there is not always a one-to-one relationship between a person's own religion and the pictures s/he employs or the places s/he stands.

Collingwood has argued that meetings among humans are seldom entirely "dialectical" (aimed at compromise, tolerance, co-existence) just as they are seldom entirely "eristical" (aimed at confrontation in which one party secures the obliteration of the other). Instead, he suggested, human relationships tend to be somewhere in between: more or less dialectical, more or less eristical. This analysis is helpful in understanding the range of statements that can be made in the language of religious markings and rituals of travel. Markings range between exclusivist (only the Buddha, or only the Virgin) and inclusivist (Buddhists who also portray Jesus or Mecca; the "Hindu" deities, with all their openness and multivalence described above, are also often present in Buddhist buses); they can be confrontational (like the popular Muslim bumper sticker/painted phrase "Read Koran: Your Last Testament") or harmonizing ("Protection of the Deity/ies!" [*devi pihitayi*], ambiguous enough to refer to any of the four religions). Likewise, some Buddhist men and women may stand only at Buddhist shrines while others may stand at the shrines of every religion (I once saw a lorry driver cross himself in front of the Vishnu image at the Buddhist Temple at Gatembe [the main focus for Buddhist rituals of travel along the Kandy-Colombo Road]). Moreover, single individuals will worship roadside shrines differently depending upon differing circumstances.[22] Some Hindus, for example, might make a point of joining the Buddhists in standing at Buddhist shrines during periods of Buddhist chauvinist attacks on the Hindu population (Hindus may likewise change body ornamentation and other marks of their ethno-religious identity [even their personal names] during such periods of danger). A modernist who does not usually pay tribute at such shrines might do so if riding with someone to whom these practices are especially important.

Whether confronting or conforming, or something in between, the bus is one field in which multireligion can occur. I suggested at the beginning that the location of my own confrontation with that fundamentalist Christian was not coincidental because I recognize that the bus in Sri Lanka is always charged multireligiously, a space made likely for religious meetings by the markings and rituals associated with it. This begs the question, why the bus?

There certainly are precedents, in all the Sri Lankan religious traditions, for making journeying a religious affair. Pilgrimage is an important dynamic in all four religions, and pilgrimages in their own ways involve religious rituals and markings.[23] More generally, all the traditions associate certain dangers with travel: the dangers of entering foreign lands, of leaving the domains that are protected by one's chosen deity, of encountering malefic forces like the evil eye. Quite apart from these somewhat abstract dangers, travel in modern Sri Lanka is dangerous in very real ways. Numerous atrocities — landmines, massacres — against bus passengers of all traditions and by adherents to all traditions have been committed in the wake of the several civil wars fought in Sri Lanka over the last decade. Even in times of comparative peace, over-crowded buses speeding along narrow winding roads spell disaster, especially given the kamikaze tactics of professional drivers. It is not at all uncommon for the people hanging onto the windows and standing on the baseboard to fly out into traffic when the driver slams on the brakes; people are regularly trampled on buses and in bus queues; rides can be one breath-takingly close call after another. During 1990—1991 upwards of twenty buses and vans fell off cliffs taking turns too quickly or meeting an oncoming driver who refused to chicken out; hundreds of lives were lost. Both abstractly and concretely, riding the bus is a dangerous activity in Sri Lanka; these problems of course are compounded for female passengers who must contend with forms of sexual abuse from unruly male passengers.

The danger, as well as the tradition of making journeys religious affairs, inspires people to protect themselves while journeying. Pre-journey rites of protection – vows to deities, prayers to saints, acquisition of amulets, chanting (Buddhist) *pirit* or (Hindu) *mantras* or (Christian and Muslim) benedictions – are common, and apparently have old roots. When we start to examine the specific shrines at which passengers stand or make offerings, it becomes clear that for adherents they constitute especially auspicious locations for travellers to access divine protection.[24] Thus the language of religious marking and rituals of travel is employed to say more than "I am Muslim" or "I am Buddhist" (or "I am a Christian who respects this Hindu deity," or, when the picture is of a beauty queen or Michael Jackson, "I am not religious"); it is employed to say "I recognize (or deny) the power of this deity/ place/structure to keep us safe on this journey"; it enacts religious belief.

So multireligion on the bus in Sri Lanka has roots in the pilgrimage practices of all four religions, and the adherents to those religions
root their multireligious practices in them by supplying tradition—
specific content to the shared forms. Yet the degree of continuity should
not be overemphasized. The shrines in question are distinctly modern
(the two most famous traveller—protecting Buddhist temples, Gatembe
on the Kandy-Colombo Road and Kalutara Dagaba along the Southwest
Coast [the Galle Road] were constructed in the 1960's and 1970's) and
so are these specific practices. Public transportation was a British innovation, and the advent of the privately—owned buses and vans (that are especially noteworthy in terms of religious marking) is post—1977 (the
ascendance of the current, capitalist, government). We cannot point to
evidence that the practice of religious marking of public vehicles or these
particular rituals of travel (enacted on journeys that are not, technically
speaking, pilgrimages) have any pre—modern roots. Nor can we point to
one tradition as "first" or "original" (precluding any possibility of treating
these practices as "syncretic" or the result of one tradition's "influence" on
another).

The dangers associated with travel help us to understand why
the bus should become a multireligious field, but it cannot serve as a
complete explanation because there are other multireligious fields in
modern Sri Lanka which do not entail protection from danger. The same
practice of religious marking, and some of the associated rituals — with
the same range of possible "statements" —is equally ubiquitous among
shop—keepers, whose shrines invoke the chosen deity's blessings for
prosperity rather than protection. The shop (*kade*) is, in rural and urban
settings alike, an important multireligious meeting place; marked multireligiously, it becomes a forum for multireligious dialogue and debate.
Likewise two pilgrimage sites—Sri Pada in the central highlands and
Kataragama in the southeast — have become multi—religious fields in
the same manner as the bus, where all four traditions share a single form
(pilgrimage) with tradition—specific content. Sri Pada is an ancient site
of pilgrimage, dating at least to the 10th century, A.D. Buddhists maintain that the enormous footprint shaped indentation at the top of this
mountain is that of the Buddha, implanted during one of his mythical
visits to Sri Lanka.[25] Hindus say it is Vishnu's footprint.[26] Christians
maintain that it belongs to Saint Thomas the Apostle. Muslims maintain

that it is the footprint of Adam.[27] The deity at Kataragama is icono-graphically Hindu, namely the war god Skanda/Murugan, son of Shiva and Parvati, brother of Ganesha. But he is conceived by Buddhists (who clearly outnumber Hindu pilgrims at the site, especially over the last dec-ade) as a Buddhist deity, and his worship is part of a larger cycle of Buddhist pilgrimage to Buddhist shrines and stupas at Kataragama plus Tissamaharama, Kirinda, Dikwella, Matara and Kushtarajagala near Weligama. Christians will also make vows to this powerful deity; there is a mosque within the sacred part of the city. It is a most remarkable mul-tireligious spectacle to see Buddhist pilgrims dressed in Shaiva garb per-forming Shaiva austerities while dancing frenetically at the mosque, then sitting for a sermon by a Buddhist monk at the foot of austere Kiri Vehe-ra, The multireligious contestation over these shared spaces bears great similarity to practices on the bus (and in the shop) — these pilgrimages become a language for the broad range of sentiments between exclusiv-ism and inclusivism, confrontation and compromise — even though they do not participate in the dangers of the road.

Airwaves constitute another example of the way that certain shared spaces become charged as multireligious fields even in the absence of a danger for religion to respond to. All four traditions sponsor radio and television shows; more intrusively, they employ P.A. systems in loud and sometimes all–night battles for hegemony over the airspace in cer-tain multireligious cities like Kandy. Muslim calls to prayer, Buddhist *pi-rit* chanting, Christian sermons, and Hindu *mantras* can co–exist in a wild cacophony of sacred words, each religion increasing the volume as the others do the same. This "loudspeaker religion" (which has not been received happily by all segments)[28] has no roots in the four traditions (loudspeakers are a recent import) even though it has been rooted in the practices of chanting sacred words that have developed in all of them.

It is clear that certain parts of cities, too, have been constituted as multireligious fields. Single street corners in Colombo sport Hindu ko-vils, Buddhist temples, Christian churches and Muslim mosques; throughout the country there are places where religious edifices have been constructed, obviously as conscious statements, opposite edifices constructed by adherents to other traditions.[29]

The list of multireligious fields known in contemporary and his-torical Sri Lanka can be extended much further. The placement of images in temples (as in the case of Vishnu [see above]), social service organization and ideology (as in the case of nineteenth century "meetings" among Buddhists and Christians [and Hindus and Muslims]; the nineteenth and early twentieth centuries left as active social organizations the Y.M.C.A., Y.M.B.A., Y.M.H.A. and Y.M.M.A.), philosophical or theological doctrines (e.g., the contested meaning of *dharma*, used by Hindus to refer to divinely–ordained duty, by Buddhists to designate [among other things, such as the constituent elements of reality] the teachings of the Buddha and, in the Sinhala New Testament, as a translation of "Logos"),[30] diplomatic meetings (e.g., the seventh–ninth century conferences of Sri Lankan and South Indian kings in which the monarchs would adjudicate "inter–religious dialogues" and debates among Shaiva *sadhus*, Jain ascetics and Buddhist monks) and holidays (there is an ongoing battle between Sunday and the full moon day as official "days of rest" in Sri Lanka,[31] where the entire yearly calendar can be seen as a multireligious field involving dialectical as well as eristical views on which days are "holy" and why) are all charged as multireligious fields in Sri Lanka.

Concluding Remarks

A catalogue of multireligious fields only scratches the surface. In each of these fields, over time, adherents to different religions have come together in a variety of ways that have had important implications for their self–identities as well as their inter–relationships. A study of the history of religions in Sri Lanka that focuses upon these multireligious fields will be more holistic than the studies of individual traditions which scholars to date have produced. We can see that the history of religions in Sri Lanka is more than an internal development of particular religious outlooks; it is the connected history of an entire society.

I suspect that Sri Lanka is not unique in this regard. Multireligious fields have been constituted wherever and whenever adherents of different religions share common space. In my view, the entire history of religions can be viewed more holistically once we begin to see the degree to which religious meetings have characterized that entire history, once we undertake serious historical study of multireligion. As a counterpart to the history of religion's myth that individual religions have remained cultural isolates, historians of religions have often characterized the nine-

teenth and twentieth centuries as the time in which religions first became globally aware of each other. The doubt I have cast upon the isolation of individual religions in history casts doubt upon the view that we
are living in a unique "age of discovery." Our own attempts at constituting
multireligious fields — formal contexts for the meeting of religions including ecumenical conferences ("Interfaith Dialogue") and scholarly discourses ("Comparative Religions") — are far from unique; they are
merely the newest forms produced out of a very old tendency among religious people to confront, challenge, harmonize and/or oppose religious
others.

Notes

1   Sri Lanka had diplomatic and economic relations with Rome as early as the first
     century, A.D.(for cites in Pliny and epigraphic sources see H. Ellawala, *Social History
     of Early Ceylon* [Colombo: Dept. of Cultural Affairs, 1969] p.136; cf. W. Rahula,
     History of Buddhism in Ceylon [Colombo: Gunasena, 1956] pp.144-5), and the
     Church Fathers possessed and disseminated some knowledge about Buddhism (for
     a review of the early Christian sources see David Scott, "Christian Responses to
     Buddhism in Pre-medieval Times," *Numen*, 32, I [July, 1985], pp. 88-100). Physical
     evidence of Nestorian Christianity in Anuradhapura has been unearthed (a large
     Nestorian Cross carved of stone in Anuradhapura style is on display at the National
     Museum, Anuradhapura). There already exists an extensive discourse on the rela-
     tionship of Buddhism to early Christianity (and other "Western" movements includ-
     ing Manichaeianism and Gnosticism), focused upon essentialized "ideas" rather than
     historical contexts, which seems to have burned itself out arguing about "who influ-
     enced whom," with each side accusing the other of exaggerating the evidence (for one
     view, with a review of other scholarship on this subject, see E. Conze, "Buddhism
     and Gnosis" in Ugo Bianchi, (ed.), *The Origins of Gnosticism: Colloquium of Messina,
     13-18 April 1966* [Leiden: E.J.Brill, 1970], pp. 651 ff). In my view it is largely the
     formulation of the problem as one concerning "influence" that accounts for the in-
     conclusiveness and unproductiveness of this discourse. The evidence needs to be re-
     examined with a view toward human agency; if we can begin to understand early
     Christians and their contemporary Buddhists as co-participants in certain multireli-
     gious fields (as defined below) we can start asking questions about the degree of co-
     participation in different areas and among different groups; the types of "meetings"
     that occurred among Buddhists and Christians; the manner in which ideas (or sto-
     ries, or cultural styles, or disciplinary codes, or types of experience) were rendered
     appropriable (and/or opposed), the political implications of appropriation and/or
     opposition.

2   E.g., Richard Gombrich and Gananath Obeyesekere, *Buddhism Transformed: Religious Change in Sri Lanka* (Princeton: Princeton University Press, 1988); Richard Gombrich, *Theravada Buddhism: A Social History from Ancient Benares to Modern Colombo* (London: Routledge, 1988); Kitsiri Malalgoda, *Buddhism in Sinhalese Society, 1750-1900* (Berkeley: University of California Press, 1976).

3   The classic critique of "religion" and "religions" is W. C. Smith, *The Meaning and End of Religion* (New York: Mentor, 1962). Unfortunately, Smith's prediction (p.175) that the term "religion" should become obsolete in serious speech and writing by 1987 has yet to materialize, and the book has had far too little impact among professional historians of religions. For a study of the Orientalist invention of "Buddhism" as "a religion" see Philip C. Almond, *The British Discovery of Buddhism* (Cambridge: Cambridge University Press, 1988).

4   My philosophy of history has developed very much out of my readings of the works of R. G. Collingwood, who stood alone at Oxford (against the Positivists) as an extender of the work of B. Croce in English historiography. I consider him the great systematic philosopher of our century and rely, implicitly and explicitly, on Collingwood's ideas and inspiration throughout this and much of my work. On the problem of mutually-exclusive categories in historical thought see R. G. Collingwood, *An Essay on Philosophical Method* (Oxford: Clarendon, 1933), "Chapter Two: The Overlap of Classes," pp.26-53.

5   On the scale of forms in historical thought see *Philosophical Method*, "Chapter Three: The Scale of Forms," pp.54-91.

6   See the *Oxford English Dictionary*, s.v. "Influence" may be one of the most widely-applied and presupposed analytic tools in the Social Sciences and Humanities, yet to my knowledge it has not been subjected to even the most basic scholarly scrutiny. (For a very preliminary critique see Smith, *Meaning and End*, p.83). I was made aware of the problems involved with "influence" in historical discourse by Ronald Inden in the *Seminar on Text and Knowledge in South Asia* at the University of Chicago, and the present discussion is little more than an attempt to state systematically what he forces all his students to grasp about "influence." Yet I still catch myself falling into the easy closing of questions that an appeal to "influence" effects, and I caution to state that readers who start looking at the way they use it, and the way it is used in the scholarship (or pulp journalism) they read, will be amazed at how deeply this magical and rather empty idea has pervaded the very structures of our thought.

7   *Oxford English Dictionary*.

8   See Carston Colpe, "Syncretism" in Mircea Eliade, ed., *Encyclopedia of Religion* 14 (Macmillan, 1988), p.218; cf. *Oxford English Dictionary*, s.v.

9   Colpe, pp.218-219; *Oxford English Dictionary*.

10   Colpe, p. 219.

11   Colpe, pp. 218-227.

12   Colpe, p.219.

13   A seminal collection of essays has been Heinz Bechert, (ed.), *Buddhism in Ceylon and Studies on Religious Syncretism in Buddhist Countries [Symposien zur Buddhismus-forschung, 1]* (Gottingen: Vandenhoeck & Ruprecht, 1976).

14   *Rethinking Buddhist Missions* (Ph.D. Diss, University of Chicago, 1992) esp. section 3.5 ("Buddhist Missions in Christian Discourse").

15   For a general overview of Buddhist thought about "God" and references to more extensive studies see my and Gunapala Dharmasiri's "God," *Encyclopedia of Buddhism*, 5:2 (1991). pp.345-47.

16   Dondra, Vishnu's "home" on the Island, apparently dates to about the 10th c. (See S. Paranavitana, *The Shrine of Upulvan at Devundara* [Oxford: Oxford University Press,1953]). *Culavamsa* of about the thirteenth century utilizes Vaishnava stories while criticizing the worship of Shiva.

17   The interested reader should see R. Inden, "Imperial Purana, Imperial Formation." forthcoming in *Post-Orientalist Approaches to the Study of South Asian Texts*, for an analysis of the very subtle, conscious *ways* in which leaders among the Rashtrakutas of the 8th-9th c. accorded Buddhism a place (however subordinate) within their Vaishnava imperial formation. The Sinhalas allied themselves, against the (Shaiva) Cholas, with the last Rashtrakuta emperor at about the time that the "Buddhist Vishnu" emerges in the historical record.

18   John C.Holt, *Buddha in the Crown: Avalokiteshvara in the Buddhist Traditions of Sri Lanka* (Oxford: Oxford University Press, 1990).

19   I have shown that Vibhishana was constituted as a divine homologue to the Sri Lankan rulers (of Gampola and Kotte) who submitted to Rama (equated during this period with the Vijayanagar Emperor); the cult of Vibhishana functioned literally as the constitution of Sri Lankan participation in the Vijayanagar Empire. See my "Vibhishana and Vijayanagar: An Essay on Religion and Geopolitics in Medieval Sri Lanka," in *The Sri Lanka Journal of the Humanities, Special Jubilee Edition (1994)*.

20   See *Philosophical Method*, "Chapter Four: Definition and Description," pp.92-103; cf. R. G. Collingwood, *An Autobiography* (Oxford: Clarendon, 1939), pp.53-88.

21   It is a great irony, in light of the fact that these are intended as protective practices (see below), that heavy traffic pulling on and off the shoulder at these shrines, or simply stopping in the middle of the road, constitute these shrines as among the most dangerous hazards on Sri Lanka's roads.

22   I am grateful to Malathi de Alwis for these insights.

23   On Hindu pilgrimage in Sri Lanka see Brian Pfaffenberger, "The Kataragama pilgrimage: Hindu–Buddhist interaction and its significance in Sri Lanka's polyethnic

social syslem," in *Journal of Asian Studies* 38 (1979), pp.253-70; on pilgrimage in Sinhala culture see John C. Holt, "Pilgrimage and the Structure of Sinhalese Buddhism," in *Journal of the International Association of Buddhist Studies* 5 (1982), pp.23–40; the Hajj is celebrated both by direct participation and simultaneous rituals back home; in recent years pilgrimage to the Christian Holy Land has developed into a major Sri Lankan industry as well.

24 Often, these shrines are associated with certain miracles said to have occurred at them, which indicate the protective presence of the deity(ies) residing in them or represented by them.

25 In the medieval period, Buddha footprints constituted a pan–Indic Buddhist phenomenon. Sri Lanka was said to possess another, at the bottom of the Kelaniya River in front of the Kelaniya Temple (cf. my *The History of Kelaniya* [Colombo: S.S.A., 1994]); other Buddha footprints were described in various parts of India by the Chinese pilgrims.

26 There is an on–going fight– which began to turn violent during 1991–1992 – over who placed the sacred footprint in Gaya/Bodh Gaya: the Buddha or Visnu? The iconography of both conceptions is virtually identical.

27 God, feeling sorry for Adam, set him down in Sri Lanka because it most resembled the Paradise from which he had been cast out.

28 During 1990–1991 several angry "Letters to the Editor" on this subject were published; it is a widespread topic for complaint among homeowners in Kandy.

29 A fine example is the Vidyalankara *Pirivena* (and Maha Bodhi Society), built directly opposite one of the most important nineteenth century Christian schools; this was a conscious challenge offered by the family of Anagarika Dharmapala. On the prominent display of saints' images as Christian counter–responses to the rise of Buddhist nationalism see R.L.Stirrat, *Power and Religiosity in a Post–Colonial Setting: Sinhala Catholics in contemporary Sri Lanka* (Cambridge: Cambridge University Press, 1992).

30 This multivalent use of "dharma" as a multi–religious (harmonizing) strategy is at least as old as the Ashokan inscriptions, 3rd c. B.C.

31 The current government's legislation prohibiting the sale of meat and alcohol–diet and drug choice is another multireligious field – on full moon days has been particularly vexing to Christians and Muslims. This has been a recent move in a veritable politics of meat, a situation in which meat choice functions as a multireligious field. Many Hindus eat no meat (or only chicken) on moral grounds, and the idea of eating beef is particularly abhorrent. Buddhists will, more often, eat meat (but as a rule they will not personally kill the animal, even if it is a chicken), although they too tend to avoid beef. Muslims on the other hand delight in eating great quantities of meat, including beef, except pork (which non—vegetarian Buddhists, on the other

hand, relish). Christians eat everything, which is made particularly public (and offensive) to practitioners of all the other religions for several days before Easter when, in order to tenderize their Easter hams, they fill the air with the squeals of pigs being beaten with sticks.

Unmooring Identity:
The Antinomies of Elite Muslim
Self-Representation in Modern Sri Lanka[1]

Qadri Ismail

"...the critique is by its very nature rather precocious, incomplete and generally endowed with all the immaturity of a thing in its formative stage. But it is this very want of maturity that drives the critique audaciously, if not prudently in every instance, to probe those fundamental contradictions of the existing system..."

—Ranajit Guha, 'Dominance Without Hegemony'

"...what political possibilities are the consequence of a radical critique of the categories of identity? What new shape of politics emerges when identity as a common ground no longer constrains the discourse...? And to what extent does the effort to locate identity as the foundation...[of] politics preclude a radical inquiry into the political construction and regulation of identity itself?"

—Judith Butler, *Gender Trouble*

Pretext

It was a bright and pleasant morning (as opposed, I suppose, to a dark and stormy night) the first time this paper— in an earlier and cruder version — was presented in Sri Lanka. Afterwards, a somewhat agitated young Sri Lankan Muslim asked: "Are you trying to take my identity away from me?" Yes, I instinctively wanted to reply. Instead, I said: No; what I would like you to do is think about the bases upon which this identity has been fashioned. And its consequences…

Introduction

How does one represent a social formation? As a seamless whole, or as a coalition of sometimes coincident, sometimes conflicting interests? As a real ("natural") entity or as a construct? Or, rather, should the question be: Why does one represent a social formation? What are the stakes involved, whose political interests are on the line, when one chooses to see a social formation as an undivided unity rather than a site of struggle or a problematic unity?

But, first, why the term "social formation," rather than those more popular within Sri Lankan identitarian discourse, "ethnic group" and "community"? The anthropological origins of the former, not to mention its racial connotations, make it suspect; and "community" is much too loose and misused a term to be useful. Both terms also smack too much of the ontological; and imply that its members have something natural in common. Whereas the term "social formation" draws attention to the socially constructed character of these identities. It is also, as Etienne Balibar reminds us, an old, if now underused Marxist term. He suggests we use it,

> to mean…a construction whose unity remains problematic, a configuration of antagonistic social classes that is not entirely autonomous, only becoming *relatively* specific in its opposition to others and via the power struggles, the conflicting interest groups and ideologies which are developed over the *longue duree* by this very antagonism.[2]

It is in this sense that the term (Muslim) social formation is deployed in this paper: to discuss a construct — as opposed to an ontological entity — whose unity is problematic; to examine the construction of that unity, of the stakes and antagonisms involved and of the many exclusions required to constitute and maintain it; to show that social formations are not stable entities but sites of struggle over which (interest) groups would achieve hegemony over the formation and thus determine the nature of its (dominant) identity. When deployed in this sense, the term allows one to point out the fissures and cracks within the Sri Lankan social formations, to see them as sites of unceasing struggle and to interrogate the class, gender and other interests involved and elided in the enunciation of an identitarian project. *It enables one, in short, not only to begin undoing the theoretical notions underpinning these constructs but also to ask what the consequences of such undoings may be and to imagine different forms of social organization.* This (anti-nationalist) task, I might add, is one of the more pressing that face the Sri Lankan left today. We have to expose the pretensions to commonality that undergird notions of community. For, it is difficult to find much emancipatory potential today, for all but a tiny elite, in any of the nationalist (identitarian) projects at work in the country.

This paper examines identity construction within the Sri Lankan Muslim social formation, to be precise within the Muslim elite, from the early years of this century to the late 1980s. I focus on the Muslim formation essentially for two reasons: out of a long-standing personal interest; and because of its arguably exemplary nature. Exemplary in both senses of the word. I hope the present work— intended as a beginning and an example—would provoke further undoings of identity formation in Sri Lanka; and that, by contributing to undoing the binary (Sinhala/Tamil) terms by which the "ethnic problem" has been constituted, by redefining the terms by which the "problem" is seen, would help enable new and better ways of conceiving "solutions."

For the purposes of this paper, I represent the Muslim social formation as consisting of two "distinct" groups, Southern and Eastern Muslims: "Southern" referring to the Muslims of the seven Sinhala dominated provinces, who form roughly two-thirds of the Muslim population of Sri Lanka; "Eastern," to those of the former Eastern Province. This distinction, as I hope will become clear later, isn't made on a purely geographic basis, though its geographics aren't entirely unimportant either. It is made for purely strategic reasons; the politics of which, I hope, become evident by the conclusion of the paper.[3] I focus on the Southern Muslim elite and its self-representation in modern Sri Lanka. I argue that this elite, of middle and upper class Southern Muslim men, represented the entire formation in its own image: as a peaceful trading community of Arab — as opposed to Tamil —origin, whose presence in Sri Lanka dates back to medieval times, and which has traditionally enjoyed good relations with the Sinhalese. I interpret this representation as resulting from the "rules" of Sri Lankan identitarian discourse, the Muslim elite's desire to safeguard its economic and other interests, as well as its fear of the forces of Sinhala nationalism and of the hegemonic Sinhala state.

This representation, like most representations of identity, is exclusive, being both gendered and classed.[4] It constitutes itself by excluding women, since trade is a practice virtually monopolized by men; and by excluding those Muslims, notably Easterners, who are not or do not see themselves as traders. This in turn raises a further set of questions: Are Southern and Eastern Muslims best seen as having substantial interests in common, as having antagonistic ones, or both? What consequences would arise from seeing Eastern Muslims as sharing more interests with Eastern Tamils than with Southern Muslims? What would be the consequences of arguing that Muslim women, since they suffer a patriarchal oppression comparable to that experienced by women in other Sri Lankan social formations, have more in common with other Sri Lankan women than with Muslim men? What these questions signify is that identities are always already overdetermined. That is to say, whenever an ethnic identity is being projected one can—must, if one is committed to undoing that project — always read in that projection class, gender and other interests which the identitarian would seek to elide.[5] That, in other words, the term "Muslim social formation" — like the Tamil and Sinhala — is an unstable one, since it hides and excludes more than it reveals or includes. To put all that somewhat differently, identity is about hegemony —not "community."[6] The Muslim social formation, therefore, is read here as an ideological construct signifying the hegemony of the (Southern, male, bourgeois, trader, etc.) Muslim elite. This is not to argue that a social formation is reducible to the interests of the elite that enjoys hegemony over it. Such hegemony is successful only because, at least at certain moments—notably when the formation is, or sees itself as being, under threat (certain) interests of subordinated groups within the formation coincide, or are seen to coincide, with the interests of the elite. Without this co—incidence, the ideological sway of the elite cannot hold.

This paper also examines changes in the categorization of Muslim identity. I argue that the Sri Lankan Muslim social formation "lost" its ethnicity in the post–colonial period; or, to be precise, "lost" its racial/ethnic identity. A loss to be noticed not on an ontological register but within the terms of Sri Lankan identitarian discourse. Once upon a time, from about the early 20th century till well into the post–colonial period, the Muslim formation was seen to have a distinct racial ("Moor") as well as religious identity; as the term "race" slipped out of identitarian discourse, it came to be seen as an ethnic group (also "Moor"); today, it is seen to have an exclusively religious identity. The importance of all this cannot be emphasized enough and not only to students of identity politics. For it points to the fact that *identities cannot be taken for granted; that they are fluid, transient, always in flux, never permanent; and that they alter (discursively) precisely because they are constructs. If they were "real" stable and eternal, they couldn't change.*

Before getting to the substance of the argument, a few words are necessary on terminology. I follow current usage and call the subject/s of this paper Muslim. I do not seek to contend thereby, or even imply, that the Muslims are in fact a religious formation: "I shall accept the groupings that history suggests only to subject them at once to interrogation"[7] Nevertheless I am also aware that by using the term one does lend credence to the construct; as Spivak argues, it "is impossible...to mark off a group as an entity without sharing complicity with its ideological definition" (GS:118). I use the term for want of a better option.

The terms "racial" and "ethnic" are sometimes used interchangeably in this paper. This is not done to negate the substantive distinction between the two; where relevant the distinction is called attention to. But, since they inhabit the same continuum, in both chronological and imaginary terms, they are occasionally conflated. I do this because the two terms possess a discursive unity (and not necessarily only in the Sri Lankan context) because, as Balibar suggests, the idea of the race always lurks beneath the idea of the ethnic group.[8] (The evidence of this in relation to the Sri Lankan Muslim instance will become clearer in the course of this paper). The term elite is deployed in the same, admittedly somewhat loose but nevertheless useful sense suggested by the Subaltern Studies Collective: it refers to the dominant group —

seen in class, gender and regional terms within the Muslim social formation.[9]

One last remark about methodology. What follows is an examination of discursive self–representation by the Muslim elite. Therefore this study is restricted to a discussion of written texts mostly produced in English, the language that marks the Sri Lankan elite in general. Such an approach seeks not merely to justify my academic training, but also to demonstrate that such a training can be useful in examining phenomena not generally considered, at least in this country, the turf of a literary critic.

Sri Lankan identitarian discourse: A note

A detailed examination of the terms used (over time) in discussions of identitarian politics in Sri Lanka is a pressing necessity; in and of itself and also because most Sri Lankan scholars — Kumari Jayawardena and Leslie Gunawardana come to mind as admirable exceptions to this general rule — are not in the habit of interrogating categories.[10] Such an examination would ask at least the following questions: Who or what do the terms race, nation, community, ethnic group, represent? Who/what do they elide? Where do they come from?[11] What do they do once they arrive? What function/s have they served within Sri Lankan identitarian discourse? How about "majority" and "minority," which many consider to be value neutral, if not purely mathematical, demographic terms without consequence. *If it is correct that, upto the early 20th century, "the Tamils...were not regarded as a minority community, but were treated as one of two majority groups,"*[12] *when and why did the Tamils attain minority status?* Why does the phrase "Sinhala, Tamil and Muslim" sound "natural"? How does it happen that, when the Sri Lankan social formations are mentioned, the dominant one ("majority") is almost always mentioned first? What is the place of the Tamil social formation within this discourse? Of the Up–Country Tamils, who until recently were not even considered Sri Lankan? Of the Veddas, relegated to the margins of the nation? How and why did the distinction between "Indian" and "Sri Lankan" Tamils come to be instituted and maintained? Whose interests were at stake here? Why are "Colombo" Tamils — seen as distinct from "Northeastern" Tamils and often victims of the pogroms of the Sinhala state

— discursively erased when the ethnic problem is discussed? Why are the many pogroms of the Sinhala state against Tamil life and property represented as (spontaneous) riots?

In what ways are this discourse gendered? Take the distinction often made between "nationalism" and "chauvinism." The logic underlying this usage is that nationalism is good — for "us"; and chauvinism bad — for "them." This usage is patriarchal, since it elides the many ways in which the nationalist project suppresses/ subordinates women. For instance, why is it that paternal identity is taken to be the exclusive marker of identity for the Sri Lankan subject? Why is a person considered Tamil if her/his father is considered Tamil, regardless of the identity of the mother?[13] How is it that certain interests and crises peculiar to (a certain class of) men have been allowed to pass, within this discourse, as pertaining to the "whole nation"? In other words, nationalism can only be seen as (unreservedly) good from a masculist perspective.[14]

I lack the time and space to discuss these and other questions here. However, a working definition of "Sri Lankan identitarian discourse" is necessary for the development of my argument. A discourse, or to be precise a discursive formation, is a regulatory device; it includes and excludes — includes by excluding — follows ascertainable rules in the constitution of subjects and objects, has a certain (not absolute) internal coherence.[15] It is not necessarily static over time, nor necessarily without its contradictions. A discourse is also a site of struggle over the constitution of subjects (and objects) within it. Thus Sri Lankan identitarian discourse would encompass many positions ("discursive events" within Foucault's terminology): the Jathika Chinthanaya ("National Ideology") position that there is no ethnic/Tamil/minority "problem" in Sri Lanka, other Sinhala nationalist positions, liberal positions which insist that Sri Lanka is a multi-ethnic country and the Tamil separatist ones.[16] This list, of course, is not inclusive and all these positions are not equal. Another way of saying this is that Sri Lankan identitarian discourse is dominated by Sinhala nationalist positions; but it is an uneasy dominance, one constantly under challenge.

My main concern here is not with Sri Lankan identitarian discourse in general as with a few of its rules: how it constitutes ("ethnic") subjects, what markers it allows and disallows in this process. As we know, Sinhala nationalist forces have dominated the Sri Lankan state and followed a quasi-genocidal policy to-wards non-accommodative sec-tions of the Tamil social formation in the post-colonial period; this has been resisted by nationalist and other sections of the Tamil social forma-tion. In the course of this often violent process, during which the Muslim elite aligned itself with the Sinhala state, the contours of Sri Lankan identitarian discourse were defined.[17] In other words, how the Tamil and Sinhalese elites defined/represented their own social formations (con-structed their identities) determined the markers of identitarian differ-ence in Sri Lanka. When Sinhala/Tamil difference was seen as racial, "blood" was represented as the chief (though not exclusive) marker of that difference; when the difference was represented as ethnic, language — an ostensibly transparent term, unlike "blood" — became the chief marker.[18] It was only within these terms/boundaries, ones already de-termined, that the Muslim elite could construct an identity for itself in the (post)colonial period. (In the colonial period, as I discuss later, the terms were determined largely by the British colonial state.) All this is not to negate elite Muslim agency; but, rather, to point to it being cir-cumscribed by the more assertive forces of Sinhala and Tamil national-ism.

I now consider two texts, produced by the International Centre for Ethnic Studies (ICES) and liberal in their logic, on "Tamil–Muslim riots" that illustrate the way Muslims are represented within Sri Lankan identitarian discourse. They not only reinforce this representation (if not suppression), but do so in ways that raise crucial questions about the in-adequacies of the liberal argument in general. ICES has sponsored two reports on clashes between Tamils and Muslims in the East, where civi-lians on both sides have been agents and victims of violence. The first, written by Frank Jayasinghe with the assistance of Nigel Hatch, investi-gated "the events that took place at Karaitivu" in April 1985[19] Jayasinghe says that he investigated these "events" (nice, neutral word) at the behest of a "group of concerned citizens [who] felt that it...[was] important to constitute independent commissions of inquiry *involving persons belong-ing to groups not implicated in the violence*" (FJ: 1, emphasis added). The logic here, that no Muslim or Tamil could be considered objective, as well as the belief in "objectivity" itself, is a classic component of liberalism. Nevertheless, Jayasinghe couldn't have been chosen merely because of his Sinhalese name; he was presumably considered capable of objectivity.

But another liberal notion — based upon a belief in the rule of law — informs this choice: that justice must also be seen to be done. Thus the exclusion of Tamils and Muslims from these "commissions." The same logic was followed by the next ICES expedition to the East, nine years later, by Shantha Pieris and Jeanne Marecek.[20]

In an appendix to his report, Jayasinghe recounts the narratives of six victims of the violence — all Tamil. "[V]ery regrettably," he explained, "our contacts with members of the Muslim community around Karaitivu were limited" (FJ:15). In other words, he didn't bother to find and interview Muslim victims — despite the desire to appear objective. Why this happened becomes easier to establish if one reads FJ with the Pieris/Marecek report. SP, too, reproduces (16) survivor narratives. It, too, fails to include a single Muslim narrative (despite, this time, interviewing several Muslim villagers). These exclusions are not accidental but point to the denial of subjectivity to Muslims (even) within (the ostensibly inclusive liberal) Sri Lankan identitarian discourse.[21] A passage in the second report makes this clear. Arguing that such "events" will end only if the "ethnic problem" is solved, the report finds that such a solution would require:

> ...political will on the part of the recognized leaders of the respective ethnic communities to meet the legitimate aspirations of the Tamil people. The grievances of the Tamil people should be met and redressed without jeopardizing the legitimate interests of all the other communities (SP:36).

The paternalism of this passage shouldn't hinder us here. What should be noted is that in this representation, while one social formation, *named as Tamil*, is said to have "legitimate aspirations" and "grievances," others, *unnamed* but presumably including the Muslims, have mere "interests" (though also legitimate).[22] The ethical — not merely semantic — difference between a "grievance" and an "interest" signifies a hierarchization of oppression (and provides further proof of the subordinate status Muslims occupy within Sri Lankan identitarian discourse). This hierarchization, this entire instance, helps illustrate the difficulty the Muslim elite has had in its attempt to intervene and assert an ethnic identity for itself within the terms of this discourse.[23]

However, as hinted at earlier, the Muslim social formation cannot only be seen as a passive victim of a discourse over which it has no control; the politics of its elite have contributed to its subordinate position too. The accomodationist politics the Muslim elite followed with respect to the Sinhala state have not only reinforced this position of subordination but also contributed to the elite's (eventual) lack of success in asserting a racial/ethnic identity for the social formation.

I conclude this section by briefly mentioning two recent collections of articles on the Muslims, published by Muslim organizations, which illustrate both the gendered nature and concerns of the Muslim elite and its accomodationist politics. The first, a typical elite Muslim text, is the product of a conference sponsored by the Naleemiah Institute of Islamic Research.[24] Since this conference is one of the few held in Sri Lanka to discuss exclusively Muslim issues, its focus is most revealing. Of the 19 papers in the book, only one (by a Sinhalese !) examines post—colonial Muslim politics. Indeed, the title says it all: "Avenues to Antiquity"; backward, not forward looking; anxious to establish the Muslim presence in Sri Lanka as ancient — but reluctant, in typical elite Muslim fashion, to face the contemporary turmoil that produces this anxiety. Predictably enough, none of the essays address women's issues (except tangentially, and from a patriarchal perspective, with reference to the law). A more recent collection of the Muslim Women's Research and Action Front takes the opposite stance.[25] Faizun Zackariya states in its introduction:

> The main objective of the workshop [that led to the book] was to organize the community around specific issues so as to bring about changes in a conscious way (CC:i).

The emphasis in this text is not just on the present, but on understanding it in order to change it. Of course, it isn't accidental that a feminist organization would have invested more in the future than in the past.

Ethnic or religious formation:
Who, What, Why are the Muslims?

"Led on by our shepherds, we have only once kept pace with li-
berty and that was on the day of its interment."

—Karl Marx

From the late 19th century onwards, the Muslim elite represented the entire social formation as a distinct "race" of Arab origin; distinct, one must repeat, from the Tamil?[26] While the term race was an
accepted part of Sri Lankan identitarian discourse this was somewhat
easy to establish. As the term slipped out of Sri Lankan identitarian discourse in the post–colonial period, to be replaced by "ethnic group," the
dominant marker of which was seen to be language, it became increasingly difficult to maintain, leave alone establish, such a Muslim identity
not based upon a notion of the religious. Eventually, these attempts not
only failed but were given up.

If it is true, though, that the Muslim social formation "lost" its
(always unstable) ethnic identity recently, the question arises: when was
it acquired in the first place? We know now that "racial," ethnic and national identities are distinctly modern constructs, not ancient phenomena. Nevertheless, *trying to place an exact date on when a group of people
acquired a certain identity is a futile endeavor. Identities do not suddenly
emerge and proclaim themselves; they evolve, slowly.* But, with hindsight, or
at least because one must begin somewhere, one could point to certain
dates/ moments/events that were crucial to the emergence of such identities. With respect to the Sri Lankan Muslim social formation, one such
date is 1883. Other dates can no doubt be found—I use 1883 partly out
of convenience. In that year the British colonial power exiled Arabi Pasha, an Egyptian nationalist, to Sri Lanka. By then, religious revivalist
movements among the more politicized sectors of the (Sinhalese) Buddhist and (Tamil) Hindu bourgeoisies had been active for many years.
Three centuries of colonial rule by Christian imperialist powers had
weakened organized Buddhism (and Hinduism); significant numbers of
upper class/caste Sinhalese and Tamils had converted to Christianity in
this period. For these and other reasons, emergent nationalist forces in

these two social formations initially mobilized around religion.[27] By the time Pasha arrived in Colombo, a similar ("religious") consciousness was emerging within sections of the nascent Muslim elite too.

Vijaya Samaraweera has argued that Arabi Pasha wasn't so much the initiator as the inspiration, "the catalyst, the symbol around which the [newly activist] Muslims could gather."[28] Inspired by his example, by the Buddhist and Hindu revivalist movements and by what some called the "backwardness" of their community, members of the nascent Muslim elite were becoming politically active.[29] Pasha's impact on the Muslim elite can be seen, for instance, in the fact that, after his arrival and example, (male) members of the elite began to publicly sport the fez—to symbolize their Arab/Muslimness — and thus assert their difference from other Sri Lankans. Five years after Pasha's arrival, in 1888, the Muslim elite made the first public claims about its distinct identity and Arab origin. Ponnambalam Ramanathan was then the British–appointed representative of the "Tamil–speaking minorities" (including the Muslims) in the Legislative Council. Ramanathan claimed, before the Ceylon Branch of the Royal Asiatic Society, that the "Ceylon Moors" were in fact "ethnologically" Tamil:

> Taking (1) the language they speak at home in connection with (2) their history, (3) their customs and (4) physical features, the proof cumulatively leads to no other conclusion than that the Moors of Ceylon are ethnologically Tamils.[30]

At this time, the colonial administration was debating an increase in the number of native representatives it nominated to the Legislative Council. Representation was based on the identitarian differences that the British saw fit to recognize. Among the new seats under consideration was one for the Muslims. The nascent Muslim elite sensed in this the possibility of a nomination for one of their own. Some of them also suspected that Ramanathan's paper, which followed an 1885 speech along the same lines to the Council, was aimed at preventing such a nomination. As things turned out, the British administration was not persuaded by Ramanathan.[31] They created a "Mohammedan"—the early colonial term for "Muslim"—seat and appointed M.C. Abdul Rahman, an upper class trader.[32] There did exist a few educated, more politically active Muslims who also desired the seat. But theBritish state, presumably motivated by the desire to further secure its own interests under the guise of increased representation- divide and role, if you will — appointed a mercantile capitalist. British colonial appointees after Rahman also came from the wealthier, more prominent, largely Colombo–based members of this trading class. Consequent to the actions of the British colonial state, the Southern male trader elite was able to secure a power base for itself: to represent Rahman and his successors as Muslim "leaders" and eventually be in a position to establish its hegemony over the whole social formation.[33]

One can only speculate on what might have happened if the colonial power decided to see the Muslims as Tamil. What needs emphasis is that, by institutionalizing Muslim difference, the British, in a crucial sense, helped "create" Muslim identity.[34] One therefore disagrees with Benedict Anderson's claim, which could be termed counter-factual, that the "real innovation of the [colonial] census–takers was…not in the *construction* of ethnic–racial classifications, but rather in their systematic *quantification*."[35] For, most significantly, the term the Muslim social formation came to refer to itself in the early modern period, "Moor," is of a purely colonial (Portuguese) derivation and construction.

Ramanathan's speech is also significant for other reasons. His contentions were eventually rebutted by I.L.M. Abdul Azeez, arguably the leading Sri Lankan Muslim ideologue of the time.[36] Azeez was President of the Moors' Union, an organization he founded in 1900 and which published his rebuttal in 1907.[37] The existence of an organization with such a name alone points to the fact of rising "racial" consciousness at the time among at least the Muslim elite. Azeez's rebuttal is a product of this consciousness, which he also attempts to articulate and consolidate. Race being the category of difference at this stage, Azeez's arguments are replete with reference to the "Arab blood" of the forefathers of the Moors.[38] But it was no ordinary "Arab blood" that ran in Sri Lankan Muslim veins. Just as much as most Sinhala and Tamil nationalists claimed grand racial antecedents ("Aryan" and "Dravidian," respectively)[39] for their social formations, Azeez would do the same for the Moors:

> [The] ancestors [of the Moors] came from Arabia pursuing commerce…[to] the place where their primitive father, Adam, was [exiled by God]…Its seaports were the centres of trade vi-

sited by...Arab merchants...Most of the ancestors of the Ceylon Moors were, according to tradition, members of the family of Hashim...less war–like and given to the peaceful pursuit of trade...At such a critical moment [when they were being persecuted at home] what other country could have been more attractive to them, as a place of refuge, than Ceylon...?[40]

Azeez makes many moves in this passage. He represents the Muslim presence in Sri Lanka as originating from a conscious migration to a place of symbolic importance to all Muslims.[41] This move is necessary for Azeez to rebut the contentions of the more rabidly nationalist Sinhala ideologues that Muslims were alien to Sri Lanka. For instance Anagarika Dharmapala, by far the most bigoted Sinhala ideologue of the time, had accused Muslim "aliens...[of] taking away the wealth of the country."[42] One can see Azeez's dilemma: he must represent the origin of the "Moors" as Arab ("foreign") in order to distinguish the formation from the Tamil; but, in response to the Sinhala nationalists, he must also invent a Muslim "right" to be in Sri Lanka (as native, not-foreign). Thus the claim of a conscious, peaceful migration and the association with Adam's Peak: it serves to legitimize the Muslim presence in Sri Lanka as somehow native, given the importance of the Peak to all Muslims[43] It also gives the group a glorious mythic origin, made even more impressive by Azeez's claim that the first migrants were Hashimites, of the tribe of the prophet: the best possible ancestry any group of Muslims could have, short of being direct descendants of Muhammad himself.[44]

Two other points must be noted about this contention. The first concerns its gendered nature. Azeez claims that only Arab men came to Sri Lanka and that they "took Tamil wives" (IL:36).

Logically, this would make the Moors "racially" mixed, a possibility that doesn't occur to Azeez, who represents women as simply reproducing the nation on behalf of men, as conduits without the power to mark. In other words, only the paternal marker of identity is allowed: an Arab masculinity is emphasized, and a Tamil femininity denied, in the originary construction of Sri Lankan Muslim identity. Put differently, it would appear that Arab men gave birth, by themselves, to the Sri Lankan Muslim social formation.[45] Both the inclusive and exclusive aspects of this representation are important: the denial of a Tamil component is required not only to emphasize the Arab "blood" of Muslims but also to enhance Azeez's claim that the Moors are racially distinct from the Tamils.[46] The second point to be noted about Azeez gets to the crux of the argument in this section. *He is blissfully ignorant of the contradiction at the heart of that passage: of seeking religious legitimacy (Hashimite) for a racial identity (Moor). In other words, a tension can be seen between the religious and the ethnic/racial in even the earliest elite Muslim attempts to construct and maintain a distinct identity for the social formation. The Muslim elite, it would appear, was never quite certain what it was.*

This uncertainty was made even worse by the fact that the Muslims were not seen to have "their own" language, at the time a secondary marker of race. This perturbed Azeez, especially since the Muslims spoke Tamil. He explained this away by claiming that Tamil wasn't the Muslims' "national language," but "a borrowed one" (IL:11); that the ancestors of the Muslims, who settled amongst the Tamils and took Tamil wives, came to speak Tamil in very much the same fashion that the "Parsees of India...speak...Gujarati" (IL:14). What one sees here, a move again consistent with the denial of a Tamil femininity in the construction of Muslim identity, is a refusal to accord the status of Mother Tongue to the tongue of the mother. Azeez could get away with placing less emphasis on the question of language, compared to that of "blood," because at this stage the category of difference within Sri Lankan identitarian discourse was "race." Recall that Denham, who was to theorize this question a few years after Azeez, believed the races of Sri Lanka were easily distinguishable, that language was just one among many markers of such difference. Denham — as metonym now for the British colonial state— can help answer one *of the most crucial questions pertaining to Muslim identity in modern Sri Lanka: why, in a country whose recent history is replete with small groups assimilating into larger ones, did the Muslims not assimilate into the Tamil social formation?*[47] Clearly, (elite) Muslims resisted assimilation, just as much as some sections of the Tamil elite encouraged it.[48] But one must also recognize that the Muslim assertion of difference *may not* have been successful without the role of the British colonial power which recognized; encouraged and institutionalized Muslim difference. In other words, "ethnic–racial classifications" were indeed constructed by the British colonial state; though of course with the acquiescence and participation of dominant groups within these "classifications." Or, to put it more precisely, these "ethnic–racial" identities got established/were constructed/emerged out of a certain process: the (patriarchal/capitalist) colonial encounter with native elites.[49]

This did not mean, however, that Muslim — "Moor" — racial distinctness was easily maintained even in this period. Tensions can be seen within the Muslim elite, between what was considered, following a colonial distinction accepted and encouraged by the Muslim elite, its "Ceylon" and "Indian" Moor components.[50] In the late colonial period (1940s), the issue was hotly debated: should the formation be identified in racial or religious terms. The issue became especially charged in 1949, when the newly independent Sinhala government of D.S. Senanayake decided to replace "Moor" with "Muslim" in the electoral register. The Moors' Association — founded in 1935 by Razick Fareed to replace the now defunct Moor Union — considered this proposal a threat to Moor identity. It argued that, since the other "races" in Sri Lanka were allowed to retain their racial identity, so should the Moors (MA:42). The Muslim League, led by T.B. Jayah and having a significant "Indian Moor" membership, argued that "a division of the [Muslim] community on a racial or tribal basis is repugnant to the principles and practices of Islam" and was for the change. Examining the two contending perspectives, one gets the impression that class interests were also at stake; though of course the whole debate cannot be reduced to one of class.[51] Fareed represented that section of the Muslim trading class who not only felt threatened by the commercial activities of the "Indian Moors" but who clearly realized that they would stand to benefit if the "Indian Moors" were expelled from Sri Lanka. Thus his insistence on a "Ceylon Moor" identity had an economic logic to it as well, as I discuss later.

This tension, this unease about identity, this uncertainty about what was a Sri Lankan Muslim, lasted for decades; only to be resolved in favor of the religious in the 1980s. But attempts were made as late as the 1970s to consolidate an ethnic identity for the Sri Lankan Muslim social formation. (By this time, the term "race" had largely disappeared from identitarian discourse.) I turn now to a 1970s text, quite remarkable in its own way, by the sociologist Mohamed Mauroof.[52] This piece too attempts to construct in the course of its writing an ethnic identity for the Muslims and is representative of elite Muslim discourse.

Maroof begins by defining the signifiers of Muslim difference:

In the urban as well as the rural areas, *the main point of social identification* of the Sri Lankan Muslim by his Buddhist, Hindu and Christian compatriots *is his Arabic* [sic] *name* and his peculiar accent in the speaking of Sinhalese and Tamil...(MM:66, emphasis added).

One can read here another instance of the difficulties facing the Muslim elite in trying to assert an ethnic identity for the social formation within the terms of Sri Lankan identitarian discourse. Maroof speaks of the "Sri Lankan Muslim" rather than the "Ceylon Moor." This could be read as an inclusionary move, of the "Malay" and the "Indian Moor," especially since he informs us that the "Muslims" comprise these three distinct categories. However, while Maroof believes that the Muslims are a trading community, he says the Malays are not one. Indeed, he finds the Malays, at least in "matters of food, dress and life-style [to] have retained their ethnic identity" — though he doesn't elaborate (MM:78). Therefore one concludes that this is merely a gesture of inclusion. *In other words, what is meant by the term "Sri Lankan Muslim" in this and other texts representative of elite Muslim discourse is what used to be meant by "Ceylon Moor."*[53] A similar exclusion can also be seen in Maroof's assertion that the main point of identification of the Muslim is his [sic] "Arab" name, rather than religion.[54] In any event, by giving "Muslim" an ethnic rather than a religious connotation, Maroof trips over his own feet. Within his logic, the term Muslim would signify a member of an ethnic group, to be identified as such by non-members of that group (remember that the Arab name, not Islamic religion, is represented as the primary marker of identity here). If that is the case, if the Muslim is an ethnic, s/he should, following Maroof's logic, be identified as such by other ethnics (Tamils or Sinhalese). But Maroof says that members of religious groups — Hindus, Christians and Buddhists — are supposed to make the identification. In other words, if identity is founded on ethnicity, one shouldn't have to resort to religious categories to define difference.

Maroof's next move is to claim that Sri Lankan Muslims have their own language — crucial for the assertion of a "credible" ethnic identity within Sri Lankan identitarian discourse:

*Arabic–Tamil [is] the true language of the Sri Lanka Muslims...*written in Arabic script, adding Arabic phonemes and morphemes to...Tamil, using Arabic words to express ideas and concepts not known to the Dravidian Tamil world–view. The syntax of its spoken version is considerably different from the Tamil spoken [by Tamils...It] has produced an impressive literature...(MM: 68).

If what he says is correct, if "Arabic–Tamil" was indeed the "true" language of the Muslims, it is arguable that Muslim political forces would have agitated to maintain Muslim education in that language. Why did this not happen? Mauroof also fails to mention that, at the time of his writing, the Sri Lankan Minister of Education was Badiudin Mahmud. The same Minister Mahmud who, arguing a few years earlier that the Muslims had no language of their own, enacted regulations allowing the children of the Muslim elite to continue being educated in the English medium.[55] (A benefit otherwise allowed only to Burghers and the children of "mixed" marriages, but denied the children of the Sinhala and Tamil elite.) The point is simply this: unlike the Sinhala and Tamil social formations, the Sri Lankan Muslims were never able to claim a language for themselves. To be precise, the Muslim social formation wasn't seen within Sri Lankan identitarian discourse as having "its own" language. In and of itself, this wouldn't matter very much. But language was and is a crucial marker of difference within Sri Lankan identitarian discourse. By the time Mauroof writes, the term "race" having disappeared from this discourse, language had become the virtually definitive marker of ethnicity. Thus his preoccupation with linguistic and other issues, whereas Azeez's major concern ("blood") was to establish a different and distinct racial origin and identity for the Muslims.[56] Therefore, the lack of a language on which a patent could be placed made elite Muslim claims to a distinct ethnicity all the more hard to establish.

Mauroof's not too subtle invocation of "culture" should also be noted. Tamil, he says, is part of a wider "Dravidian world—view"; this implies that the language of the Muslims is part of an "Arab" one. Again, note the assertion of a Muslim identity in opposition to a Tamil other. But the most remarkable facet of this text is its very last sentence where Mauroof, if not contravening his previous arguments, seems to sense their implausibility: "If the Muslims of Sri Lanka lose the faith that they have in their religion, there would be very little left of them as a community"(MM:83). Again one can see that Mauroof, though claiming that Sri Lankan Muslim difference is founded on ethnicity, resorts to the religious in the final analysis. For, if Muslim identity in Sri Lanka, following Mauroofs logic, was indeed based upon a claim to a distinct ethnicity, then the "community" cannot disappear even if all its members became atheists. Which brings us back to the question: What is a Sri Lankan Muslim? An ethnic, or a religious person? The point, quite simply, is that *the content of Muslim identity - and the same holds for Tamil and Sinhala identity—cannot be defined.* But more than this, Mauroof is also caught in the same vice that has trapped all elite Muslim ideologues trying to assert an ethnic identity for the social formation: they must contend with the terms of a discourse which renders such claims inappropriate or unacceptable; terms the Muslim social formation, occupying a subordinate position within this discourse, has little power to change — despite the (admittedly weak) attempts of its elite to do so.

As argued earlier, the basis of elite Muslim identity is also constitutively gendered. Once more, MM — an exquisitely contradictory text that would have had to be fabricated if it did not exist — helps illustrate:

> The Muslim…villages are residential, housing the traders and bureaucrats who work in the towns…During an ordinary day one runs across many more women…than adult males. While the women stay home, fetch water, do the cooking and conduct the gossiping and visiting that forms the basis of the social life of the village, the men are at work (MM:79).

There is something more going on here than a masculist refusal to see domestic labor — fetching water, cooking — as "work." Domestic labor, in this passage, is aligned with "gossiping and visiting" and represented as "social" (private) activity—as opposed to the truly productive (public/economic) activity performed by men. This representation, of women as unproductive—indeed as counter—productive gossipers — is necessary for the representation of men as productive. The former derives its signification from the latter. In other words, it produces—not just reproduces — a certain representation of men and women (not to mention a certain notion of the public and private) that helps further reinforce the subordination of Muslim women within identitarian discourse: the logic here being that those engaged in purely private activities cannot mark the public.

As I said earlier, by the late 1980s the Muslim social formation was seen to have "lost" its ethnic identity — one that, as should by now be clear, it had great difficulty in maintaining from the beginning. I want now to briefly note a text that serves to mark this loss, by A.M.M. Shahabdeen, a bureaucrat turned businessperson:

> In a multi—religious society there is bound to be unity and diversity in the tenets of the different religions and social attitudes based on them...The adherents of the different religions should therefore respect divergences and learn to be tolerant of the beliefs and value systems of each other.[58]

Shahabdeen, talking of contemporary Sri Lanka, sees the Sri Lankan polity in religious, not ethnic, terms. It is the multi—religious, not multi—ethnic, nature of the polity that he emphasizes. This is consistent with his representation of the Sri Lankan Muslim social formation, throughout his text, as a religious group. That it might have, or might have had, an ethnic identity, is a question he doesn't address. Given its representative nature, this text signifies that, by this time, religion had become the sole marker of Muslim identity in Sri Lanka.

An explanation of this can be found within Sri Lankan identitarian discourse. After 1983, after that is both the Sinhala state sponsored pogroms against the Tamils and the emergence of Tamil militancy as a potent force within the Sri Lankan polity, relations between (nationalist forces within) the Sinhalese and Tamil social formations became even more polarized. In this context, the most significant marker of public difference between the two formations came to be represented as linguistic: a Tamil/ Sinhala person, within this discourse, was one who had a Tamil/Sinhala father and spoke Tamil/Sinhala. A Tamil (Sinhala) person was also expected to be Hindu (Buddhist) or Christian; but religion was not a primary marker of identity. Not having their "own" language, what made the Muslims most publicly different was religion. Indeed, within the terms of Sri Lankan identitarian discourse, the Muslims now followed a reverse ("inappropriate," in Arjuna Parakrama's terms) logic: what they were represented as having in common was not language, like

Tamils and Sinhalese, whose elites largely defined the terms of the discourse, but religion. Consequently, they came to be seen within this discourse as a religious, not an ethnic group.[59] By the late 1980s, the Muslim elite stopped contesting this representation. By then, Muslim distinctiveness was recognized and its content did not matter any more. By then, in any case, the elite had given up the battle as lost and, given the Sinhala state's actions against the Tamils, genocidal in intent, the Muslim elite had more pressing battles to fight.

The myth of the businesslike native

As mentioned before, the Muslim elite represented the entire social formation in its own image as a trading community. The logic behind this is a combination of the patriarchal (male dominance), the economic (class interest) and the political (hegemony). In this section, I investigate the emergence and continuance of this identification of an entire social formation with an economic practice of its elite.

Mohamed Mauroof has theorized the relationship between Muslims and (mercantile) capital, arguing the case for three "ideal—types" of Muslim traders: the gem trader, the urban entrepreneur and the village boutique—keeper. This move virtually mythologizes the elite. For instance, Mauroof represents the gem—traders as being

> ...traditionally known all over the island for their philanthropy.
> They...recognize the God—givenness of their wealth, as taught
> in Islam, and are rather meticulous about...[sharing it with]
> their fel-low-beings (MM:69).[60]

The gem—trader here must be read as a metonym for all Muslim traders and therefore of the elite. And the question that arises is not whether all Muslim traders are in fact generous, but why Mauroof represents them thus. If one recalls Dharmapala again, it becomes easier to argue that Mauroof too responds to the image of the Muslim (trader) as exploitative; an image sustained by Sinhala nationalists even in the contemporary period.

But the identification of Muslim with trader arose in the colonial period and Denham, author of the first comprehensive colonial census on Sri Lanka, provides a good place to begin. He found that 60 % of

Muslim men and 15 % of the women were "earners" in 1911 (EB:457); that is to say, they were integrated into and could be accounted for by the logic of a colonial economy. Most Muslim women, he says, were either agriculturalists or weavers (in other words, they were not significantly engaged in trade). This definition of labor is of course both patriarchal and capitalist: the vast majority of Muslim women were (and still are) engaged in domestic labor or house—work, activities not seen as productive by Denham.[61] Denham doesn't, for reasons unexplained, have comprehensive figures for the composition of the Sri Lankan workforce in 1911. Thus one is unable to figure out what percentage of the adult male Muslim population was seen to be engaged in trade. He does, however, list those occupations "in which the largest number of male dependents between 20 and 30 are found in each native race" (EB:460). The ratio here of Muslim men working on the land to those in the trading sector is 5:2. Denham concludes: "Ceylon Moors for the most part are small farmers cultivating their own lands" (EB:466). Nowhere does he claim that the Muslims were essentially a trading community,[62] despite the prevailing British colonial belief to that effect.

Sixty years after Denham, quoting Central Bank statistics, S.W.R. de A Samarasinghe and Fazal Dawood inform us that in 1973 28% of the Muslim workforce was engaged in trade and 35% of it engaged in agriculture.[63] Nevertheless, Samarasinghe and Dawood blithely label the Muslims a "business community." As noted before, this is how the Muslim formation is usually represented within Sri Lankan identitarian discourse. *But if it is the case that less than a third of the (gendered) Muslim workforce participates one way or another in trade, why is the entire social formation represented as a trading community* — or business community for that matter? Why is it that the Sinhala social formation is never called an agricultural, or farming, or peasant community within this discourse—even though three-fourth's of its (gendered definition) labor force work the land? The answer is to be found in assertions like Samarasinghe's, that the Muslims possess a "cultural bias towards trading and self-employment."[64] An assertion that has its origin in the colonial period; which the British, the Muslim elite and later the (ideologues of the) Sinhala state were to foster, albeit for different reasons.

Despite Denham and his "correct" reading of the figures, there was another, more powerful colonial tradition at work in representing the Muslims (and the other social formations) in terms of a Protestant-patriarchal-capitalist logic. Ameer Ali has noted that British colonial writers on Sri Lanka used the following adjectives to describe Muslims: "active, energetic, industrious, laborious, enterprising, adventurous, thrifty, calculating..." and so on.[65] These attitudes were most clearly articulated — one could say theorized — by James Tennent, one time Colonial Secretary in Sri Lanka. The influence of his two volume *Ceylon*, the classic colonial history of the country, was widespread amongst the Sri Lankan elite: it served as a model for future histories and helped establish, within the native elite, a colonial way of seeing themselves.[66] To Tennent the Muslims ("Mahometans") were petty traders; after calling them "energetic," "industrious," "busy" and "ambitious," he says:

> ...these immigrant traders became traders in all the products of the island...At no point were they either manufacturers, or producers in any department; *their genius was purely commercial, and their attention was exclusively devoted to buying and selling* what had been previously produced by the industry and ingenuity of others.[67]

One should note in passing the racism here: the Muslims were not manufacturers; only Europeans were capable of such ingenuity or industry. But the more important point concerns the colonial (contribution to the) construction of (Muslim) identity. In Tennent — as in British colonial discourse generally — Sri Lankan social formations are identified/characterized purely in terms of their economic function; or, to be precise, in terms of their relation to a certain patriarchal capitalist logic. A similar logic was at work in other British Asian colonies as well, as S.H. Alatas has argued. This is how, he says, "colonial capitalism defined useful labor" in Malaya:

> ...the labor of traders, money making through commerce, selling goods through and from colonial European countries, or later in the nineteenth century managing cash crop plantations..[68]

Groups engaging in such activity were considered industrious, looked upon positively, by the British. A similar argument can be made with respect to the British colonial representation of Muslims in Sri Lanka, one that the Muslim elite was only too eager to accept, encourage; in short, to be complicitous with, since it served the hegemonic interests of that elite.

The complicity can be seen, as should by now be expected, in a text as early as Azeez, who often quotes Tennent to back up his claims. One has noted before that he represented the Hashimites, who supposedly originated the Muslim presence in Sri Lanka, as being "less war—like and given to the peaceful pursuit of trade" (IL:11). Like fathers, like sons: the "trading instinct" of the Hashimites, he says, were "transmitted to their descendants, the Moors of Ceylon" (IL:9). That is to say, from the beginning the Muslims came to Sri Lanka to trade, not to colonize or plunder the country. This representation also contains an implicit response to the arguments of Dharmapala and his ilk; for Azeez adds that the Muslims came to dominate the trading sector in Sri Lanka in the pre-colonial era because "our Sinhalese friends were not traders, they hated commerce and gave themselves up to agricultural and other pursuits" (IL:12). This dominance continued into the late colonial period:

> Mr Ramanathan has thought it sufficient to refer to the Moors as petty traders, peddlers, boutique keepers, boatmen, fishermen, agriculturalists and coolies, but...had he been a little more candid he would have said that they included wholesale merchants, large shopkeepers, planters and wealthy landed proprietors, and, in point of wealth, they were only next to the Sinhalese...(IL:3).

From Azeez to Shahabdeen, the Sri Lankan Muslim elite not only represented itself as capitalist but as being successful, too, a representation necessary to justify its accommodationist politics. The subtext here, at least in the post-colonial period, goes something like this: all Muslims are traders and successful because we, the Muslim leadership, worked with the Sinhala state (unlike, again, the Tamils). In other words, as I discuss at greater length in the next section, the Muslim elite had to represent the entire social formation as traders in order to safeguard its own interests.

An actively passive politics

No good study exists of Muslim politics in modern Sri Lanka. I cannot remedy that admittedly important lacuna; it is only necessary for the purposes of the present argument to discuss what 1 have called the accommodationist politics of the Muslim elite in slightly greater length than above. The focus will be on a few key events in post-colonial Sri Lankan history.

As noted before, the Muslim elite represented the entire social formation as one which traditionally enjoyed good relations with the Sinhalese; consequently, it not only followed an accommodationist politics with respect to the Sinhala state but also took great pains to represent itself as so doing. Such a politics was required, as is hopefully clear by now, not just to safeguard the trader elite's economic (and other) interests; it was also compelled by *a fear concerning its physical safety.*[69] A fear that grew in the post–colonial period as the Sinhala state actively oppressed non–accommodative sections of the Tamil social formation; and sometimes indeed followed a quasi–genocidal policy against the Tamils. I argue that this fear of being suppressed, if not of being exterminated, also made the Southern Muslim elite accommodate itself to the Sinhala state.[70] Accommodation, however, had an "unintended" consequence: it reinforced Muslim subordination within identitarian discourse (making it even more difficult, as argued above, for the elite to establish its claims to a distinct ethnicity).

The Southern Muslim (elite) itself was the victim of the first big "riots" in modern Sri Lanka, in 1915. This is the only event in Sri Lankan Muslim history that has been studied in any depth by the academic community — presumably because Sinhalese were involved. Hardly any of the pieces, however, discuss Muslim perspectives or the impact of this on subsequent elite Muslim politics.[71] I cannot here discuss either the actual events or their causes at any length; my concern is the elite Muslim response to it. But this much must be said: *they were not riots.*[72] All too often in both academic and popular writing in Sri Lanka this word, which implies a spontaneous happening, is used to depict what in fact is organized violence: in Kandy, Colombo and other towns in May–June 1915 organized groups of Sinhala men — their class background varied from place to place — attacked the property of Muslim traders and in some places destroyed mosques. As several of the commentators mentioned before have noted, these attacks were mostly, though not exclusively, directed at "Indian Moors." But, given that some of their property was attacked too and, as mentioned before, that Muslims in general were represented in this period as ruthlessly exploitative foreigners, the Muslim elite panicked.

This panic grew in the period immediately after the riots, as many Sinhala nationalist ideologues attacked the Muslims. Dharmapala, for instance, would continue to insist upon the alienness of all Muslims soon after the events:

> the "Muhammadan…[is] alien to the Sinhalese by religion, race and language. He traces his origin to Arabia, whilst the Sinhalese traces his origin to India and to Aryan sources…..[T]here will always be had blood between the Moors and the Sinhalese. The peaceful Sinhalese have at last shown that they can no longer bear the insults of the alien. The whole nation in one day has risen against the Moor people" (quoted in KJ 1:14, emphasis added).

One might note in passing the "Aryan" anti–semitism here; but more important is the threat of continuing bloodshed against a group here denied membership in the nation. Elite Muslim fears were not ameliorated, either, by the actions of Ramanathan, then the only "elected" Sri Lankan member of the Legislative Council, who ardently supported redress for the Sinhalese; especially those members of the Sinhala elite who were arrested by the British colonial state, which saw the attacks on the Muslims as a prelude to a general Sinhala nationalist upsurge.

The events of 1915 led to two developments that concern me here. The treatment the politically active members of the Sinhala elite received at the hands of the British, until then looked upon as benign rulers, propelled the movement for Sri Lankan self–governance.[73] But, given that this movement was led by the same Sinhala elite that at best ignored Muslim victimization during and after the "riots" and, at worst, saw the Muslims as alien, the Muslim elite was completely alienated from this movement. Consequently, the elite aligned itself with the British colonial state, in the hope no doubt that the state would prevent further attacks on Muslim life and property.[74] It was not till the 1940s, when self–governance looked inevitable, that the Muslim elite shifted its allegiance, though not without misgivings, to the Sinhala elite, which seemed certain to control the new Sri Lankan state.

Among the first acts of the new state was to disenfranchise those it considered non–Sri Lankan nationals, a move primarily designed to evict "Up–Country Tamils," brought from South India to serve as indentured labor in the plantations by the British colonial state. As mentioned before, this also affected some 35,000 ("Indian") Muslims. The disenfranchisement of people mostly born in the country who suddenly found themselves labelled foreign (an early attempt at "ethnic cleansing") was consistent with the Sinhala nationalist logic of the state. Razick Fareed, by now the dominant elite Muslim politician/ideologue, supported this move wholeheartedly (as did other elite Muslim parliamentarians). He did so not only because he wanted to be seen as accommodative of the interests of the Sinhala state; the interests of his class were also involved, since the citizenship of many "Indian" Muslims were also at stake. On the day the Citizenship Bill came before the Senate Fareed was scheduled to leave on pilgrimage to Mecca. Nevertheless, he found the time to get to the Chamber and speak:

> ...the Ceylon Moors have suffered most in the past for want of a Citizenship Bill. We...have been treated very badly by certain people under the guise of Muslim brotherhood.

In another talk later that year, he explained what he meant by bad treatment and identified the people unnamed above:

> The Ceylon Moors had a flourishing trade in... Pettah barely 40 years ago; but today you find the whole of the trade in Pettah, even the property which the Moors owned... in the hands of non-Ceylon traders.[75]

Again, note that Fareed does not identify the "Indian Moors" as such; it is their"non–Ceylon"–ness, which is meant to distinguish them from native Muslims, that is called attention to here. And one might also mention that, within the narrative logic of capitalism, the economic vicissitudes of the "Ceylon Moor" should have been understood, and accepted, in terms of competition (fair or otherwise). But the Muslim elite stood to gain economically from co-operating with the Sinhala state in the eviction of "Indian Moors." So, it did.

The next important act of elite Muslim appeasement of the state came in 1956, when it supported 'Sinhala Only.' This time, it had less directly to gain. The replacement of English with Sinhala only (as opposed to Sinhala and Tamil) as the sole official language of Sri Lanka was the first major move against "Sri Lankan Tamils" by the Sinhala state. Fareed's speech on that occasion is a quite remarkable instance of toadyism.[76] He had this to say on the question of parity of status for Tamil:

> ...it is most unfair to ask parity of status for Sinhala and Tamil only, because [if one does so] there should [also] be parity for English, in respect of the Burghers and Englishmen; for Malay in respect of the Malays; and Arabic in respect of the Moors.

This is at best a specious argument. Apart from the fact that hardly any Sri Lankan Muslims spoke Arabic, the only other language for which parity of status was being demanded then was Tamil.[77] But Fareed contradicted himself in virtually his next breath:

> I will not keep it a secret from this House that the mandate to vote for this Bill was given to me on the assurance given by me to my community that English will continue...Ceylon Moors must retain the use of English not merely because they are a commercial community but also because it is a mode of access to the abundant wealth of Islamic literature...

Since only elite Muslims spoke English, Fareed is being explicit about the interests of his class here, at the expense this time of Eastern Muslims. In the course of the same debate, Eastern Muslim Members of Parliament would argue passionately for parity — because Sinhala Only would hurt their interests too. But Fareed, though he admitted to a difference of opinion on the subject between Muslim MPs, strove to negate the difference; a move necessary to successfully represent himself as articulating the interests of the entire Muslim formation. Without this, his arguments could not effectively appease/convince the Sinhala state.

One can also read in such a move the construction of a (Southern) Muslim identity by constitutively excluding Eastern sensibilities. For Eastern Muslims were, among other things, too close to the Tamil language. I cannot in this paper do more than contrast Fareed with the views expressed by one Eastern Muslim MP. For instance, M.M. Musta-fa, a Muslim elected on the Federal Party ticket from a predominantly Muslim electorate not only voted against "Sinhala Only" but actively re-butted Fareed. He also claimed that "we [Muslims] in the Eastern Prov-ince" don't speak "Arabic—Tamil" but "the purest form of Tamil."[78] In other words, at least some Eastern Muslims saw no contradiction in identifying with the Tamil language. Indeed, many call it their mother tongue.[79] This identification, the Southern Muslim elite could not allow, thus Fareed's move to suppress it. It is therefore predictable that Fareed would choose to appease the Sinhalese by demonizing the Tamils:

> I do not wish to be a party to the political genocide of my race...by another race, the Tamil...which is stretching its trea-cherous tentacles to draw us into the whirlpool called the Ta-mil—speaking nation.. [80]

What is amazing about this statement, quite apart from its coun-ter—factual nature, is that Sinhala violence against the Muslims is com-pletely erased. It had to be; for, after saying that his "vote is not a humble gesture to placate and pay homage to the majority community by a weak minority," Fareed did just that, explicitly admitting that the Muslim elite would accept Sinhala hegemony:

> We do not want any master, but *if we must have a master let it be one master only...the Sinhalese.* We are prepared to serve under them...[W]e have suffered enough under the Tamil yoke (em-phasis added).[81]

Fareed, again, didn't bother to detail this suffering. The Muslims were never under the "Tamil yoke" to begin with; and therefore couldn't have suffered as a result.[82] But, as should by now be clear, terminological inexactitude was not something Fareed had a problem with.

The next text I want to discuss is by Lalith Athulathmudali — delivered, appropriately enough, under the auspices of the Razick Fareed Foundation. Athulathmudali began his speech on 'The Future of the Muslims in Sri Lanka'[83] by negating the argument for Tamil being made an official language:

...the biggest controversy, or rather shall I say the Maypole around which we have danced for the last 30-40 years is a May-pole called the 'Language Crisis' (LA:26).

By this kind of ridicule, by comparing the official language issue to a dance, and a "foreign" one at that, Athulathmudali seeks to dilute its seriousness, a move that is brazenly Sinhala nationalist. But Athulath-mudali has to represent 'Sinhala Only' as unimportant in order to make his next point, that only the Muslims were

...prepared to learn every possible language that was taught in this country, unrelentingly, without any hang—ups, without feel-ing that their identity was being lost (LA:26).

Athulathmudali earlier defined the Muslims as "a community re-ferred to by religion." If that was the case, if religion and not language de-termined Muslim identity in Sri Lanka, then of course they would be "prepared to learn" any language, since doing so would not place their identity at risk. But this argument is directed not so much at the Mus-lims as at those Tamils resisting Sinhala state oppression who, correctly identifying the suppressive intent behind 'Sinhala Only', rejected it.

After making the absurd claim that, for the Muslims, "Tamil is the language of religion, Sinhala is the language of commerce and Eng-lish is the language of education" — which reveals that his argument is pertinent, if at all, only to a certain class of Muslim - - Athulathmudali gets to the crux of his argument:

...there is a solution to the language problem of Sri Lanka along the lines which the Muslims have consciously or unconsciously shown us (LA:26).

The "language problem" is metonym for "ethnic problem;" this is made quite clear by Athulathmudali's claim that the "Muslims have been treated [by the Sinhalese] in SriLanka with...tolerance..." That state-ment can of course be disputed; but the point is in the subtext. To the Tamils who resist Sinhala hegemony, it says: accept our hegemony and we will stop trying to exterminate you.[84] And to any Muslims who may have difficulties with continuing to accept Sinhala hegemony: if you don't, we will treat you like we have treated the Tamils. The threat, though implicit, can nevertheless be clearly read in this passage. And helps explain why, the Muslim elite consistently feared the same Sinhala state it collaborated with.

Given its accommodative politics, the Muslim elite generally repressed this fear. But it surfaced sometimes and can be noted even in the speeches of Fareed. For instance, Fareed told parliament when Sri Lankan self—government (Sinhala control of the state) appeared imminent:

> ...the Moors of Ceylon...are as much dear children of Mother Lanka and as much Ceylonese as my Sinhalese brothers and sisters. The Moors and the Sinhalese have lived together for centuries in this blessed island home of ours in amity and accord. *Mistakes have been made in the past*, but I do not want them to be repeated. That is my earnest hope, that is my fervent plea (quoted in KM 1:469, emphasis added).

The "mistakes" euphemistically alluded to here presumably are the "riots" of 1915. Such (was) is the extent of elite Muslim fear of Sinhala (state) oppression that they are never expressed explicitly. But, beneath the diplomatic language, an anxiety can be detected. Thus his plea to the Sinhalese to accept the Muslims, too, as "dear children of Mother Lanka." Fareed's use of the gendered metaphor is quite consistent with the masculist logic of this breed of identitarianism. By claiming that all Sri Lankans have a common mother, he draws attention to the essentially fraternal nature of the national community; or, rather, to what the national community should be.

A slightly more explicit articulation of this fear can be seen in a speech, clearly addressed to the Sinhala state, that Badiudin Mahmud made in late 1983 (after the pogroms against the Tamils). After repeatedly asserting that the "loyalty and allegiance of the Muslims to their homeland Sri Lanka" has been exemplary throughout the centuries, he says:

> *The Muslims of Sri Lanka...have not made any fantastic or extravagant demands. We do not stand for the division of the country in any form*, nor do we support or encourage separatist tendencies. As a minority we feel that we should be fully at home in the country to which we belong (BM:10, emphasis added).

This is Fareed more diplomatically put. Here, too, one can read the Muslim elite desire to both make itself "fully at home" within Sinhala hegemony and to define its politics against the Tamils. For Mahmud argues that the Muslims have behaved "loyally" — unlike, implicitly, the Tamils —never having made "fantastic or extravagant" demands of the state. The logic behind this move is not mere class interest. When one takes into account the timing of his speech, one realizes that the subtext is fear: that the Sinhala state, having just instituted a pogrom against the Tamils, would now turn on the Muslims; that even a consistently accommodative politics wouldn't prevent this. A fear that can be seen most clearly in the following lines:

> We don't want to harm anyone nor do we expect anyone to harm us. We only wish to live in peace with the rest of the people who take pride in calling themselves citizens of Sri Lanka (BM:14).

The "rest of the people" refers of course to the Sinhalese; the Tamils being seen by the Sinhala state — to whom Mahmud addresses his remarks — as separatist, trying to make themselves citizens of another (their "own") country.[85]

Conclusion

But, so what?

I have, thus far, discussed the bases upon which elite Sri Lankan Muslim identity was constructed, the historical circumstances under which this took place and the interests and agencies involved. I have also pointed out, though not discussed, the interests and agencies that were excluded, *that had to be excluded*, for the Muslim elite to represent the entire social formation in its own image.

However, as we know, hegemony is never complete; it is always resisted. In other words, some Muslim women and Eastern Muslims, at least, have contested the definitions of Muslim identity fashioned for, and sought to be imposed upon, them. I shall in future work discuss these contests. I want here just to note two texts that signify the incompleteness of hegemony.

The first is a poem by Khalida Lebbe titled 'Our Kind':

A knock on the door
Inside
Confusion
Soft patter of feminine feet
Veiled heads whisper together
Gently
A curtain moves
Imperceptibly
Then
Jubilation
Why it's our cousin
Ahamed
Girls, come here
Open the door
It's one of our kind.[86]

This poem instantiates the process of identification. On the surface, it appears to describe an instance of identification along Muslim
(religious? ethnic?) lines. But it does much more, questioning such an
identification along gender lines. It draws attention to the fact that not
just the spaces but the very worlds of Muslim women and men are separate. Why are the "girls," inside the house, "confused" by a knock on the
door? Because something out of the ordinary is happening. A Muslim
man, supposed to be outside at that time of day, wants to come inside. As
imperceptibly as the curtain moves within the poem, Lebbe draws attention to the fact that cousin Ahamed, "one of us" on a religious or ethnic
register, is not on a gendered one; if he was, obviously, he would be inside
with them. A point reinforced by the poem's exaggeration of femininity:
the women are confused, their feet patter softly, they whisper gently and,
finally, are jubilant at what is, after all, a banal discovery. What Lebbe's
text shows is that, like I said before, identity is always overdetermined: at
the same point that a commonality is being identified and constructed, a
difference is also being identified and called attention to. What does it
mean, Lebbe makes us ask, for the "girls" (and Muslim women, generally)
to identify the commonly–named Ahamed (and Muslim men, generally),
free to roam outside, unveiled, as one of them? How much, indeed, do
Muslim men and women have in common?

The second text I want to note is by M.I.M. Mohideen. Mohideen is the product of, among other things, both Sinhala state and elite Muslim neglect of eastern Sri Lanka. Which perhaps explains his willingness (if not need) to articulate Muslim "grievances" in public. He lists seven issues on which, he claims, the entire Muslim formation has grievances, paying the most attention to language and land settlement, of peculiar interest to Easterners. He then argues that the Muslims were and are not a trading community. Finally, he takes on that elite responsible for this representation, stating that a tiny minority of "rich businessmen"

> ...controlled the destiny of the Muslim community as a whole during the last half a century. But *this minority group, enormously rich, lacked the educational enlightenment and political foresight to lead the community in the right direction. As a result, the Muslim community...is educationally backward, politically insignificant, economically retarded and culturally isolated.*[87]

Mohideen's text is an instance of the sensibility out of which the Muslim Congress was to emerge; it not only challenges the Muslim elite but insults it. Since Mohideen wrote, circumstances have worsened dramatically for most Eastern Muslims; the challenges facing them today have never been greater. Thousands of Easterners are refugees in various parts of the country; hundreds have been killed and those still in the East live in fear, especially of the LTTE; the Sinhala state has been generally unsympathetic to their plight.[88] Under these circumstances, where the identities of all Eastern social formations have been strengthened by confrontation, suggestions that call for new politics on a non—identitarian basis run the risk of sounding hopelessly utopian. But Sri Lanka today is a situation that calls for the taking of risks.

The point is simply this: if identities are always constructed, then they can also be deconstructed, perhaps even reconstructed. Though not of course into anything one chooses. If, to paraphrase Marx, people make their own identities, they do not do so just as they please; they must contend with their circumstances, which impose limits on their agency and alternatives. In the current context it is, for instance, impossible — leaving aside the question of desirability — for Sri Lankan Muslims to be-

come Sinhala or Tamil. But more enabling alternatives, that take
ence into account without fetishizing it, are also imaginable.

Such a project, however, or projects, must move alongside undoing hegemonic identities; ones that, as I have been arguing throughout
this paper, are not enabling, and indeed disable those groups subordinated by such identitarian constructs. In a word, one cannot redo without also undoing. Therefore, I seek to provide one out of many possible
answers to the 'But so what?' question by radically shifting my focus,
from the south to the east, from analysis to something verging upon advice.

Joan Scott has argued that identity isn't "a reflection of some essential reality but a matter of political allegiance."[89] Identity isn't exclusively a matter of political allegiance; but, if one is willing to see one's
political allegiance as an expression of one's interests, then one can also
see that identities can and will change if interests change or are rede-
fined. Such a redefinition is among the more pressing challenges facing
Eastern Muslims today.

Ameer Ali has noted in a recent article that the Muslim social
formation is very much a divided one:

> ...the appearance of the SLMC...exposed for the first time that
> the so—called unity of the Muslims under the religious banner
> is...superficial...[B]eneath that banner there are real issues
> which encourage centrifugalism...[T]he interests of the Mus-
> lims...in the Sinhalese areas are fundamentally different
> from...[Eastern] Muslims. While the vast majority of the Tamil
> district are farmers and landless peasants, those living in the
> Sinhalese areas are mostly petty businessmen, artisans and ur-
> ban workers. Linguistically also...the Muslims have become a
> divided community.[90]

This of course has been the argument throughout this paper.
But, while Ali mourns this development, it represents for me a potentially progressive opportunity: it carries with it the potential that Eastern
Muslims, at least, can move away from identitarian politics as we know
it. And, in so doing, provide an example to us all.

To repeat Butler's question with which I began this paper:
"What new shape of politics emerges when identity as a common

ground no longer constrains the discourse?" In other words, what political possibilities can Eastern Muslims envisage if they see themselves as having interests, desires, futures, in common not with Southern Muslims but with other Easterners? More than one, of course. But it is only one possibility that I would like to foreground here.

Even if the materialities of current politics militate otherwise, other materialities, of geography and economics, arguably point to the necessity of Eastern Muslims, Tamils and Sinhalese living together. The emphasis here would be, in Jean—Luc Nancy's terms, on "being—in—common," not "common being";[91] upon a recognition of what could be termed necessity — of shared interests, not a shared identity. At the time of this writing, it is hard to claim that the social and political conditions for such an alliance exist. At the same time, it is also true that there are (still?) people in the East who have not disavowed the possibility.[92] Who are, in fact, working towards such alliances. They allow, in however limited a fashion, an optimism of the will. I add my voice to theirs.

Notes

1. This paper is conceived of as beginning a comprehensive study of Muslim identity in Sri Lanka. Many important questions — pertaining to women, the East, the rise of the Muslim Congress, the impact of international Islamic nationalisms on Sri Lanka, the colonial period and so on — are barely touched upon here. My most grateful thanks to Pradeep Jeganathan, Sanjay Krishnan, Laura Lomas, Joseph Massad, Yumna Siddiqui, Jyotsna Uppal, Milind Wakankar, Tim Watson and especially Colleen Lye for their extremely useful criticisms of earlier versions of these arguments. Without their comments, this paper would make very sorry reading. (But then, what are friends for!) I must also thank Pavi Kailasapathy, Radhika Coomaraswamy, Kumari Jayawardena and the SSA for other help in making it possible.

2   Etienne Balibar, 'The Nation Form' in *Review* XII, 3, (Summer 1990), p.334.

3   The reference here is to Gayatri Spivak, who defends the "strategic use of positivist essentialism in a scrupulously visible political interest," in *In Other Worlds: Essays in Cultural Politics* (Routledge: New York, 1988), p.205; hereafter, GS.

4   Joan Scott and Judith Butler argue that a "radical contestation of" the foundations of identities would "expose the silent violence of these concepts as they have operated not merely to marginalize certain groups but to erase and exclude them from the notion of 'community' altogether"; that such a contestation would "establish exclusion as the very precondition and possibility for 'community,'" see 'Introduction,' in Scott and Butler (eds.) *Feminists Theorize the Political* (Routledge: New York, 1992), p.xiv.

5   For an excellent (ethnographic) illustration of this, see Pradeep Jeganathan, "All the Lord's Men? Ethnicity and Inequality in the Space of a Riot," in Michael Roberts (ed.) *Sri Lanka. Collective Identities Revisited* (2nd edition) vol 2. (Colombo: Marga Institute, 1998).

6   The term hegemony is used here in the Gramscian sense, as being constituted by persuasion as well as coercion.

7   Michel Foucault, *The Archaeology of Knowledge and the Discourse on Language* (Pantheon: New York, 1971), p.26. Hereafter, MF.

8   See Balibar and Immanuel Wallerstein *Race, Nation, Class: Ambiguous Identities* (Verso, New York, 1991), pp. 96–100.

9   For a definition of this usage, see Ranajit Guha, 'On Some Aspects of the Historiography of Colonial India,' *Subaltern Studies I* (Oxford UP: New Delhi, 1982), p.8.

10   It is perhaps unfair to cite as instance of this an essentially journalistic work, S. J. Tambiah's *Sri Lanka: Ethnic Fratricide and the Dismantling of Democracy* (U of Chicago Press: Chicago, 1986). But the Harvard anthropologist's definition of the Muslim social formation is typical: "The Muslims…are distinguished as an ethnic category on account of their religion alone" (p.4). That "ethnic" and "religious" signify very different things has clearly escaped the notice of Tambiah.

11. For instance, Werner Sollars convincingly argues that the term "ethnicity" — related to but not to be confused with 19th century ideas of "ethnology" — is a post–1940s U.S. coinage that "took" in the early 1970s. (*Beyond Ethnicity: Consent and Descent in American Culture* [Oxford: New York, 1986] pp.20–24.) This is the period of U.S. global dominance, and the appearance of the term within Sri Lankan identitarian discourse in the late 1970s cannot be coincidental.

12   K. M. de Silva, 'Muslim Leaders and the Nationalist Movement,' in M. A. M. Shukri (ed.) *Muslims of Sri Lanka*, p.458. Hereafter, KM1. Even more astounding than to find de Silva, always an unabashed ideologue for the Sinhala state, saying this, is the fact that nobody has investigated this crucial issue further.

13   This way of seeing identity has very material consequences, including the way citizenship laws have been framed in Sri Lanka.

14   For a general account of the relation between woman and nationalism, see Flora Anthias and Nira Yuval–Davis. 'Introduction,' *Woman–Nation–State* (Macmillan: London, 1989).

15   The above is derived from Foucault, mainly MF.

16   Despite the facts, so to speak, the followers of *Jathika Chinthanaya* manage to insist that Sri Lanka is not multi–ethnic,–religious,–cultural. It is at moments like this that the limits of a purely positivist intellectual intervention — as David Scott's essay in this volume also suggests — become painfully apparent.

17 Izeth Hussain has made a similar argument: "Ethnic discourse is for the most part written by majorities and rebellious minorities" 'The Sri Lankan Muslims — the Problem of a Submerged Minority' (unpublished paper, p.7); hereafter IH. He also notes the subordinate position of the Muslim formation within this discourse: "The impression is given [by most writers on the ethnic problem] that the Muslims...are peripheral to the main ethnic problem" (p.8). Hussain, it should be noted, does not use the term discourse in its Foucauldian sense.

18 A detailed discussion of Sri Lankan identitarian discourse would chart the history of the deployment of these terms; paying attention, among other things, to their co-lonial and neo–colonial genealogies.

19 *Report* (privately published, 1985). Hereafter, FJ.

20 *The Welikanda Massacre* (ICES: Colombo, 1992). Hereafter, SP.

21 Jayasinghe and Pieris are in distinguished company; as I discuss later, most academic work on the 1915 "riots," the first occasion on which Muslims were victims of orga-nized violence in Sri Lanka, does not grant the Muslims subjectivity either.

22 Note that the distinction SP draws between the (Tamil) "people" and (Muslim) "community" serves to reinforce that already made between the Tamils and Muslims.

23 Arjuna Parakrama has theorized the question of the difficulties of "subaltern linguis-tic intervention," albeit in a very different context, much better than I can: "Subaltern linguistic intervention... represents... 'inappropriate' or 'unacceptable' discourse which cannot be taken into account by the normative standard. In fact, the "proper" discourse...must systematically exclude these "mistakes" or "deviations" (or ridicule them...in terms of its own criteria of acceptability decided upon by those elites who can make their "meaning" stick) if it is to remain coherent and viable." *Language and Rebellion: Discursive Unities and the Possibility of Protest* (Katha: London. 1990), p.7.

24 *Muslims of Sri Lanka: Avenues to Antiquity* (Naleemiah Institute: Beruwela, 1986); hereafter, MS.

25 *Challenge for Change: Profile of a Community* (MWRAF: Colombo, 1990); hereafter, CC. Three of the 13 articles in this collection address issues specific to Muslim women; two of these are written by Sinhala women and the other by a Muslim man.

26 A terror exists in elite Muslim discourse: of being identified with the Tamil and, consequently, facing Sinhala state oppression.

27 For more on the early period of Sinhala nationalism, see for instance Gananath Ob-eyesekere, 'The Vicissitudes of Sinhala–Buddhist identity through time and change,' (hereafter GO) in Michael Roberts (ed.) *Collective Identities. Nationalisms and Pro-test in Modern Sri Lanka* (Marga: Colombo, 1979) and Kumari Jayawardena, 'Some Aspects of Class and Ethnic Consciousness in Sri Lanka in the late 19th and early 20th centuries; in *Ethnicity and Social Change* SSA (eds.) (SSA: Colombo, 1985).

28 'The Muslim Revivalist Movement,1880—1915' (hereafter, VS) in Roberts, p.247.

A revised version of this paper, one of the very few good pieces of academic work on the Muslims, appears in MS. For more on Pasha's impact, see Samaraweera's 'Arabi Pasha in Ceylon: 1880.1901,' in *Islamic Culture*, vol XLX, 1977; and Ameer Ali, 'The 1915 Racial Riots in Ceylon (Sri Lanka): A Reappraisal of its Causes' in *South Asia*, December 1981; hereafter, AA 1.

29   "Backwardness" in this context should probably be interpreted as pointing to the significantly small Muslim presence, and therefore influence, within the tiny native colonial elite of the time; a lack the Muslim elite realized could hurt their political and economic interests.

30   'The Ethnology of the "Moors" of Ceylon,' in *Journal of the Royal Asiatic Society (Ceylon)*, vol X, 1888, p.262. Hereafter PR. It should be noted that Ramanathan doesn't use the term "race"; it wasn't in public currency at the lime. The term was first officially used in Sri Lanka by the (British) Census of 1911 to replace 'nationality". Census author E. B. Denham explained the change in terminology thus: "[T]he word nationality…cannot be regarded as an appropriate description of the various peoples in Ceylon. "The races in Ceylon are clearly differentiated — inter–marriages between them have been rare; they have each their own particular religion to which the large majority belong, and they speak different languages." *Ceylon at the Census of 1911* (Govt. Printer: Colombo, 1912), p.194. (Hereafter, EB.) By 1911 "race" was already a part of identitarian discourse: the leading Sinhala nationalist ideologue of the time, Anagarika Dharmapala, writing in English, described the Sinhalese in 1902 as the "sweet gentle Aryan children of an ancient historic race." (Quoted in GO:302).

31   It is quite possible that part of the reason for this lay in the belief dominant amongst British colonials in India that Hindus and Muslims were essentially different. Hardly any work exists, though, on the influences of British colonial attitudes and policy in India on Sri Lanka.

32   The use of the term "upper class" isn't entirely accurate here, since class formation in Sr Lanka was just beginning in this period. It is deployed for want of a better term.

33   Over the next decades this elite continued its collaboration with the state and further consolidated its power and hegemony. It cannot be stressed enough that, in the post—colonial period, all the "leaders" of the Muslim social formation, or more precisely those recognized as such by the Sinhala state (and the Muslim elite) didn't just hail from this elite but were selected by Sinhala political parties (both the UNP and SLFP). Elected to parliament from electorates with a Sinhala majority, they owed their political fortunes to those same Sinhala parties.

34   So, not incidentally, did the Dutch, the first to introduce a systematized code of Islamic law to govern Sri Lankan Muslims. The code, imported from Batavia in 1770, was of the Shafi school of Islamic jurisprudence. Since then, most Sri Lankan Muslims have considered themselves Shafi. For more on this, see T. Nadaraja, *The Legal*

System of Ceylon in its Historical Setting (E. J. Brill: Leiden, 1972).

35   *Imagined Communities* (Verso: London, 1992), p.168. The phenomenal influence of this text is not something I have ever understood. For more on the contradiction at the heart of Anderson's thesis, see Partha Chatterjee, *Nationalist Thought and the Colonial World* (Zed: London, 1986) and my 'Rethinking the Post-Colonial Nation: The Importance of Frantz Fanon,' in *An Introduction to Social Theory*, R. Coomaraswamy and N. Wickremasinghe (eds.) (Delhi:Kornak, 1994).

36   Within post-colonial elite Muslim discourse, the Ramanathan-Azeez debate is often represented as constituting the founding moment of Muslim political identity in Sri Lanka. For instance, M. L. M. Aboosally wrote in 1985: "Ramanathan asserted that the Ceylon Moors were Tamils by race and Muslims by religion. Offended by this misinterpretation of the origin of the Ceylon Moors, I.L.M.Abdul Azeez...was able... to prove... that the Ceylon Moors were descended from Arab traders." ('Introduction,' M.M.M.Mahroof, et. al. (eds.) *An Ethnological Survey of the Muslims of Sri Lanka* (Razick Fareed Foundation: Colombo,1986), p.x; hereafter ES. This text, like MS, shows a marked interest in the past, but contains no account of Muslims in Sri Lanka in the post-colonial period.

37   It is worthy of note that Abdul Azeez, or any other Muslim, wasn't invited to reply by the Royal Society.

38   Azeez must have been pleased by Denham, who would write four years later: "the Moorman...bears little resemblance to the Tamil. They must...be very closely intermixed, but the original Arab blood has left its mark on the race..." (BB:237).

39   On the incorporation of "Aryanness" into the Sinhala social formation, see Leslie Gunawardana's brilliant, 'The People of the Lion,' in *Ethnicity and Social Change*, (*op.cit*). Unfortunately, there is no similar work on the Tamil formation.

40   'A Criticism of Mr. Ramanathan's "Ethnology of the 'Moors' of Ceylon" (MICH: Colombo, 1957), p.11. Hereafter, IL.

41   The best piece of work on the origins of the Muslim communities in Sri Lanka is A. C. M. Ameer Ali's excellent, 'The Genesis of the Muslim Community in Ceylon (Sri Lanka): A historical survey,' in *Asian Studies*, Vol XIX, Apr—Dec 1981. Ali argues that permanent Muslim settlements in Sri Lanka were by–products of those on the Malabar coast in India, established over many years by traders from the Arabian peninsula, Persia and East Africa who integrated into the local, southern Indian, population.

42   Quoted in Kumari Jayawardena, *Ethnic and Class Conflicts in Sri Lanka* (Centre for Social Analysis: Colombo, 1985), p.12.

43   Is it too much to read Azeez 's representation of the origin of the Muslims in Sri Lanka, as resulting from the (peaceful) pursuit of commerce, as being in opposition not just to the (alien) colonial conquerors but also to earlier migrants (Tamils) who

may also have come to Sri Lanka as conquerors?

44 What influence, if any, the presence of Pasha and his entourage had on the Muslim elite's insistence on its grand Arab origin is a question that needs further study.

45 For more on this question, see Marilyn Lake, 'Mission Impossible: How Men Gave Birth to the Australian Nation,' in *Gender and History* vol 4, No. 3, 1992.

46 In this connection it is important to realize that another "tradition" pertaining to their origin was also current among Sri Lankan Muslims at the time, locating their origin in southern India (VS:261, EB:234). Azeez, not surprisingly, actively suppresses this: "Let me state at once that there is no tradition in Ceylon that the ancestors of the Ceylon Moors came from Kayal [in south India]...nor have I heard that such a tradition exists at Kayal" (IL:24). Methinks the gentleman protests too much.

47 This question was put to me by Gananath Obeyesekere. It could, of course, be premature.

48 Indeed, many Tamil nationalists tried to maintain an ostensibly inclusive "Tamil speaking people" identity until the late 1980s. For more on this, see K.Sivathamby, 'The Sri Lankan Ethnic Crisis and Muslim–Tamil Relationships: A Socio–Political Review' in Charles Abeysekera and Newton Gunasinghe (eds.) *Facets of Ethnicity in Sri Lanka* (SSA: Colombo, 1987), p.193; hereafter, KS.

49 This is of course a tentative, incomplete answer. There exists hardly any theoretical work on the colonial (contribution to the) construction of identities in Sri Lanka. Such work is a very pressing necessity; and should perhaps be inspired by, among other essays, Gyanendra Pandey's excellent 'The Colonial Construction of 'Communalism': British Writings on Banaras in the Nineteenth Century' in Ranajit Guha (ed.) *Subaltern Studies VI* (Oxford: Delhi, 1989). R.L.Stirrat and Elizabeth Nissan, both anthropologists, make a somewhat bland attempt to discuss the topic in 'The Generation of Communal Identities' in Jonathan Spencer (ed.) *Sri Lanka: History and the Roots of Conflict* (Routledge: London. 1990). They claim that "British rule substantialized heterogeneity," formalized "cultural difference and... [made] it the basis for political representation"; however, they conclude that this was done not out of a "wish to 'divide and rule'...[but] out of misguided 'liberal' sentiments..." (p.29). This is a conclusion informed by the spirit of Macaulay. I must also remark upon another aspect of the Stirrat/Nissan piece; "While the British were present there was relative calm; but only eight years after independence communal violence broke out between Sinhala [sic] and Tamils for the first time" (p.34). This representation is not the consequence but the cause of the denial of divide and rule. One might add that the distance from here to Bishop Heber is not very long.

50 This distinction was institutionalized by the British in the 1911 census, when "Indian" and "Ceylon" Moors were enumerated differently. One can, again, only speculate as to what might have occurred if this wasn't done.

51   Indeed, the issue that dominated Fareed's election campaign in 1952 against M. C. M. Kaleel, then leader of the Muslim League, was whether the formation was a racial or religious one. Kaleel was the UNP nominee for the multi–member Colombo Central constituency and, when denied the UNP nomination, Fareed challenged him as an independent. The Muslim voters of Colombo Central, in their wisdom, sent both to parliament.

52   'Aspects of Religion, Economy and Society among the Muslims of Ceylon,' *Contributions to Indian Sociology*, no. 6.1972. Hereafter, MM. This paper has been published in several other places, including T. N. Madan (ed.) *Muslim Communities in South Asia* (Oxford: Delhi, 1976).

53   It must be noted that within Sri Lankan identitarian discourse today, the "Indian Moors" have been assimilated within the category "Muslim."

54   This argument finesses questions about "Moor" names like Macan Markar, Marikar Bawa, Sinne Lebbe and Kariapper, which are not Arab. An 1816 list of Sri Lankan slave–owners proves interesting reading in this connection. Among the many Muslims names listed here are Pakkier Tamby, Cadolebbe Vidahn, Koos Kanie and Sabo Masthan Saybo (ES:69). Even accounting for British errors in transcription, hardly any of them are recognizably "Arab," which raises the question as to when Sri Lankan Muslims consciously Arabized their names.

55   Mahmud would repeat this to Vasundara Mohan, in 1981: "The Muslims of Sri Lanka have nothing which we could call our mother–tongue," in *Identity Crisis of Sri Lankan Muslims* (Mittal: Delhi, 1987), p.41; hereafter, VM.

56   It is also important to recall that, to Azeez, Muslims spoke Tamil, the same language spoken by members of the Tamil social formation, not "Arabic–Tamil."

57   Mauroof also fails to realize that the identity of the Muslim social formation is based on exclusion as well as inclusion, on difference: a Muslim is also neither Tamil nor Sinhalese.

58   'Islamic Revivalism in International Perspective and its Impact on Sri Lanka,' in CC; hereafter, AS.

59   Sivathamby makes a similar argument: given "linguistic nationalism in Sri Lanka, where Sinhala and Tamil constitute distinct language cultures, the identity of the Muslims has necessarily to be expressed and maintained through their religion..." (KS:200).

60   The compatibility of Islam and capitalism is a theme present in most instances of elite Muslim discourse. AS, for instance, insists upon it too. However, these various writers do not do so for the same reasons, aren't always responding to the same historical pressures.

61   As Zillah Eisenstein argues, "the social relations of society define the particular activity a woman engages in at a given moment." ...What "one woman does in the

home of another, or what she does when hired by a man is seen as domestic work and is paid, but what a woman does as a wife or mother in her own home is considered a labor of love, is not defined as work by the society..." see 'Some Notes on the Relations of Capitalist Patriarchy,' in *Capitalist Patriarchy and the Case for Socialist Feminism* (Longman: New York, 1981), p.47.

62　Though he does say that they were successful traders and excelled in it (EB:236).

63　'The Muslim Minority of Sri Lanka: A Business Community in Transition,' published in MS; hereafter SW. The authors neglect to tell us what or where this "business community" is in transition to. Indeed, reading SW one discovers that the Muslims are neither a business community nor in transition. Again it must be noted that the Bank does not consider women's housework to be "work."

64　It cannot be stressed too much that the subtext here —discussed in the next section — is that the Muslims are also a wealthy community. Samarasinghe, for instance, implies this by quoting figures which "show" that per capita income among the Muslims was the highest for all Sri Lankan social formations. Interestingly enough, Nimal Siripala uses the figures of the same Central Bank but comes to radically different conclusions (in 'Muslims of Sri Lanka: Aspects of Income Distribution,' in CC). Siripala argues that there are severe disparities in income between urban and rural and between upper and lower class Muslims and presents a complicated picture of the economic welfare of the Muslim formation, thus revealing the ideologicat impulse behind the use of only per capita income figures by Samarasinghe.

65　'Muslims and Capitalism in British Ceylon (Sri Lanka): The Colonial Image and Community's Behavior,' in *Journal of the Institute of Muslim Minority Affairs*, vol. 8 no. 2, 1987, p. 312; hereafter, AA2.

66　For more on this, see Yasmine Gooneratne, *English Literature in Ceylon 1815—1878* (Dehiwela: Tisara Prakasakayo, 1968). especially chapter 6.

67　*Ceylo*, vol. I (Dehiwela: Tisara Prakasakayo, 1977 [1859]), p.534, emphasis added. It should he noted that, for Tennent, the Muslims were a "tribe," not a "race" and he found the term "Moor" a "meaningless designation," p.532.

68　*The Myth of the Lazy Native*, quoted in AA2:314.

69　Partha Chatterjee argues that: "Hegemonic power is always a combination of force and the persuasive self–evidence of ideology. To the extent that the persuasive apparatus...necessarily and invariably fails to match the requirements of direct political domination...[hegemonic] rule is always marked by the palpable, indeed openly demonstrated, presence of physical force." (*The Nation and its Fragments* [Princeton UP: Princeton, 1993].p.56.) In my reading, fear is the elite Muslim response to the threat of force.

70　It should be noted here that class interest and fear are inextricably linked to the geographical distribution of the Muslim population. Unlike Eastern Muslims, who re-side in concentrations in the former Eastern Province, the Southern Muslim tion is scattered throughout the Sinhala dominated parts of the country. This, too, has contributed to the accomodationist politics of the Muslim elite; though, of course, its politics cannot be reduced to purely geographical factors.

71 Except for K. M. de Silva, however, manages to do this without once mentioning Anagarika Dharmapala, blaming Ramanathan for the subsequent behavior of the Muslim elite. *The Journal of Asian Studies* carried a symposium on the riots (vol XXIX.2, February 1970): Kumari Jayawardena's 'Economic and Political Factors in the 1915 Riots,' is a fine examination of the events in Colombo; Charles Blackton, in an otherwise unremarkable piece ('The Action Phase of' the 1915 Riots') does note that the Sinhala nationalist representation of these events focuses not on acts against the Muslims but on the subsequent acts of the British colonial state against the Sinhala elite, thus making the Sinhalese victims of 1915 and completely erasing the Muslims (even as participants, leave alone victims); P. T. M. Fernando's 'The Post Riots Campaign for Justice' follows the logic of Sinhala nationalism — the "justice" he is concerned about is limited to the Sinhala elite. For a good, though not entirely unproblematic Muslim perspective on these events, see AA1. Michael Roberts has an intriguing piece discussing the role of British colonial law in enabling the events: 'Noise as Cultural Struggle: Tom–Tom Beating, the British and Communal Disturbances in Sri Lanka, 1880s–1930s,' in Veena Das (ed.) *Mirrors of Violence* (Oxford: Delhi, 1990). His is an argument I am mostly in sympathy with. I would have ignored John Rogers' narrative of the events in *Crime, Justice and Society in Colonial Sri Lanka* (Curzon: London, 1987) were it not for its (neo) colonial sensibility; he documents riot after riot, without appreciating any difference between them, in very much the style of the colonial administrator one thought was by now dead and buried. I would strongly urge him, though without much hope, to read Pandey.

72 When one reads K.N.O. Dharmadasa, however, who labels these attacks "Sinhala-Muslim clashes," one comes to have less antipathy to those who use the term "riots". (It should be noted here that Sinhala life or property was not harmed by Muslims during these "clashes".) Dharmadasa's insidiousness, though to be expected from an apologist for Dharmapala, needs to be rebutted. For instance, he describes Gampola as "a one-time capital of the ancient Sinhalese kingdom, which in modern times had come to shelter a sizeable Moor population" (*Language, Religion and Ethnic Assertiveness: The Growth of Sinhalese Nationalism in Sri Lanka* [U of Michigan Press: Ann Arbor,1992], p.143). One can see here distinct echoes of Dharmapala: the Sinhalese are ancient; the Moors, recent — implicitly, alien — and being "sheltered" by the Sinhalese. This, presumably, should lead to Muslim acceptance of Sinhala hegemony, to Muslim acceptance of any Sinhala maltreatment.

73 One might mention here that the close nexus between the Sinhala independence movement and attacks on Muslims has escaped the notice of most commentators.

74   K.M.de Silva has noted this, albeit with a spin I do not share: "For a decade or more after the riots the mood of the Muslim community was a mixture of fear and suspicion of Sinhala nationalism and in that mood they were eagerly receptive to the blandishments of the British administration" (KM I:457). Ameer Ali gets closer to the point: "If there was any lesson that the Muslim community learned from that episode [1915], it was the fact that Sri Lanka... is a Sinhalese country and that to confront the Sinhalese... is...risk[y]..."('Politics of Survival: Past Strategies and Present Predicament of the Muslim Community in Sri Lanka,' in *Journal of Muslim Minority Affairs*, vol. 7.2, 1986. p.154; hereafter, AA3.) One might add here that the "lesson" was "learned" not so much by the Muslim community as by its elite.

75   The above quotes are from AA3:156.

76   *Hansard*, 12 June 1956, pp.1626-1638. The following quotes are all from that speech.

77   It should be noted that Fareed's lukewarm endorsement of Arabic (unsupported with a demand for it to be made an official language too) coupled with his support of "Sinhala Only," helped further reinforce the fact that the Muslims did not have "their own" language.

78   (*Hansard* 11 June 1956, pp.1229).

79   It is also necessary in this connection to note the remarks of Y.Ahamed, an Eastern civil servant, who wrote in the late 1980s, after, that is, Tamil-Muslim relations in the East had got seriously polarized: "By whatever name the Tamil speaking Muslims are called...for reasons of national harmony or political expediency, their way of life and their history are intimately and fondly harmonized in the totality of [the] Tamil heritage." (Quoted in *Land, Human Rights and the Eastern Predicament: UTHR Report# 11*, April 1993, p.43; hereafter, UT11.)

80   Within the terms of this discourse, derogatory remarks of Ramanathan are to he expected, and Fareed delivered, saying that the "Tamils today are trying now what Sir Ponnambalam Ramanathan tried in 1885."

81   Here, Fareed could have been unconsciously echoing another Muslim "leader," Mohamed Macan Markar, who said in 1938: the Muslims "do not want equal representation with the Sinhalese... [W]hat we want is adequate representation and good government. I prefer this country to be ruled by the Sinhalese" (quoted in VM:25). This was in response to a demand by some Tamil political organizations, when the idea of self–government was first being mooted by the colonial power, for power sharing between representatives of all the Sri Lankan social formations. Not incidentally, both Fareed and Macan Markar, another upper class trader, were knighted by the British for services rendered to the crown.

82   It should perhaps be noted that, despite his current stature, Fareed didn't always succeed in getting himself elected to parliament, even though he switched parties more

than once. Indeed he was more often appointed to parliament by a Sinhala political party than he was elected (by largely Sinhala voters). In 1947 he even deserted his constituency, Colombo Central, hoping to be elected from Pottuvil, in the East; he was defeated by a local notable. Many Southern Muslim "leaders," fearful of their fate amongst a largely Sinhala electorate, have often run for parliament from Eastern (predominantly Muslim) constituencies. In the post–colonial period only one did so successfully. It would appear therefore that Eastern Muslim voters, at least, never had much faith in their Southern Muslim "leaders."

83   Razick Fareed Foundation: Colombo, 1986; hereafter, LA.

84   The flip side of this argument. which Athulathmudali doesn't quite address but is implicit in his comments, is that the Muslims have benefited from accommodating themselves to Sinhala hegemony. It is in this context also that Samarasinghe's remarks that the Muslims are the "wealthiest" community must be read. K.M.de Silva makes this point explicitly and details the "benefits" the Muslims have received from the Sinhala state (in KM I): nebulous educational scraps, the recognition of (the very patriarchal) Muslim personal law and permission for Muslim employees to receive two hours leave on Fridays to attend *kothuba*. Consequently, de Silva argues that the creation of a separate Muslim political party "is fraught with perils for the Muslims. There is nothing that such a political party can do for the Muslims that they cannot do as members of national [sic] political parties." 'The Muslim Minority in a Democratic Polity – Reflections on a Theme' in MS, p,447; hereafter KM2. One might add here that arguments similar to de Silva's have been made by the Muslim elite, too.

85   One might note in passing that such statements almost explicitly deny the possibility of a Sri Lankan state where power is shared.

86   *New Ceylon Writing # 5*, 1984, p.24.

87   *Sri Lanka Muslims and Ethnic Grievances* (Privately published: Colombo, 1986), p.12, emphasis added.

88   For a good account of the circumstances of Tamils and Muslims in the East in early 1993, see UT11.

89   *Gender and the Politics of History* (Columbia: New York. 1988), p.88.

90   'The Sri Lankan Ethnic War: The Muslim Dimension,' in *Tamil Times* 15 November 1992, p.14. Hussain, too, makes a similar claim: "The Moor identity may have to suffer fission in the future as a result both of a linguistic and a political division" (IH:4).

91   *The Inoperative Community* (U of Minnesota Press: Minneapolis, 1991).

92   UT11 mentions many Muslims and Tamils from the East arguing this as late as 1993.

Authorizing History, Ordering Land: The Conquest of Anuradhapura[1]

Pradeep Jeganathan

"The conquest of India was a conquest of knowledge."
—Bernard Cohn[2]

Introduction

Central to this essay is the argument that knowledge and authority are linked in a recursive way: fields of knowledge produced by authoritative social agents become authoritative knowledge. Linked with this assertion is the argument that authoritative knowledge, and the epistemological formations that encompass them, are not merely intellectual positions, nor purely discursive or textual fields. Rather, I wish to suggest that authoritative forms of knowledge simultaneously produce discursive, as well as non-discursive objects; that is, physical, concrete objects. These non-discursive objects in particular produce startling "effects of the real." This is not to deny the reality of discursive objects; rather, it is to stress the particular effects of non-discursive objects.

Yet, epistemological interventions through their own rules of existence erase their beginnings, their histories, and their conditions of possibility. If we are to unmask the constructed nature of authoritative knowledges - not to demonstrate them false, for they are true given their own conditions but to show through their workings, their consequences, and their implications with other projects of power - then we must write the history of such authoritative fields of knowledge.

This paper is concerned with writing such a history: a history of the production of authoritative knowledge about a particular subject - history- in a particular space - what is now called Anuradhapura, Sri

Lanka. What follows is not then a history of Anuradhapura; rather it is a history of knowledge about Anuradhapura, and the practices that produced that knowledge. Nor does this history span all time, from what ancient historians might call the 'very beginning.' On the contrary, I am only concerned here with a history of modern knowledge about Anuradhapura, because my argument is that the 'very beginning,' or point of origin of contemporary, authoritative forms of knowledge about Anuradhapura is recent. The 'very beginning' was only 'the day before yesterday.' My point is this: the authoritative epistemology of Anuradhapura, that is the field of power and knowledge it is located in today, was created in a radical rupture in the nineteenth century. And hence, Anuradhapura is as old as that rupture.

But, the reader will protest, Anuradhapura is ancient; we have always known of its existence. For even when it had fallen into rack and ruin, pilgrims still made their journey; it was named in indigenous texts throughout all time. There are many who will make this claim, with varying degrees of sophistication. Take for example, such a sophisticated, recent attempt by Steven Kemper, who in a carefully hedged scholarly text about the modernity and ancientness of Sinhala historical practice, writes suddenly, and explicitly: "[t]he prize among the Buddhist sacred places in the island has always been Anuradhapura."[3] There are many assumptions in this one line that are worth interrogating, from the point of view of this essay. There is the implicit claim here of the *existence* of "Buddhist sacred places," over the long *durée*. And in as much as these were sacred places, Anuradhapura has *"always"* been the prize among them. Now a "Buddhist sacred place," for Kemper, is defined by an argument about restoration: sacred places are those which are continually restored; and restoration is a "genuinely ancient practice in Sri Lanka."[4] So for Kemper, the Nationalist "campaign in the 1890s to protect religious places in Anuradhapura," is a recent manifestation of this ancient practice; nor is he surprised that Anuradhapura is chosen by Sinhala Nationalists as a site suitable for this ancient practice of restoration, because, if I may paraphrase him gently: "Anuradhapura... has always been... the prize."

I seek to contest these statements, in two related ways. First, I write a historical account of the discursive and non-discursive epistemological practices– for me, historical, archaeological and aesthetic practices –that produce a modern site like Anuradhapura. These are practices that Kemper contains under the sign of 'restoration': he marks them as ancient, and therefore without a significant modern history. Second, in an effort which ties in with the first, but is yet different, I will write the history of the conditions of possibility, of a statement such as Kemper's. Or in other words, I will expose the fields of power and knowledge that have made such previous statements appear true.

Read in this vein, this essay is much closer to, but yet is differently focused from Elizabeth Nissan's important work on Anuradhapura.[5] On the one hand, I am in agreement with much of Nissan's argument: Anuradhapura was made in the nineteenth century; its ancientness is indeed "a new creation."[6] I also agree that there is a remarkable similarity between colonial constructions of Anuradhapura and nationalist readings of the site. On the other hand, my disagreement with Nissan lies with the theoretical reasoning she uses to arrive at this conclusion. Take this key sentence: "In this paper…I concentrate on the congruence, or 'elective affinity', between European ideological commitments and some of the material available to Orientalist scholarship in Sri Lanka."[7] In this formulation, "the material available," and the Orientalizing of that material, given "European ideological commitments" seems to take place in a field that is devoid of relations of power. Rather, the movement from the first field of knowledge — "the material available" — to the second, orientalized field of knowledge is theorized as possible given a "congruence" or "elective affinity" between the two fields of knowledge. But it is my view that any object of knowledge is also a dense point in a field of power; orientalized objects are particularly so, produced as they are in a field of colonial power. This is so, in the logic of my argument, because the production of an object of knowledge entails the making of truth claims, and such claims have a recursive relationship with authority. While this claim is a general one, making it also allows for the production of a specific, new history of Anuradhapura which is crucial to our understanding of that object. And that is the project of this essay.

In order to analyse these fields of knowledge and power, I will use two Foucauldian constructs. The first, "regime[s] of truth" which are for Michel Foucault "the ensemble of rules according to which the true and the false are separated and the specific effects of power attached to the true."[8] In other words, a "regime of truth" orders and organizes knowledge, allowing for truth claims to be made. The second construct, disciplinary formation,—as in "historiographic/spatial formation" is an adaptation of Foucault's "discursive formation."[9] For me it is a bundle of discursive statements, as well as a structured set of non-discursive practices, that construct objects, both discursive and non-discursive, by their operation. A disciplinary formation, then, structures and gives coherence to the internal logic of both statements and practices that are produced as "true" by the "regime" at hand.[10]

In the pages that follow, I shall focus on the operation of several such formations: the major division is the 'historiographic formation' on the one hand, and a 'spatial formation' on the other. I use the name 'spatial formation' as a marker for two formations that take 'order' as their 'regime', and the 'landscape' as their object. They are an 'archaeological formation'[11] and an 'aesthetic formation.' These formations, then, simultaneously produce knowledge and authorize the re-making of Anuradhapura in their operation.

The Historiographic Formation

To appreciate the colonial epistemological field that authorizes Anuradhapura, I first analyse the "regime of truth" of its historiography and then move to its concretization in mid-nineteenth century Ceylon. The kind of historiography which concerns me here is a nineteenth century construct; what Collingwood calls "positivistic historiography."[12] This epistemological/theoretical position formed the 'regime of historiographic truth' of the Royal Asiatic Societies (of GB & I, and of Bengal, founded in 1784). The production of knowledge about conquered lands and peoples was a crucial moment in the colonization of South Asia. And knowledge of history was quite central in these efforts: to know the 'past' was to control the 'present.'[13]

The rules of a 'regime of truth' inherent in the discourse of nineteenth century positivist historiography concern chronological narratives of events:

(1) These 'events' must remain 'natural' i.e., within the bounds of 'scientific knowledge': for example, no 'fantastic miracles' are allowed. (2) The narrative of 'history' flows continuously forward from the 'past' to

the 'present.' If the narrative covers a long period it is divided into epochs. Each epoch has a 'beginning' and an 'end.' (3) This time frame within which 'history' moved had to be bounded by the existing 'scientific' conceptions of the age of the world and its people. (4) 'History' is teleological: it is 'progress' —from 'barbarism' to 'civilization' or vice versa, 'degeneration.' (5) This teleological narrative produces, for the historian, the contemporary moment as well. That is, the contemporary moment is seen as a logical culmination of the narrative of history and is crucial for the 'understanding' of that moment. As it may be already becoming clear, several general epistemological 'rules' are inherent in this view of history. In this epistemological field, 'knowledge' transcends reality, it is not constituted by, and constitutive of, its socio-cultural context. Knowledge is 'objective' as opposed to 'biased.' In fact, knowledge represents reality perfectly: the neat, dominant metaphor is the mirror. The claim of perfect re-presentation is also a 'truth' claim and a very strong one: only one version of the 'truth' can exist.[14]

Not surprisingly, given this 'regime of truth,' the imperial historian in South Asia found it difficult to find indigenous texts that could be treated as 'authentic historical accounts.' This was not, of course, for the want of 'source materials.' Texts which were recognized as 'ancient' such as the Vedas, Brahmanas, Puranas or 'Epics' like the *Mahabharata*, and the *Ramayana*, were dismissed as ahistorical fictions: these texts did not meet the dominant conditions of 'truth.'[15] As James Mill argues in a text that was to become 'hegemonic'[16] in the field: "This people, indeed, are perfectly destitute of historical records:"[17]

The Sri Lankan case was quite similar in the early period of European colonization. European accounts available from the seventeenth century through the early nineteenth century are unanimous that no texts that can be read as historical (in the sense set out above), can be found among those available in the island.[18] John Davy's writings[19] are representative of these accounts: "The Singalese... possess no accurate records of events, are ignorant of genuine history, and are not sufficiently advanced to relish it."[20] A remarkable rupture, however, takes place in the late 1830's. A set of ancient, indigenous texts, that are 'read' as a chronological narrative are 'excavated.' These texts reach the threshold of the 'regime of historiographical truth': they become 'authentic history.' Two names appear in the space of this rupture, but it is George Turnour's translation that becomes authoritative.[21] In an effort to locate Turnour and this rupture socially, let me pause here to outline the contours of the British colonial social formation in Sri Lanka during the early nineteenth century.

The British crown became the first European power to establish control over the *entire* island in 1815-1820, after the conquest of the Kandyan Kingdom in the central hills of the island. While the initial transfer of power in 1815 was a negotiated one, a major indigenous uprising in 1817–18, met with a strong military response. Subduing and maintaining control over the newly acquired Kandyan territory was the paramount project of the time. Militarily, judicial and executive authority was not clearly separated and often resided in the same official. These officials, then, were required to be competent in many fields. Attempts by officials to construct a sociology and history of the colony were considered necessary and useful, yet such attempts were hampered by a lack of knowledge of indigenous languages. [22] As such, the published accounts of indigenous history and sociology of the time, in their conclusive statements, fall back into received, authoritative assumptions about the 'East.' Even exceptions to this rule appear to be rare, and George Turnour who was learning both Sinhala and Pali from local Buddhist monks, is certainly an important one. On the one hand, Turnour's efforts must be located in the practical necessities of colonial administration: for example, he was required to adjudicate a dispute between two Buddhist factions over the control of Sri Pada, a sacred mountain, in 1825-6, a project which may have required the construction of a 'history of Buddhism,' and *perhaps* inspired his interest in Pali texts.[23] On the other hand, Turnour must also be located in the larger intellectual formation of the Royal Asiatic Society of Bengal [RAS/B] (also intimately linked with the colonial project), where his efforts were presented via the mail and critically debated.

In the 'moment' just after translation, the claim Turnour would like to make for the 'authenticity' of this history is an extremely provocative one, for it flies in the face of received wisdom. However, by 1838, the major text in question the *Mahavamsa*, becomes *the* authoritative 'historical' text of 'Ceylon.' There are three important levels of this transformative operation which I want to mark before I proceed further with my narrative.

(1) From oral to textual: Available evidence indicates that the *Mahavamsa*, together with its commentaries, was not read as a text i.e., from the physical manuscript, at the time of its 'discovery' by Turnour.[24] Multiple, indigenous conceptions of the past clearly existed at the time and while some conceptions overlap with the textual material, others do not. Furthermore, I would suggest that these conceptions of the past, constituted a debate that was meaningful in its social context. Different positions within the debate contradicted each other.[25] Importantly, these conceptions were constituted by and constitutive of categories, conceptions of the world, and epistemological fields that were different from those that can be read from the texts in question.

(2) From text to positivist history: In its translation from Pali to English, the *Mahavamsa* undergoes a set of violent transformations. Some of these transformations are linguistic and stylistic: errors in translation and inattention to the poetic, metrical style of the original. But most importantly, the major transformations are epistemological. The dominant regime of positivist historiography read out all conceptions of the world and epistemological positions that were contrary to it. That is, notions of incalculable, non-linear time and 'fantastic miracles' that could be regarded as central to the text, were marked in translation as unimportant, biased, 'ahistorical' and 'untrue.' Both these indigenous fields of knowledge— oral and textual, become what Foucault calls "subjugated knowledges."[26]

(3) From claim to acceptance: The first reading of Turnour's initial claim for the 'historical' nature of the *Mahavamsa* before the RAS/B, in 1835, produced an opinion, shared by Turnour, that the text could be read as illuminating the history of *Indian* Buddhism. An extremely important archaeological identification, crucial for the entire 'chronology' of Indian history, as it is being constituted at the time, is made given this reading and the existence of the text. Yet, by 1838, after the intervention of James Princep (Secretary of the RAS/B), and a great deal of petty suppression and editorializing on his part, Turnour's *Mahavamsa* is read only as providing an internal chronological history of Sri Lanka, which is then thought to be tangential to the history of India.[27] This transforma-

tion, continues to have extraordinary implications for authoritative conceptions of Sri Lankan history: The history of Sri Lanka, is always seen as a separate analytic field from the history of India, from the earliest times to the present day.

Let me now return to my narrative, and the larger question: why were the Pali Vamsa texts read as authentic histories? The 'common sense' answer is that the reasons lie in the texts themselves: they are 'chronological narratives' or 'histories.' Even though this assumes that ancient 'Sinhala' writers were positivist 'historians' and ahistorically collapses the nineteenth century epistemological 'moment' into that of ancient Sri Lanka, it remains the dominant view in contemporary scholarship to this day. But, as I have already noted at length above, this reading does considerable violence to the texts in question. The explanation, then, can not be reduced to the nature of the text alone.[28] Among a complex of causes that are undoubtedly operative here, I tentatively suggest one possibility: the availability of 'sights/sites' on the ground, that the text referred to, considerably reinforced Turnours' truth claim and in general that of the translated text. In fact, Turnour himself writes that "the authenticity" of the translated "annals" are "attested" by the "remains" of "many stupendous works, the remains of which still exist…"[29] and similar links are repeatedly drawn between 'the ruins' and the 'historical texts' as the claim for their authenticity is made."[30] By the middle of the nineteenth century these claims had been accepted: the Pali chronicles had a great deal of authority as authentic historical texts.[31] By 1859 Sir James Emerson Tennent could claim that "Ceylon..[is]…in possession of continuous written chronicles, rich in authentic facts" that present a "connected history of the island…"[32]

The social context that allowed the production of a text such as Tennent's (1859), and also William Knighton's *History of Ceylon* (1845)[33] which appears a little earlier, is also important. By the middle of the nineteenth century, commercial considerations, rather than purely military ones seem dominant in the government of the colony. This reflected the labour of workers on coffee plantations that had been setup in the previous two decades and the resultant surpluses that circulated in the colony. Administrative and military authority was now separate and organized, and also the mercantile capitalists and planters were important segments of the colonial bourgeoisie. At the level of serious intellec-

tual production, diverse elements from all segments of the colonial bourgeoisie united in the formation of the Ceylon Branch of the Royal Asiatic
Society in 1845, which was modeled on existing parent societies in London and Calcutta. The aims were to "collect scattered rays of information
possessed by different individuals" and to "encourage a literary and scientific spirit... in the island."[34] Many of the major producers of the knowledge I am excavating here were active members. Sir James Emerson
Tennent, Colonial Secretary at the time was the founding Vice-Patron
and William Knighton, a planter, was the Secretary. Tennent's text in
particular drew heavily on the intellectual resources and specialized
knowledge of the members of the Society. As such it is a magnificently
detailed, magisterially documented work that leaves no subject unexplored. It produced an authoritative field of specific knowledge about
'Ceylon' that remained unquestioned throughout the nineteenth century.
It sold widely, with two new editions being printed within two months of
its first production.[35] The newly excavated 'history' culled from the *Mahavamsa*, framed by the 'regime of positivist historiographic truth' was an
important formation of knowledge for the society. Throughout the nineteenth and early twentieth centuries, efforts were made to translate additional texts and to 'improve' existing translations of Pali and Sinhala
chronicles: for example, the additions (*The Culavamsa*) of Wijesinha in
1889, and Geiger's version of the *Mahavamsa* in 1912.

The nineteenth century (European) debate on the newly discovered 'historical' texts was, indeed, a lively one: skeptical positions were articulated. For example, a leading scholar of things Indian, Vincent Smith
was vehement in his opposition to a *part* of the text: "the Ceylonese
chronology prior to B.C. 160 is absolutely and completely rejected, as being not merely of doubtful authority but positively false in its principal
propositions."[36] Quite apart from noting that Smith's position was a minority one, and that he softens it later,[37] we must remember, more importantly, that this opposition was voiced within the dominant terms of
debate: always defined by the authority of the *Mahavamsa* and the 'Pa-
li/Sinhala chronicles.' Any oppositional position was an argument with
this authority.

Let me now present some of the salient theoretical positions and
concrete 'facts' that are embedded in this specific 'historical' narrative as

read through the positivist regime of historiographic truth. My exposition here will be out of the versions of Knighton (1845) and Tennent (1859), the authoritative voices in this field. First, in general, the theory and epistemology of this 'history' does not deviate much from the the rules of the 'regime of historiographic truth' sketched out earlier. Details from the texts that do not 'fit' but have survived translation are repressed in the retelling or are noted as 'false.'

What we have here is a history of kings and battles, plagues and famines. This historical narrative intersects with nineteenth century theories of 'race'. The initial 'moment' is the story of the invasion of the island and the colonization of the native inhabitants by 'Bengalis' from (North-East) India in 543 B.C. This group then metamorphasizes into the 'Singalese.' The major narrative then becomes that of the '[C]/Sing/[h]ala' kings and peoples who throughout this history battle Tamil/Malabar kings and peoples (from South India) for the control of 'Ceylon.'

This historical narrative is presented in two sections, first of progress, from 543 BC to 302 AD, and then of degeneration and decline from that point to the nineteenth century. This is quite different from an earlier position that I located in a quote from John Davy (see above), where a narrative of an almost unchanging 'barbarism' is assumed. The 'moment' of the 'new' golden past, which occurs at the end of the progressive period, is dwelt on at some length. Knighton, for example, compares this zenith to that reached by Greece and Rome.[38] Romantic comparisons with Greek and Roman 'civilization' can proceed comfortably here, because the degradation/decline of the 'Sinhala civilization' and the ascendency of British 'civilization' in the *contemporary* moment is an authoritative fact.[39] Anuradhapura, in its golden age, represents the midpoint of the master narrative of history; its glorification in the textual narrative does not change the teleology of the narrative. It is important to realize that this degenerate contemporary moment, as is teleologically produced by the narrative of the *Mahavamsa*, fits neatly with the social fact of British colonial rule in the island. This then is the master narrative of Sri Lankan 'history.'

The Spatial Formation

Nuwarakalaviya, the administrative province where Anuradhapura is located, was not very important to the indigenous kings of the early nineteenth century. In 1803, Prince Muttusami (brother-in-law of the late King Rajadhi Rajasinha), a would-be British sponsored claimant to the throne of Kandy, is asked to cede a province of the Kandyan Kingdom in exchange for assistance. During secret negotiations he refuses to cede Sabaragamuwa, because it (1) brought substantial revenues and (2) would lead to the loss of Sri Pada, "the sacrilegious cessation of which would bring down on him the wrath of heaven and the curses of mankind." The prince, however, makes a counter proposal: he is willing to cede the province of Nuwarakalaviya instead. This is, roughly, what is now called the NCP, and it doesn't seem to worry the prince that he will lose control of Anuradhapura.[40]

For the British colonial project in Ceylon, at the beginning of the nineteenth century, the major spatial typology that emerges is the opposition of the coastal low lands to the 'interior.' Much of the coast, was well 'known' to and 'ordered' by Portuguese and Dutch colonial projects of conquest and rule that began in the early sixteenth century. When in 1815, British colonial rule extended to the Kandyan Kingdom in the 'interior,' a new project of 'ordering' the landscape of the whole island begins. The mountainous, and therefore, supposedly inaccessible terrain of the central region of 'Ceylon' was seen by the British as a signifier of the ability of the indigenous people to rebel and resist colonial rule successfully. Therefore this project, in which cartographic practices and the building of transportation networks were linked, was a priority. Since the centre of indigenous authority was seen to be in Kandy, it was the south-central region surrounding the city, that first intersected with these practices. Specifically, after the widespread rebellion of 1817-18 a concerted effort was made to build a road from Colombo to Kandy in the central hills to facilitate the movement of troops. This project was a difficult one and was only completed in 1831.[41] In its course, the areas to the west and south-west of Kandy were mapped and networked.

At this time, however, there was another region of the newly colonized territory that remained 'unknown' and unordered by the colonial project. This region, which is central to our discussion, was to the north and north-east of Kandy. In cartographic representations of the period it was referred to as an "unexplored district" or an "unknown mountainous region."[42] This region became important for the colonial project only after the setting up of large coffee plantations in the central hills in the mid 1830's. It was important because large groups of wage labourers needed to be transported from South India to the central hills to work on these plantations. The swiftest route of migration was through this hitherto unordered region to the north of the central hills. The project of ordering land, then, moved to the Nuwarakalaviya, which later became the 'North-Central Province'. Yet, as noted in my narrative above, the excavation of the *Mahavamsa* was simultaneous with this project of colonial order. Together with the colonial cartography that emerged here, then, was a different cartographic image, culled from the *Mahavamsa*: an entire 'landscape of ruins' emerges from the reading of the text. Let me note here Tennent's map,[43] which superimposed this landscape on the contemporary cartographic image. This map divided the island into the Rajarata, Mayarata and Rohanarata. The 'landscape of ruins,' that the *Mahavamsa* was read as referring to, was located primarily, in the *Rajarata* (land of kings), which was the same physical territory, Nuwarakalaviya, that was being mapped and networked in the larger colonial project at this time.[44] The shift in the meaningful constitution of the 'ruins' of the Nuwarakalaviya after the 'excavation' of the 'historical' texts is remarkable. Hurriedly jotted diary notes are re-examined and special expeditions are made to the site of the ruins and quite extensive, careful observations are made and published.

Before I move to the details of the reception and reconstitution of clusters of ruins at this 'site,' I will first provide a telling example of the narrativization of Anuradhapura, through the semantic construction of its proper name. The 'site' that I have referred throughout this paper, as Anuradhapura, is written in different transliterated forms in the various colonial accounts 1 have been reading. While some of this variation is attributable to the problems inherent in translating an unfamiliar word, I suggest that there is more going on here. To explain: the two semantic poles that emerge throughout the early nineteenth century accounts are Anurajapura and Anuradhapura. One can see the increasing use of the second term with the growing authority of the *Mahavamsa*. Now, in

Sinhala, Anurajapura could mean, Anu[wa]-ninety, raja-king, pura-city: The city of ninety kings. In the seventeenth century Robert Knox refers to the city as a place where ninety kings ruled.[45] The Portuguese historian, Fernano De Queyroz, also writing in the seventeenth century, is even more explicit: he refers to the place as Anu Rajapure, which he translates as the "Mansion of Ninety Kings."[46] By the nineteenth century, however, the authority of the *Mahavamsa* begins to overide this semantic construction: we can read this hierarchization in Jonathan Forbes: "It is the general belief of the *uneducated* natives that the name of the city is derived from Anuraja (ninety kings).."[47]

This semantic construction is displaced by the operation of the *Mahavamsa*, which refers to the city as Anuradhapura, giving two versions of its *founding*: (1) By a person named Anuradha; (2) under the constellation Anuradha. By the middle of the nineteenth century the semantic construction becomes fixed as Anuradhapura. Note here that Anuradha is a proper name, linked to founding; it has *no* connotation of ninety. This transformation is not merely semantic; it provides a brief glimmer of what must be a much larger series of epistemological transformations, of the same nature that I mapped when writing of the authorization of textual history, which are now being inscribed on the land. To explicate somewhat crudely, the construction Anurajapura refers to a place where a version of the past may be located in space; the construction Anuradhapura, captures the *founding* moment of a narrative of history.

Let me now proceed to the content of the cluster of ruins at Anuradhapura and its reconstitution. Two major clusters of 'ruins' attract the attention of colonial officials: 'tanks', which are an interconnected system of artificial reservoirs, and 'monuments/dagabos' which are (physically) very large brick domes. Each cluster is seen as being embedded in a disordered 'state of nature' but the 'tanks,' conspiring with 'Nature' are inscribed with historical causality: "Here [in Anuradhapura] the air is heavy and unwholesome, vegetation is rank, and malaria broods over the waters, as they escape from the broken tanks..." [48] Jonathan Forbes' account of an 1828 visit, which he writes up in the late 1830's, links the "desertion...consequent decay and present desolation" of Anuradhapura, to the then widely believed environmental theory of decline. The "warm and damp nature of the Ceylon climate," Forbes argued, "excites an activity of vegetation, which the indolence and apathy of native character are not calculated to struggle against..."[49]

This degenerate state of nature is always juxtaposed against a former glorious state, in some detail: arguing against James Mill's assertion that other reservoirs similar to these were merely 'holes in the ground,' the romantic William Knighton stresses the significance of the 'tanks' as markers of a great civilization. He quotes Edward Upham, a contemporary Orientalist, to note that the "forming [of] immense lakes for facilitating the operations of agriculture...[were] extraordinary excavations [that] rivalled the most remarkable labours of antiquity, *and were hardly surpassed by the kindred wonders of Egypt*."[50] This juxtaposition is then taken to its logical conclusion: a call for (British) imperial intervention to restore this past 'glory' is made. These policies and actions take shape as Anuradhapura intersects with the larger project of 'ordering land': cartographic practices, the building of transportation and communication networks, which I outlined earlier.

Lt. Thomas Skinner, a military officer, cartographer and engineer is an interesting figure here. In 1832, he 'opens' a road from the northwest coast (from Mannar), to Anuradhapura in the 'interior': "about which less appeared to be known than about the most recently discovered lake in Central Africa."[51] Skinner 'encounters' Anuradhapura in quite the same way other colonial officials and Orientalists of the period do (in a degenerate state of nature) but in contrast to these passing visitors, he is a man of action, the man on the spot. As he begins to see Anuradhapura as the degenerate signifier of a golden age, he calls for its restoration in a letter to the Governor written in 1833.[52] Even though the lack of funds prevents the proposal from becoming active immediately, Skinner's vision begins to take shape by the late nineteenth century. By the 1870's "the renewal of interest in irrigation began to gather momentum," and by 1878 "work ...[was] going on vigorously upon hundreds of tanks in the North-Central Province."[53] This is our first example of the topographical inscription of the 'excavated history' of the *Mahavamsa* on the landscape. I will leave the excavation of the 'tanks' of Anuradhapura here, and move to a parallel development: the excavation of monuments.

These are very large brick mounds, smaller temples, and palaces. Once again, the glorious state of the city as described in the *Mahavamsa*, which remarks on "temples and palaces, whose golden pinnacles glitter[ed] in the sky...the palace..[had]...large ranges of buildings, some of them two and three stories high"[54] is important here. The present condition of the monuments is seen once again, as a signifier of degeneration, signs of battles fought and lost with 'Tamils' and 'Nature:' "all the ruins at Anuradhapoora, even the lofty monuments which contain the relics of the Buddha, are either entirely covered with jungle, or partly obscured by forests...."[55] Yet, even though these 'monuments' are seen as 'obscured' by Nature, the colonial gaze is able to penetrate this first layer. With the *Mahavamsa*, and the 'historical' texts in hand, each mound begins to be identified. Once identified, the monuments are presented in the chronological narrative of their construction. In fact, the authority of this chronological narrative is so strong in the early period of the colonial encounter with Anuradhapura that it determines a radical shift in expository mode from 'travel narrative' to 'great historical narrative.' That is, there is a shift from the usual 'travel narrative' mode which lists sights on the landscape in the order they are seen by the traveler during his (rarely her) journey to a 'historical narrative' where the order of the physical journey is repressed to present the sights as they are presented in the chronology of the *Mahavamsa*: the chronology of their construction. For example, Knighton passes the Ruwanwelisaya (a large dagaba) three times moving up and down one street in Anuradhapura waiting for the right 'historical' moment in his retelling of the *Mahavamsa* before he describes it.

Furthermore, a 'micro-historical narrative' is located at each physical ruin of the cluster: the story of its desecration (by Tamils/ heretical[Sinhala] kings), and rebuilding (by orthodox Sinhala kings), are told in detail, up to the final abandonment to 'Nature.' By the late nineteenth century this narrative hardens into a 'racial' one, with the 'racial' wars of 'Sinhala' against 'Tamil' being inscribed on the landscape. This history, in turn, is projected onto the contemporary (late nineteenth century) moment. John Ferguson, editor of the important *Observer* newspaper, surveys Anuradhapura from where "the Tamil invader, Elara, fell to the sword of the Sinhalese monarch, Dutugemunu, and the tide of Damilo

[Tamil] progress southwards was arrested —at least temporarily."[56] Not only is this history now simply Sinhala vs. Tamil; it is linked crudely and unselfconsciously with the present. Ferguson, refering to the yearly movement of Indian Tamil labour along this route, remarks upon the "determined and constant... southward flow of the successors of the old South India invaders." Given this "influx of Tamils" he asks ominously, "[w]ho can calculate the final results of this ebb and flow, bat more flow than ebb."[57/58] This is my second example of the topography of history: here, the teleological logic of the 'regime of historical truth' is complete as it is inscribed on the land: it explicates the present.

(a)   **The Archaeological Formation**

Simultaneous with these efforts to authoritatively date and meaningfully encode each sign on the landscape, with a 'history' from the *Mahavamsa*, is a cluster of disciplinary archaeological practices. Once again, here, as in the case of the historiographic formation, it is the will to scientific knowledge that guides the colonial officials here. The 'regime of truth' of the archaeological formation, analogous to the regime of the historiographic formation, presupposes a knowing, seeing subject that is independent from the object of his study. In its practice, this formation seeks to produce objectified signs that can be authoritatively examined: measured, classified and labelled. The effort to restore these objects to a previous, "authentic" condition of existence is central to this practice. Once restored, the viewing of such objects is further enabled in an archaeological site or a separate museum.

We can see in the early colonial encounters of Anuradhapura 'soft' versions of the 'regime' of archaeological practice that would increasingly 'harden' through the nineteenth century. The practice of measuring: heights, widths, lengths, breadths, and related calculation of square areas and volume can be noted from the earliest 'post-*Mahavamsa*' accounts.[59] The next step in the logic of this regime is classification. In an early account Chapman presents a crude typology of the 'dagabos': "they. ..may be divided into two classes, *viz*. Those of moderate height, and having rows of pillars around them; and those of considerable height, surrounded by granite platforms of great extent."[60] Such attempts change dramatically over the period of the nineteenth century to produce typologies acceptable to the regime of (disciplinary) archaeological practice. To grasp this shift more completely, I will now present an overview of the larger set of institutional changes that create this archaeological formation. By 1868 a Commission of Inquiry, The Archaeological Commission, was appointed by the Governor. The appointment of this commission led to plans for the 'clearing' of ancient monuments at Anuradhapura. As this clearing took place 'new' monuments were 'discovered.' In 1870, photographs were taken for the first time. A complete survey of all that was 'known' in Anuradhapura was completed in 1873-75. Systematic collection of (ancient) inscriptions at Anuradhapura began in this period "and detailed plans and sections, indicating architectural measurements, and drawings of the ancient...dagabas, were made. Lithographic copies were sent to the British Museum for the reference of scholars."[61] Also in 1875, a museum was built in Colombo and ancient sculptures and remains from Anuradhapura were exhibited. Inscriptions from stone epigraphs dating from the 3rd to the 13th century were copied, translated and deposited in the Museum Iibrary.[62] Archaeological excavation began for the first time in Anuradhapura in 1884.[63] Up until 1890 the Government Agent of the district was responsible for this work, but in that year, H. C. P. Bell was appointed the first 'Archaeological Commissioner.' Wage and prison labour was then employed in the work of exploration, clearing, and excavation.[64] Interestingly, much of the wage labourers were immigrant Tamils.

It is important to realize that these practices re-constituted the 'landscape of ruins' at Anuradhapura, both materially and meaningfully. For example, reading George Capper's account of the measurements of the 'dagabos' of Anuradhapura after the 1875 survey, which took place in the wake of much 'clearing and cleaning up,' we see that the heights of the 'dagabos' are now different since earth has been removed from their bases. This leads to a new hierarchy of heights of the dagabas and authoritative tables of the 'height from platform to the ground,' and 'height from platform to [the top of the] ruin.'[65] This new, 'scientific' information, together with other recently excavated indigenous 'architectural' texts, in turn, led to a comprehensive theory of classification of the dagabas in general, which informed the understanding of the Anuradhapura monuments. Six basic dagaba types were accepted, and complicated theories relating to the relative proportions of each section of a specific type to its other sections were advanced.[66]

Another shift in the structure of the meaningful constitution of Anuradhapura took place in the wake of disciplinary archaeological practice. After the first layer of 'debris' was cleared, H.C.P. Bell wrote in 1890 that the "ruins... must be divested... of from 4 to 5 feet of soil before any comprehensive grasp can be attained of their general plan..."[67] It was in this announcement of the extent of the 'depth of ruins under the surface' that Anuradhapura began to be seen as a 'buried city.' Note that this notion is quite different from the earlier construction I traced out: the city embedded in a 'state of nature.' This 'buried city' is not a smelly, malaria infested jungle, riddled with wild animals and rebels that might be physically difficult to negotiate. On the contrary, 'the buried city' presents an adventurous opportunity to the "wealthy but idle men of Europe" who are perhaps, "longing for a chance of distinguishing themselves..."[68] As we can see, the product of the practice of disciplinary archaeology is being inserted into the practices of an imperial bourgeoisie. This move, I suggest, marks the emergence of conditions that make the commodification of Anuradhapura possible.

(b)   The Aesthetic Formation

Intersection of the ruins of Anuradhapura with an 'aesthetic formation' links it even more forcefully with the process of commodification. The regime of aesthetic formation shares epistemological similarities with the regime of disciplinary archaeology. Yet, at a practical level, its categories are somewhat distinct from those produced by the archaeological formation. Here, 'correct' proportions, 'elegance,' and 'fine' details produce the category of 'beauty;' breathtaking size produces 'sublimity;' and the availability of a sanitized, ordered state of nature produces the 'picturesque.' The 'ruins' produced by the aesthetic formation are not only for serious, scientific orientalists. Crucially, the objectified signs produced here are on display and are to be consumed by international tourists from the metropolis: thus the value of commodified history is realized. From the first (serious) encounter with Anuradhapura, in the 1830's, the European gaze unanimously perceived a superior "elegance and unity of design," and found "beauty" in the "minute sculptures on its tall, slender and graceful columns" of the Thuparamaya, the 'oldest' of da-gabas.[69] This dagaba is often compared to classical Greek architecture; what this implies, of course, is that this 'sight' meets the classical Euro-pean aesthetic regime. This is interesting in light of the general Indian example where new categories had to be introduced to the aesthetic re-gime to assimilate many indigenous architectural forms.[70]

The Thuparamaya remains a key 'site/sight' of beauty through-out the nineteenth century, yet once again it is transformed by archaeo-logical practice. Later accounts contrast the newly restored dagaba's "snow white, bell-shaped, pointed form," with the earlier vision of a "top heavy mass," and othe runrestored dagabas, such as the Jetavanaramaya, constituting it as a "thing of beauty," because of the contrast in this new context. The modern reconstructions also produce another important shift in meaning: Anuradhapura moves from being 'ruined' to 'ancient.' This move parallels the move from a "degenerate" site to the "buried city" traced out in relation to archaeological practice. An "ancient city" doesn't exist in a malarial swamp; rather, it displays the 'authentic' past in a con-text of civilization and order, much like a museum. These conditions bring in the eyes of an observer, a "vivid realization of how beautiful the great pyramid dagabas must have looked when covered with fine po-lished chunam, their vast masses gleamed white against the sky...."[71] I find the trope of the 'museum' here useful to capture the simultaneity of 'beauty' and 'ancientness' that emerges in Anuradhapura at this time. The 'museum,' an abstract category, also captures the abstraction inherent in the commodification of Anuradhapura: it is now equivalent with other museumized landscapes which have been produced in other parts of the world.

Furthermore, the clearing and cleaning of Anuradhapura also marks the emergence of the city as a 'picturesque' site, suitable for paint-ing and picnics.[72] The unrestored Jetavanaramaya' s "forest-clad sides and old burnt-brick tower" are thought to be a "dream of beauty" suitable for painting. "Beautiful pictures" of this scene, one commentator boasts, "have been recently painted by an English artist-visitor, whose work may possibly adorn the walls of 'The Academy' next year..."[73] The banks and bunds of the now-restored tanks become especially suitable sites for pic-nics which overlook their clear, clean expanses of water.[74]

Unjungled, measured, marked, sanitized and aesthetisized, Anuradhapura as a commodity was now ready for large scale consumption:
tourism. By the end of the nineteenth century several guide books appeared, notable among them Caves' *Ancient Cities of Ceylon*, and Bur-
rows' *Buried Cities*. The Fergusons, newspaper and book publishers,
would at regular intervals give "accounts of the progress made [in 'Ceylon'] since 1803," so that the "resources awaiting development by capitalists, and the unequalled attractions offered to visitors" would be widely
known in the metropolis. In their late nineteenth century accounts Anuradhapura was listed under "Attractions for the Traveller and Visitor."[75]
The easy intersection of Anuradhapura with transportation networks
within Sri Lanka, was stressed. "The trip to the ancient capitals of Anuradhapura and Polonnaruwa… ninety to sixty miles to the north and
east [from Kandy], can easily be arranged for the visitor," the guide suggests, also neatly remarking on the city's intersection with an international communication network: "from amid the ruins of Anuradhapura
(2,000 years old) one can despatch a telegram to friends at home in Eng-
land or America…"[76]

To summarize then, the narrative history read from the *Mahavamsa* remains largely stable throughout the nineteenth century. Anuradhapura, as perceived in the first colonial encounter in the 1830's and
40's, is seen as representing an age of decline and fits easily with the ascendency of Europe, and the British conquest of the island. The intensity
of disciplinary archaeological practice after the 1860's, however, trans-
forms the 'site/sight' both materially and meaningfully. At the centre of
the archaeological project is restoration: remaking Anuradhapura, and
perceiving it in its 'ancient glory.' Anuradhapura is now *not* degenerate: it
is an 'ancient,' 'aesthetic' commodity. It has emerged as a "sign of the modern."[77]

Nationalizing Anuradhapura

Until the end of the nineteenth century, the 'ancient' landscape of
the North Central Province is not important discursively or materially as
a sign for anti-colonial struggles. For earlier uprisings, eg., in 1818 and
1848, it is the space and sign of the last indigenous Kings of Kandy, in
the central hills, that is important. The other major uprising of the nine-

teenth century takes place in the urban concentrations of Colombo and Galle, in 1866.[78] The importance of the 'historical' landscape of the *raja rata* is a product of the intensity of colonial archaeological practice that begins in the 1870's and the simultaneous rise of modern Sinhala-Buddhist nationalism. To a large extent, the Sinhala nationalization of the textual and material history produced by the Colonial project proceeded on that very colonized terrain. As the Anagarika Dharmapala (1864-1933; the son of a rising Sinhala furniture merchant), who became the major figure of Sinhala-Buddhist nationalism in the late nineteenth and early twentieth centuries[79] argues, there is no other *"nation on earth* which could boast" of "most authentic and ancient of historical records," such as the Mahavamsa of the Sinhalese, *which according to Sir James Emerson Tennent,* 'stands at the head of the historical literature of the East, unrivalled by anything extant in Hindustan...'"[80] Note the authoritative reference to Tennant and the construction of the uniqueness of this 'history', which is linked to the extraordinary prominence given to it in nationalist ideology.

It is Dharmapala's close associate, the Brahmachari Walisinha Harischandra, who led the first attempt to nationalize the 'Raja Rata.' In 1899 Harischandra founded a branch of the Maha Bodhi Society in Anuradhapura. He was involved in several disputes with colonial officials and was arrested (and later tried and acquitted), after a violent uprising in the city in 1903. Yet his post-uprising texts (1904, 1908), in the main, also accept and reinforce the core 'regimes of truth' produced by the colonial intervention. The historiographic regime of truth is not in question: Harischandra reads the *Mahavamsa* within this regime. This 'history' is inscribed on the ordered land of Anuradhapura in some detail.[81] No objections were made to the wider regime of disciplinary archaeological practice: measuring, marking, dating, excavating, and restoring and the production of objectified, classified 'ruins.' In fact, throughout the text, Harischandra called for 'better' archaeologists than H. C. P. Bell and his associates, whom he described as being incompetent to work at the 'sites' of Anuradhapura. For Harischandra, the practice of 'monumental' archaeology is welcome for it allows the aesthetisization, and commodification of history. For example, the Thuparamaya was for

Harischandra, too, the site/sight of great 'classical... elegance,' and he cites colonial writers and officials for authority.[82]

Harischandra was also supportive of the commodification of history: the last section of his text is a straightforward tourist guide.[83] He notes that the extension of the railway to Anuradhapura in 1904 makes travel much easier, and then goes on to present the "best way to see the shrines and ruins... within easy access... within a limited time, without the interference of unqualified guides, who relate absurd stories...."[84] It is an account for wealthy travellers, very much like the accounts of John Ferguson I quoted earlier. In fact, Harischandra supports the consumption of the commodity of the 'picturesque' by international tourists. He recommends a walk to the "bund of the Abaya Wewa" where "the cooling breezes that waft from this tank will, ...no doubt refresh the tourist,"[85] and also advises visitors to take a "refresh[ing] drive over the grand bund of the Nuwara Wewa."[86] Harischandra's text also articulates the colonial racial categories of Sinhala and Tamil —inscribed earlier on the landscape— with the 'racial' and 'religious' exclusivity of his nationalism. Harischandra, like Ferguson before him, notes the mark of Tamilness in 'ancient' Anuradhapura at Elara's tomb, and objects to this sign. He suggests that there is no "proof whatsoever to accept" that this mound is "Elara's tomb," and argues therefore, that the internal road, now called "Elara Road," be renamed "Isurumuniya Road".[87] Harischandra also objects to the Tamil proper name "Baswakkulama," being used for an Anuradhapura reservoir because the name is "foreign to the history of Anuradhapura."[88]

Today, Anuradhapura is a site of convergence for Sinhala Buddhist pilgrims, nationalist ideologues in search of a backdrop, and also international tourists looking for 'ancient culture.'[89] And all this has contributed heavily to the mechanical reproduction of images of nationalized Anuradhapura: on post cards, posters, greeting cards, school texts and television clips. Anuradhapura, then, from the end of the nineteenth century to the present day, remains an authoritative, collective representation of a particular kind of Sinhala Buddhist history.

In this paper I have attempted to write the history of that authoritative, collective representation dwelling on the formations of knowledge— historiographic, archaeological and aesthetic– that continue to be at its core. The very 'self-evidentness' of Anuradhapura today, as ancient, aesthetic and ethnic, is a product of these knowledges; or, in other words, it is the real effect of the authoritative epistemological conquest of the nineteenth century. Hence, I argue, the near unshakability of its dominant meaning in popular, as well as scholarly writings. Nevertheless, it is important not to conflate a collective representation with a consensual one: there are many of us, both Sinhala and non-Sinhala, who are critical of such a collective representation of history. These contestory positions are important in an on-going effort to build a peaceful, democratic Sri Lanka: my efforts, in the pages above, have been an attempt at such a contestation.

Notes

1   This is a revised version of my master's thesis which was submitted to the Department of Anthropology, University of Chicago, in Spring 1990. I'm grateful to Benedict Anderson, Bernard Cohn, Jean Comaroff, Malathi de Alwis, Ronald Inden, Qadri Ismail, Kumari Jayawardena, Partha Mitter, Gyanendra Pandey, Vijay Prashad, John Rogers, David Scott and Jonathan Walters for commenting on earlier versions.

2   Bernard Cohn, The Command of Language, and the Language of Command," in *Subaltern Studies V*, Ranajit Guha (ed.) (Delhi: Oxford University Press, 1986), p. 276.

3   Steven Kemper, *The Presence of the Past: Chronicles, Politics and Culture in Sinhala Life* (Ithaca: Cornell University Press, 1991), p.148.

4   Kemper, *The Presence...* , p.133.

5   Elizabeth Nissan, "History in the Making: Anuradhapura and the Sinhala Buddhist Nation" in *Social Analysis* vol.25 (1989), pp.64-77.

6   Nissan, "History...," p.67.

7   Nissan, "History...," p.68.

8   Michel Foucault, "Truth and Power," in *The Foucault Reader*, Paul Rabinow (ed.) (New York: Pantheon, 1984), p.73.

9   Michel Foucault, *The Archaeology of Knowledge*, A.M. Sheridan Smith (trans.) (New York: Pantheon, 1972), pp.31-39.

10   Foucault however, does not extend his work to the conditions of the formation and development of colonialism, a project which is simultaneous with the historical periods he has chosen to excavate. For an extended critique of this neglect, see Gayatri Chakravorty Spivak, "Can the Subaltern Speak?" in *Marxism and the Interpretation of Culture*, Grossberg and Nelson (eds.) (Urbana: University of Illi-

nois Press, 1988), pp.271-316.

11   I use 'archaeology' here to capture a formation that some may think of as non-unitary: while I'm centrally concerned with 'archaeology' as the modern disciplinary practice of excavating ancient sites. I'm also concerned with the restoration of other 'ancient ruins', such as irrigation systems which may not be usually thought of as part of an 'archaeological field.' In as much as this formation shares structural similarities with strictly archaeological practices, I think it correct to capture them with this term.

12   R. G. Collingwood, *The Idea of History* (Oxford: Clarendon Press, 1956), pp.127-133.

13   This is different from the way some African societies were constructed, where, in the absence of any kind of written texts, knowledge of entire peoples were dismissed as "lying beyond the day of self-conscious history...enveloped in the dark mantle of night" in G.W. Hegel, *The Philosophy of History* (New York: Dover, 1837/1956), p.91.

14   See R. G. Collingwood, *The Idea...*, and Bernard Cohn, "Anthropology and History in the 1980s: Towards a Rapprochement," in *An Anthropologist among the Historians and Other Essays*, (Delhi: Oxford University Press, 1988), pp.50-1, for epistemological and theoretical overviews of European history. For an analysis of European epistemology in relation to knowledge produced about 'things Indian' see Ronald B. Inden, *Imagining India*, (Oxford: Basil Blackwell, 1990), pp.7-43, and Partha Chatterjee, "History and the Nationalization of Hinduism" in *Social Research*, vol. 59 No. I (1992), pp.111-149. Alternatively, this 'regime of truth' can be reconstituted by re-reading against the grain, Imperial dismissals of Indian 'historical' texts. James Mill, *The History of British India*. (Chicago: University of Chicago Press, 1817/1975), pp.192-3 and G.W.F. Hegel, *The Philosophy...* , pp. 162ff., would be sufficient points of entry..

15   These texts were, of course, 'read' into other discursive formations and then operated upon by the dominant regime of truth in those formations.

16   For a characterization of the *History of British India* as a 'hegemonic' text see Inden, *Imagining...*, and for further discussion see Chatterjee, *History..*, p.137.

17   Mill, p.33. Or take the celebrated philosopher of history, G.W.F. Hegel, pp.161-165, for similar views, but a different theoretical interpretation.

18   For example: Robert Knox, *An Historical Relation of Ceylon*, (Dehiwala: Tisara Prakasakayo, 1681/1966), pp.115-6; Valentyn (1725), p.60 quoted in Sir James Emerson Tennent, *Ceylon: An Account of the Island, Physical, Historical and Topographical*, 2 vols. (London: Longman, Green, Longman and Roberts, 1859), p.311; 'Philalethes' (1817) quoted in The Hon. George Turnour, The Epitome of Cingalese History" in *Eleven Years in Ceylon* 2 vols, (Major) Jonathan Forbes,

Appendix. (London: Richard Bentley, 1832/1841) and John Davy, *An Account of the Interior of Ceylon*, (Dehiwala: Tisara Prakasakayo, 1821/1969), p.215. For contemporary scholarship on this point see Yasmine Goonaratne, *English Literature in Ceylon, 1815-1878* (Dehiwala: Tisara Prakasakayo, 1968), pp.74-6 and also John Rogers, "Historical Images in the British Period", in Jonathan Spencer (ed.) *Sri Lanka: History and the Roots of Conflict* (London: Routledge, Chapman & Hall, 1990), p.88.

19 Davy, M.D., F.R.S. (1770 - 1868), was a military doctor with the British troops in the island and was incidentally the brother of the celebrated inventor Sir Humphrey Davy.

20 Davy, *An Account...*, p.215. Note here, apart from the major point being made, that an evolutionary view of the indigenous society is being presented: "...not sufficiently advanced to relish [history]."

21 Turnour "The Epitome..." The Hon. George Turnour (1799-1843), grand-son of the first Earl of Winterton, was a British colonial official who began his career in 'Ceylon' in 1818. He started learning Pali in 1826 while administrating the district of "Saffragam" (Sabaragamuwa), in the Kandyan territories, and continued, with better access to learned priests and libraries, after a transfer to Kandy in 1828. See Tennent vol.1, p.312, fn.3, and Kithsiri Malalgoda, *Buddhism in Sinhalese Society, 1750-1900*, (Berkeley: University of California Press, 1976), p.179 fn.24.

22 Kingsley M. de Silva, *A History of Sri Lanka*, (Delhi: Oxford University Press, 1981), pp.254-64.

23 See Malalgoda, *Buddhism...* p.86.

24 See Tennent, *Ceylon...* pp.267-8.

25 This suggestion is substantiated by the contradictory nature of different European accounts of Sri Lanka's past available from the (pre-Turnour) period, and also the availability of such multiple conceptions and debates within them in contemporary Sri Lanka, in my own experience and also as documented in the ethnographic literature. See Robinson, "The House of the Mighty Conqueror," in *Dialectic in Practical Religion*, Edmund Leach (ed.) (Cambridge: Cambridge University Press, 1968) and Gananath Obeyesekere, "The Myth of the Human Sacrifice: History, Story and Debate in a Buddhist Chronicle" in *Social Analysis*, vol.25 (1989), pp.78-93.

26 Foucault, 1984, p.82

27 I am grateful to Walters for bringing this point to my attention: the summary above is from his work. See "Apendix: Colonial and Nationalist Readings of the Pāli Vamsas" in R. Inden, J. Walters & D. Ali, *Querying the Medieval: texts and the history of practices in South Asia* (Oxford: Oxford University Press, 2000),pp.154-164.

28 Readings of the 'Pali chronicles' of Lanka, have remained largely within the framework generated out of the nineteenth century 'regime of truth' until the contemporary period. This position as I have suggested above is flawed. While an extended reading of the *Mahavamsa* is tangential to my argument, here, my understanding of it is indebted to Jonathan Walters' pathbreaking essay (*op.cit.*) that analyses the 'positivist moment' of initial translation, and reads the texts as constituting and constituted by the epistemological and socio-cultural fields of their production.

29 Turnour, "The Epitome...," p.273.

30 For example (Major) Jonathan Forbes: "I am pleased to think that, in visiting all the ancient cities of note mentioned in their [Cingalese] records, I have been the means of furnishing many new proofs of the authenticity of the native annals..." in *Eleven Years...* pp.5 and ff... Also William Knighton, *The History of Ceylon, from the Earliest Period to the Present Time*, (London: Longman, Brown, Green & Longmans, 1845), p.168: "If Ceylon were not at an exceeding remote period civilized and refined, whence came the vast ruins of Anuradhapoora...?"

31 The greatest authority on this matter also soon falls into line, H.H. Wilson, *History of British India*, vol. 8 (Oxford: Oxford University Press, 1855), p.86, who in his revision of James Mill's classic writes of "Ceylon...where native princes continued to rule over the remnants of an ancient kingdom, whose origin is traceable through credible records, for over two thousand years..."

32 Tennent, *Ceylon...*, p.266.

33 Knighton, *The History...*

34 From the first presidential address, delivered in 1845 by Justice Stark, quoted in Goonaratne, p.59. For further details of the founding of the society, see Goonaratne, op.cit.

35 Goonaratne, p.80.

36 Vincent A. Smith, *Asoka, the Buddhist Emperor of India* (Oxford: Oxford University Press, 1900), p.57.

37 Vincent A. Smith, *Early History of India* (Oxford: Oxford University Press, 1908), p.9.

38 Knighton, *The History...p.16.*

39 cf. Rogers, "Historical Images..."

40 Colvin R. de Silva, *Ceylon Under the British Occupation, 1795-1833* (Colombo: Apothecaries & Co., 1953), p.100.

41 Tennent, *Ceylon...* vol. 1, p.18, fn. 1.

42 Tennent, *Ceylon...* vol. 1, p.11, fn. 1; vol. II, pp.407-408.

43 Tennent, *Ceylon...* vol. 1, p.319

44 This is not to say that 'ruins' were not noted outside this region. For example, a cluster in Kelaniya, a few miles north of Colombo is important. However, many of these sites had been irreducibly destroyed by early, particularly Portuguese, colonialism. The notion that the 'raja rata' was the repository of 'ruined Ceylon' was not only constituted from a reading of the *Mahawamsa*, it was also a product of other historic interventions.

45 Knox, *A Historical...*, p.10

46 Fernano de Queroz in *The Conquest of Ceylon* (Colombo: Apothecaries & Co, 1688/1930), pp.13. This text was only translated from the Portuguese in 1929, and seems to have not been read by British colonial officials of the nineteenth century.

47 Forbes, *Eleven Years...*, p.189, fn. 4, my emphasis.

48 Tennent, *Ceylon...*, vol. 1, p.611.

49 Forbes, *Eleven Years...*, p.188.

50 Knighton, *The History...*, p.169, emphasis in original.

51 Major Thomas Skinner, *Fifty Years in Ceylon*. (London: W. H. Allen & Co., 1891), p.162.

52 Skinner, *Fifty...*, p.167.

53 K. M. de Silva, p.301 ff. For the entire complex of possible motives that guide the colonial revival of the irrigation system see Michael Roberts, "Irrigation Policy in British Ceylon during the Nineteenth Century," in *South Asia*. vol. II 1972, pp.50-1.

54 Tennent, *Ceylon...*, pp.493-5

55 Forbes, *Eleven Years...*, p.192

56 John Ferguson, *Ceylon in the Jubilee Year* (London: John Haddon, 1887), p.389.

57 Ferguson, *Ceylon...*, pp.389-390. Ferguson is referring here to the movement of South Indian labour to the tea plantations in the central hills.

58 This racial theory was already mixing with the contemporary theory of 'Aryan racial' origin. For a discussion in relation to India see Partha Mitter, "The Aryan Myth and British Writings on Indian Art and Culture" in *Literature and Imperialism*, Bart Moore-Gilbert (ed.) (Roehampton: Roehampton Institute, 1983). This European theory is appropriated more by indigenous Sinhala-Buddhist revivalists, than British colonials in the specific case of 'Ceylon.' For a discussion of how the work of Muller and Maine were appropriated by the (Sinhala) orientalist James D'Alwis, and the Buddhist revivalist (The Anagarika) Dharmapala, see R. A. L. H. Gunawardana, "The People of the Lion: Sinhala Consciousness in History and Historiography," in *Ethnicity and Social Change*, SSA (ed.), (Colombo: Social Scientists' Association, 1984), pp.33-42.

59   I. J. (Capt.) Chapman, "Some Remarks on the Ancient City of Ananarajapoora," in *Transactions of the Royal Asiatic Society,* vol III: (1832), pp.463-495, and "Additional remarks on the Ancient City of Anuradhapura" in *The Journal of the Royal Asiatic Society of Great Britian & Ireland,* vol. XIII: (1852), pp.164-79. Also, Forbes *Eleven Years...*; Knighton, *The History...*

60   Chapman, "Some Remarks..., p.473.

61   B. Bastiampillai, *The Administration of Sir William Gregory,* (Dehiwala:Tisara Prakasakayo, 1968), p.152.

62   Bastiampillai, *The Administration...,* pp.149-152.

63   This is simultaneous with the restoration of the ancient irrigation systems and reservoirs I touched upon earlier.

64   C. E. Godakumbura, "History of Archaeology in Ceylon," in *Journal of the Ceylon Branch of the Royal Asiatic Society (n.s)* vol. 13(1969), pp.1-38; R. H. de Silva, "Archaeology," in *Centenary of Education* vol. II. (Colombo: Dept. of Education, 1969); James T. Rutnam, *Some Aspects of the History of Archaeology in Sri Lanka,* (Jaffna: Jaffna Archaeological Society, 1975).

65   John Capper, "The Dagabos of Anuradhapura," in *The Journal of the Royal Asiatic Society,* ns, vol. xx: (1888), p.180.

66   For example. Henry Parker, *Ancient Ceylon,* (London: Luzac & Co, 1909), pp.336-345.

67   Bell reprinted in Ferguson, *Ceylon in 1893,* (London: John Haddon &Co., 1893), p.371.

68   Ferguson, *Ceylon in 1893* pp,349-50.

69   Forbes, *Eleven Years...,* p.201.

70   cf. Partha Mitter, *Much Maligned Monsters.* (Oxford: Oxford University Press, 1979), p.120.

71   John Ferguson, *Ceylon in the Jubilee Year,* p.397

72   See Partha Mitter's *Much Maligned...,* pp.120-136 for a discussion of the emergence of this category in European discourses on Indian 'sites,' in an earlier period.

73   Ferguson, *Ceylon in 1893...,* p.363.

74   Ferguson, *Ceylon in 1893....*

75   Ferguson, *Ceylon in 1903...,* pp.100-117.

76   Ibid., pp.l14-15.

77   See Nicholas B. Dirks. "History as a Sign of the Modern," in *Public Culture,* vol 2 no. 2 (1990), pp.25-31.

78   See John Rogers, 'The 1866 Grain Riots in Sri Lanka," in *Comparative Studies in*

Society and History, vol. 29 (1987), pp.493-511.

79 For the socio-biographical background of Dharmapala, see Gananath Obeyese-
    kere, "Personal Identity and Cultural Crisis: The Case of Anagarika Dharmapala
    of Sri Lanka," in *The Biographical Process: Studies in the History and Psychology of
    Religion*. F. E. Reynolds and Donald Capps (eds.) (Paris: Mouton, 1976)

80 The Anagarika Dharmapala, 1897 in *Return to Righteousness*. Ananda Guruge
    (ed.) (Colombo: Government Press, 1965), pp.481-596, my emphasis.

81 The Brahmachari Walisinha Harischandra, *The Sacred City of Anuradhapura,
    with Forty Six Illustrations* (New Delhi: Asian Educational Services, 1908/1985),
    pp.1-60.

82 Ibid., p.26.

83 Ibid., pp.105-130; cf. Nissan.

84 Harischandra, *The Sacred...* pp. 103-7.

85 The Brahmachari Walisinha Harischandra, *The Sacred City of Anuradhapura,
    with Five Illustrations* (Colombo: Mahabodhi Society,1904), p.25.

86 Harischandra, *The Sacred*, 1908/1985... pp.130.

87 Ibid., pp.119.

88 Ibid.. pp.116.

89 See E. Valentine Daniel "Afterward: Sacred Places, Violent Spaces," in Jonathan
    Spencer (ed.) *Sri Lanka: History and the Roots of Conflict* (London: Routledge,
    Chapman & Hall, 1990).

Gender, Politics
and the 'Respectable Lady'*

Malathi de Alwis

Positioning

On May 6th 1993 a stunned Sri Lankan public watched Hema
Premadasa propose the vote of thanks on behalf of her family, at the
State funeral of her husband President Ranasinghe Premadasa who had
been killed by a suicide bomber. This was a daring and spectacular act.
Mrs Premadasa was breaking with 'tradition' in many ways: not only does
Buddhist etiquette forbid women to speak at funerals; in addition, she
dared to 'talk politics.' And it was a kind of politics that left the newly
sworn-in President and his ruling party greatly perturbed. Mrs Premadasa's concluding message to the people was: "Please do not think you
have been left helpless and uncared for. Remember, I have resolved to
tread the path chosen by my husband...to be a refuge unto you...I appeal to you all to extend to me your continued support to carry forward
my husband's noble mission."[1]

Hema Premadasa's proclamation may not surprise analysts of
the South Asian political scene now almost too familiar with women
stepping in to continue patriarchal dynasties of leadership at the death of
their husbands or fathers: Sirimavo Bandaranaike in Sri Lanka, Indira
Gandhi in India, Benazir Bhutto in Pakistan and Begum Khaleda Zia in
Bangladesh, to name a few.[2] Yet, what infuriated the majority of Sri Lankans was that unlike her predecessor Sirimavo Bandaranaike, Hema
Premadasa had violated the code of conduct that governs 'respectable la-
dies' and she was vilified as being too bold, greedy and ambitious. A scurrilous fax entitled *Enter the Imelda Marcos of Sri Lanka* which was circu-

lated around this time compared Hema Premadasa to Imelda Marcos and attempted to sexualize and morally degrade her.

This moralistic backlash against Hema Premadasa seems centrally premised on the fact that if a woman does not conform to the norms of 'respectability,' she is a whore. Such a binary positioning is also surprisingly reminiscent of Partha Chatterjee's formulation of the bourgeois woman in post-Independent India who was de-sexualized and spiritualized by the nationalists who displaced all their notions of promiscuous sexuality on the lower classes and the 'Europeanized' 'others.'[3] In fact, notes Chatterjee, it was the bourgeois woman's 'spiritual' qualities of self-sacrifice, benevolence, devotion and religiosity, manifested under the sign of the mother or goddess that enabled her to traverse the public sphere without endangering her femininity.[4] Such an essentialization of bourgeois womanhood as 'spiritual,' I suggest, needs to be problematized and complicated. It is my contention that despite bourgeois women's efforts to embrace the markers of spirituality or what I prefer to refer as, 'respectability,' they are constantly prey to counter-discourses that may simultaneously sexualize them. Such sexualization is especially foregrounded in the discourses that centre on women who are constantly in the public gaze. In this paper, I shall attempt to explore the discourses and practices that make and unmake 'respectability' by focusing on the careers of two political women very much in the Sri Lankan public gaze today: Sirimavo Bandaranaike and Hema Premadasa.

Making Respectability

What are the characteristics of a 'respectable lady'? What is the genealogy of such an identity? How does such an identity enable women to transcend the 'private' but yet circumscribe their participation within the 'political/public sphere'? George Mosse, one of the first writers in modern times to articulate the relationship between nationalism and sexuality, defines 'respectability' as "indicating 'decent and correct' manners and morals, as well as the proper attitude toward sexuality."[5] Tracing the history of respectability in nineteenth century Europe, he points out that it was nationalism in alliance with bourgeois morality that "helped respectability to meet all challenges to its dominance."[6] Thanks to the pioneering work of social historians and feminists, we are also familiar with the fact that along with the sexual division of labour i.e., linking women with domesticity and the 'private', respectability came to be enshrined within the 'home' and embodied by 'woman'.[7]

However, in South Asia, as has been pointed out for Africa as well, 'the home' has long been "a crucial, and hitherto neglected focus of European efforts to colonize," and I may add, 'make respectable'.[8] And as the work of many anthropologists and historians have demonstrated, the colonizers' involvement in these projects of 'domestication' and 'making respectable', also provided them with an important avenue to radically transform the relations of power between genders and classes within these colonial societies.[9] However, Comaroff and Comaroff also rightly underscore the danger of assuming that a "full-grown, stable model of 'home life' was exported from Europe to the colonies" or that the "concept of the 'domestic domain' can be freed from its particular historical context and used as universal."[10]

In Sri Lanka, where much of the nationalist rhetoric was, and continues to be phrased in terms of a Motherland and a mother tongue, the idealisation of womanhood signified through the construction of the 'respectable lady', the repository of tradition and domesticity, is based on a valourisation of motherhood: as the creator and protector of the home, as the chaste and industrious wife and as the iconic representation of the nation.[11] As Partha Chatterjee's powerful and provocative essay delineates, the demarcation of the 'domestic' as an arena of retreat from, as well as resistance to, colonialist intervention and influence involved the positing of an idealised opposition between the feminized 'private' and the masculinized 'public'.[12] In Sri Lanka too, the predominantly middle class Sinhala Buddhist nationalists who perceived themselves to be the legitimate heirs of the nation, sought to define and regulate their women's lives by relegating them to the 'domestic'. Debates between the missionaries/British colonialists and the Sinhala Buddhist nationalists over women's roles in society and the family were not really about changing the status of women but rather, about re-casting a specific kind of middle class Sinhala Buddhist womanhood that was appropriate for, and emblematic of an emerging nation state. Thus, these women were not only coded as signifiers of community/tradition/ culture and the upholders of morality and spirituality, but even more importantly, as the protectors and disseminators of it through their primary responsibility as the progenitors and nurturers of future generations of middle class, Sinhala Buddhist nationalists.[13] As Dipesh Chakrabarty notes, the 'domestic' became such an inseparable part of the national that the "public sphere could not be erected without reconstructing the private."[14/15]

Female Education

The envisioning of the family as the "unit of the nation" and the home as the "cradle of its citizenry" however, meant that even the 'domestic' role ascribed to these women could not conclusively shield them from the discourses of progress and modernity: education became central to the 'Woman Question'.[16] Nevertheless, as I have noted elsewhere, the education of the middle class female was also circumscribed by a concern for propriety and practicality —one of the few issues on which both the missionary and nationalist educationists concurred.[17] A major component of the curriculum, therefore, consisted of subjects that would not only "add to the charm of a girl's home life" but also lead to "a considerable saving in household expenditure."[18] The transformation of domestic work into a *science* enabled such 'housewifely skills' as hygiene, needlework, accounting and child care to be introduced within the classroom under the umbrella of 'Home Science.' Such bourgeois virtues of femininity and domesticity that the ignorant native girls may not have learned at home, they were surely going to be taught in school (often with the exhortation that they share this knowledge with their uncouth mothers steeped in primitive traditions). This scientization and professionalization of domesticity was especially instrumental in the transformation of the middle class Sinhala woman from an "index of social malady" into a "symbol of 'national' greatness" for in her seeming 'emancipation' reposed an entire nation's regeneration and 'modernity.'[19]

The system of education that was bequeathed to the new nation of Ceylon along with its Independence, in 1948, was one that reflected the persistent and continuous inputs of Sinhala and Tamil nationalist agitators and educationists, and the recommendations and enactments of a large number of missionary educationists and colonial bureaucrats — some enlightened, and unfortunately, many others quite the opposite.[20] During the ensuing years, though the school curricula have steadily become more Sinhala Buddhist and nationalist in content, many of the

structural elements of the old system continue to be retained and reproduced despite the change of governments, and educational policies in col-
location with such changes. The perpetuation of gender stereotypes and
inequalities through the "home economics syndrome" that has continued
to dominate the secondary school system, is one such example.[21] However, it was in the practices of disseminating such ideologies of domesticity
that the post-colonial state in Sri Lanka drastically differed from its former colonisers. Foremost among the state strategies of dissemination
was (1) The standardization of the major medium of instruction in
schools through the declaration of Sinhala as the official state language
in 1956, (2) The provision of free education from elementary to university level from the 1940s onwards and the nationalisation of almost all
schools in the island in the early 1960s (3) The disbanding of all examinations con-ducted by foreign institutions, and the introduction of a Sri
Lankan version of the British Ordinary Level and Advanced Level national examinations in the 1960s.

When Sinhala was declared the national language of Sri Lanka
and almost all the schools in the island were nationalised, the system of
education which hitherto had been divided along the colonialized lines
of privately-funded, exclusive English-medium schools (mainly Christian, but a few Buddhist and Hindu as well) and poorly-equipped gov-
ernment-run vernacular schools, was largely 'democratised.'[22] It drastically
changed the political dominance of the anglicized Sinhala elite and the
hegemony of the few exclusive English-medium schools. With the introduction of the locally conducted national examinations, the passing of
which were crucial to the procurement of any job with adequate pay,
even the few Christian and Catholic private schools that had managed to
stave off the government take overs and continued as fee-levying institutions, had to prepare their students for these exams and follow the sylla-
bii put out by the state. As Laclau and Mouffe have aptly noted, every
hegemonic formation is "constructed through regularity in dispersion."[23]
The ramifications within female education were equally telling. For the
first time, girls from a variety of class backgrounds met in the same
schools, conversed in the same language and learnt from the same books.
All girls sitting for the Ordinary Level Examination were required to sit
for papers in Home Science and Health Science and use standardized
government textbooks. This ethic of service and 'motherhood' that was

propagated through the national curriculum was reconciled with the increasing capitalisation of the Sri Lankan economy by relegating the majority of women to a continuation of their domestic chores in the 'public' domain —teaching, doctoring and nursing the sick, providing secretarial services, and more increasingly from the late 1970s, cleaning and serving in tourist hotels, making garments in export-oriented factories, using their 'vocational' skills at home rather than being agricultural producers, and migrating abroad (mainly to Singapore and the Middle East) as housemaids and nannies.[24]

Social Service

Another manifestation of the propagation of this ethic of service was the consistent promotion of 'social service' as a 'respectable' and appropriate vocation for upper and middle class women. Their participation in the 'public' domain in this context was coded as being a continuation of their 'housewifely duties' in the 'private' and an essential service to the nation and humanity. In the same vein that the missionary mothers had counseled their Christian flock of women to pursue the noble task of social service, many Sinhala Buddhist nationalists too had exhorted women of the new bourgeoisie to donate the six yards of cloth that was needed to sew a *saree* to lower class women, and firmly noted that their responsibility as Sinhala Buddhist women was to work towards the 'upliftment' of their less fortunate Sinhala Buddhist sisters.[25] Therefore, being philanthropic was closely associated with religious virtue and the power of pious and moral women to demonstrate by example.[26]

This extension of 'housewifely duties' for both the converted Christian woman and the 'new' Buddhist woman usually centred on the 'upliftment' of the ignorant peasant women in the rural hinterlands or more frequently, their more accessible, yet equally benighted working class sisters in the urban slums and shanties. Often, these bourgeois philanthropists viewed these women "from a social height which precluded any specific sense of female solidarity" but rather, saw them as "potential agents of domesticity, the means by which working class men might be brought home off the streets."[27] It was in the rural village and slum then, to paraphrase Stallybrass and White, that the bourgeois spectator surveyed and classified her own antithesis.[28] This 'respectable lady,' schooled in the sciences of domesticity, the embodiment of moral virtue, spiritual strength, prosperity and nurture, became the iconic representation of an energetic and forward-looking nation that had finally broken free of its colonialist shackles. I would suggest, that it were new social responsibilities such as this most valourized and genteel of all vocations —social service, which by associating "the task of female emancipation with the historical goal of sovereign nationhood," bound women to a new, and yet "entirely legitimate subordination."[29] This new national role for women was best articulated by Sirimavo Bandaranaike, the world's first woman Prime Minister:[30]

> I feel most strongly the home is a woman's foremost place of work and influence and looking after her children and husband duties of highest importance for her to perform. But women also have their vital role in civic life, they owe a duty to their country, a duty which cannot, must not be shirked, and some at least of their time should be devoted to social welfare work.[31]

Coming from an upper class feudal family, Sirimavo Bandaranaike had been groomed from childhood to be involved in social service activities on her father's estates in Balangoda. Once she moved to Colombo after her marriage, she became an active member of one of the oldest and largest women's social service organizations in Sri Lanka — the Lanka Mahila Samiti.[32] Though her politician husband had shrewdly enrolled her in several women's organisations, soon after their marriage in 1940, and faithfully paid her subscriptions every year, Mrs Bandaranaike chose to concentrate her attentions on a single organisation.[33] She "shunned the limelight and worked quietly and unostentatiously" holding office as Treasurer, Vice-President and President of the Samiti until her resignation from the organization when she took up politics.[34]

The Lanka Mahila Samiti[35] which was formed in 1931 (the year Ceylonese women received the right to vote), was founded by Mary Rutnam a Canadian doctor who was inspired by the Women's Institutes of Canada which trained rural women to run their own organizations and instructed them on nutrition, health, first aid, child care, dairy farming, sewing etc.[36] The spawning ground of many prominent social workers such as Cissy Cooray, Violet Rajapakse and Lady Evelyn de Soysa, the

Mahila Samiti proved to have a lasting influence on Mrs Bandaranaike's life. "I owe my own beginnings as a public speaker to the Samiti" noted Mrs Bandaranaike who went onto acknowledge that joining the Samiti was a landmark in her career for it "helped to shape her penchant for service into a meaningful mould."[37] It was the contacts she made with rural folk as well as public officials during over a quarter century of social service, that gave Sirimavo Bandaranaike confidence to reply: "I was known as S.W.R.D's wife but I was also very well known in my own right...I had gathered my own experiences in public life through several years...." when questioned why she was running for political office in 1960.[38] However, the majority of people's reaction to the news of her being sworn in as Prime Minister was best captured by her husband's relative, Sir Paul Deraniyagala: "What does she know of politics? In Solla's [her husband's] time Sirima presided over nothing fiercer than the kitchen fire."[39]

　　More contemporaneously, Hema Premadasa, the wife of former President[40] Ranasinghe Premadasa, has also used her social service activities to establish a separate identity for herself that superseded the one of First Lady. Coming from a lower class, lower status background, Mrs Premadasa did not have the schooling or grooming of a 'respectable lady' nor the leisure to indulge in social service activities until her husband had sufficiently risen in the ranks of his political party. However, when her husband was elected President in December 1988, Hema Premadasa inherited a social service organisation unrivalled in its possible scope and magnitude — the Seva Vanitha Movement.[41]

　　Inspired by the Dharma Vanitha Movement in Indonesia, the Seva Vanitha Movement (SVM) was founded in June 1983 under the auspices of the wife of the then President of Sri Lanka, J.R. Jayawardene and is estimated to have over 250,000 registered members. Though it calls itself a non-political national movement, the SVM is funded by the President's Fund and its members comprise of the wives of all government officials from the grass-roots level to that of the Ministries.[42] The President's wife is automatic head of the SVM,[43] while the wives of each of the Cabinet Ministers is the head of that Ministry's SVM and so on.[44] With its main objective "to harness the support of Sri Lankan women in National Development projects through service," the SVM was mainly involved in promoting charitable projects such as opening day care centres, training centres and welfare shops, maintaining hospital wards, distributing goods to displaced persons and the armed forces etc., during its early years under the stewardship of Mrs Elena Jayawardene.[45] Yet, much of the work done by the SVM during these years was not known to the public due to Mrs Jayawardene's aversion to publicity and thelimelight.[46]

However, the SVM went through a rapid transformation with Mrs Premadasa's assumption of its Presidency. Consider this news item which appeared on the front page of a government-owned daily: On July 12th 1990, during a lull in fighting between the Sri Lankan army and the Tamil militants, Madam Premadasa flew to the battlefront in the north to spend a few hours with the soldiers. Accompanied by all the high-ranking members of the Air Force Seva Vanitha Unit, she went armed with "delicious lunch packets" and other gifts for the soldiers. While the troops feasted on the special lunch that had been brought for them, the First Lady and her entourage of elite women insisted that they should be served the usual camp diet. During her flight back to Colombo that same day, Madam Premadasa proudly exclaimed: "Next time we won't take cooked food…we will go there and do the cooking for these men ourselves"[47]

This type of publicity stunt and military morale booster epitomised Hema Premadasa's use of the SVM to project a particular identity for herself —that of the nurturing 'Mother of the Nation.' She recognized the potential of her husband's populist projects such as the *Gam Udawa* (village upliftment) and *Janasaviya* (poverty alleviation) schemes and organized her own versions which ran parallel to those of his government. During the latter half of President Premadasa's regime, he and his wife rarely appeared together but Mrs Premadasa continued to share in the limelight due to her busy schedule organized around the SVM. In keeping with her attempts to create the image of a nurturent and beneficient 'Mother of the Nation,' much of this centred on the activity of 'distribution': wall clocks, wheel chairs, umbrellas, sarees, sewing machines, milch cows, coconut scrapers, houses…. the list was endless. It is not surprising that she became legendary for "her infinite capacity to donate every conceivable item on earth and to have her photo in the newspaper for doing it, to boot."[48] Yet, in her interview with the BBC World Service on March 7th 1993, Hema Premadasa was adamant that the SVM was not dispensing charity but "dignifying women."

However, Hema Premadasa's most astonishing feat during her Presidency of the SVM, was her hijacking of the International Women's Day celebrations which had until then, been the preserve of a few feminist groups and left parties in the country.[49] Like her husband, Hema Premadasa understood the allure of the spectacle and harnessed it with consummate skill to entice mammoth crowds to the International Women's Day celebrations of the SVM. These celebrations were obviously inspired by and imitated the Independence Day celebrations that were overseen by her husband. She often 'borrowed' the services of various stunt riders and acrobats from the armed forces who would perform on Independence Day, and in the same way that the President inspected the troops on Independence Day and took the salute, Hema Premadasa too inspected the female Cadet Corps and took the salute on International Women's Day. However, she often came up with innovations of her own as well. One that surpassed them all was the air drop of cash vouchers to the value of Rs 100,000 over the stadium in which these celebrations were being held at precisely 3.42 pm on March 8th 1993.

Hema Premadasa's involvement with the SVM Was so wholehearted and so well publicised that she often eclipsed and marginalised the more retiring and less dynamic Minister for Women's Affairs and Health —Renuka Herat. This became such a source of embarassment to the Minister and other officials in her Ministry that they began to boycott the events organized by Mrs Premadasa during the latter part of her presidency. Despite Mrs Premadasa's hunger for publicity and her infatuation with the spectacular, she did envision a more radical agenda for women than her predecessor in the SVM and colleagues in the present and past governments including Mrs Bandaranaike.[50]

Unmaking Respectability

Both Hema Premadasa and Mrs Bandaranaike, through their 'respectable' roles as 'housewives of the public,' used it as an opportunity to escape a life that was bounded by the physical confines of home. Mrs Premadasa even went one step further by using her powerful position as the wife of the President, to cultivate a separate space and identity for herself within the 'public' even before running for political office. However, such 'victories' were not achieved without considerable sacrifices. The more these women were the focus of the 'public gaze,' the more they were subject to intense scrutiny. As Pradeep Jeganathan and I have suggested elsewhere, the positioning of women in the public gaze and thus public discourses as well, is markedly different to that of men; it is usually women's physical attributes, sexuality and morality that is foregrounded rather than their intellectual capabilities and achievements.[51]

Sexuality, noted Foucault, is an "especially dense transfer point for relations of power...not the most intractable element in power relations, but rather one of those endowed with the greatest instrumentality"[52] The instrumentality of sexuality in relations of power was best illustrated in 1960 when Sirimavo Bandaranaike was elected leader of her party and headed the campaign at the general elections. Though she attempted to win the sympathy of the people through her widowhood and as a mother of 3 fatherless children, a counter discourse of rumours and cartoons in newspapers, engineered by the ruling party, the UNP, portrayed her as having fathered her children out of wedlock and as sleeping with a leader of a Left party with which she was hoping to align her party.[53] The international press did not seem to do any better. Yasmin Gooneratne describes how the newspapers in Lausanne carried pictures of Mrs Bandaranaike "her face pale, her eyes rimmed with dark shadows campaigning from public platforms in Ceylon... They used the terms *volupteuse* and *seducteuse* to describe [this] placid lady."[54] It were such possibilities of 'tarnishing' that would have to be faced by a woman in the public gaze that led Sir Paul Deraniyagala to roar: "...She'll end by *spoiling* her personal reputation and *ruining* the family name."[55] Or as M.L.A. Samad, a mill worker, put it more mildly: "Mrs Bandaranaike is a respectable lady and an exemplary housewife...Politics is a dirty thing. I think she had better keep out of it."[56]

However, Mrs Bandaranaike also often manipulated her domestic identities to her advantage in the 'public' sphere. Her major platform was that she was merely carrying out the political pledges her husband had made to his beloved voters, like any dutiful wife. At the Non-Aligned Conference in Belgrade in 1961, she "electrified her audience" by speaking to them "not only as the Head of a Government, but even more as a woman and mother."[57] But, this identity could also be used against her, for example, when Sirimavo Bandaranaike was unable to keep to her 1970 election pledge that she would increase the free rice subsidy to two *serus* (measures), the opposition party circulated a pamphlet in which a mother sings a lullaby about her inabilities to provide her son with food.[58] In a similar vein, when Mrs Bandaranaike's government brutally put down a popular youth uprising in 1971, the opposition came out with various *kavi kola* (poetry broadsheets) that referred to the mother who shot her own children.[59] The fact that all three of her children, as well as her brothers and their wives and many other close as well as distant relatives, were given posts in her 1970 government led to many snide comments that even in politics, Mrs Bandaranaike's family came first! However, Neville Kanakaratne, the Sri Lankan Ambassador to the USA in 1972, gave these insinuations a slightly different valence when he noted: "Friend and political foe alike agree that the woman, the wife, and the mother are all still in her and have not been allowed to take second place to her position as her people's elected leader."[60]

Similarly, though Hema Premadasa attempted to project herself as the 'Mother of the Nation' through her succour of soldiers at the Front as well as those disabled, as the uplifter of destitute and widowed women and the nurturer of malnourished children, a counter discourse of rumours, 'juicy' snippets in the alternative press and finally, even scurrilous, anonymous faxes attempted to sexualise and morally degrade her. While much of the concern regarding Mrs Bandaranaike's entry into politics centred on the fear that her 'respectable' status would be 'tarnished,' most objections to Mrs Premadasa entering politics were premised on the very fact that she was *not* a 'respectable lady.' Not only was she lower class and of lower status but her continued prominence in the 'public sphere' as the President of the Seva Vanitha Movement had provided ample opportunities for the foregrounding of a sexualizing counter-discourse. In addition, she had the misfortune of constantly being compared with her predecessors: (1) the former President of the SVM, Elena Jayawardene, the epitome of respectability and gentility who not only shunned publicity but was convinced that woman's place was in the home and (2) Mrs Bandaranaike, the placid and dignified widow who had to be repeatedly coerced by her husband's constituency and party to run for political office. As one anonymous fax pointed out "Mrs Bandaranaike did not have

Hema's bad character and despicable reputation"; the new generation of educated and intelligent youth will not tolerate "a cock teaser...to be their leader."[61]

Mrs Premadasa's lower status and lower class position, were rarely verbalized in these discourses but were nevertheless the lynchpin. Even her body stood as a signifier of such proletarianity. For example, when she wore the *osariya* —a particular style of saree drape which is associated with upper caste Kandyan women—middle class men and women snorted at her presumption but focused more on the gaudiness and ostentatiousness of her sarees and large puffed-sleeved jackets; a not so subtle commentary that was premised on the fact that the lower classes have no taste. When TV cameras captured Mrs Premadasa weeping uncontrollably beside the body of her dead husband, the upper/middle classes shuddered and pronounced her "inability to control her emotions" rather "distasteful" and "hypocritical"[62] while others went to the extent of declaring that it was "typical of *that* class."[63] However, after spending a year more or less in seclusion, interpreted by many as a fitting punishment for her 'unlady-like' conduct at her husband's funeral, Mrs Premadasa's reappearance in the political arena as a 'subdued' and 'helpless' widow has been greeted with much more sympathy. When her attempts to contest her husband's constituency at the General Elections on August 16th 1994 were cleverly outmanoeuvred by members of her own party, even many of her more vociferous critics cried "shame."

Afterword

Respectability, enshrined in the 'home' and embodied in 'woman' through the confluence of patriarchal, capitalist, religious and nationalist relations of power, continues to be reproduced and to hold hegemonic sway over our society. While we are constantly reminded of women's passivity and subjection within the 'home,' we must also remember that hegemony does not merely exist as a form of dominance but that it is continually resisted and challenged.[64] In this essay, I have briefly explored how bourgeios women have sought to escape the physical confines of 'home' by using the very identity of respectability with which they were tied to the 'home;' they simultaneously straddled both the 'private' and the 'public' through their philanthropic roles as 'missionaries of the respectable' and 'housewives of the public.' However, as these very terms suggest, such a genteel vocation merely replicated and publicized the 'private' and thus continued to be circumscribed by notions of respectability, and the 'domestic.'

However, as I have also suggested in this paper, social service did facilitate as stepping stones to positions of leadership that encompassed the 'domestic' but also extended beyond it. The Mahila Samiti was an important prop for Sirimavo Bandaranaike, the world's first woman Prime Minister; "I was very well known in my own right" she always claimed.[65] Similarly, it was Hema Premadasa's involvement with the Seva Vanitha Movement she recalled when claiming the right to succeed her husband as President; "Both of us have worked for the people."[66] This theme was also re-echoed in an excellent cartoon that appeared in the alternative newspaper *Yukthiya*. It depicted a beaming Hema Premadasa weeping crocodile tears running to stake her claim in the political arena. In one hand she holds a pennant which delineates her husband's legacy she hopes to perpetuate and in the other, a ladder. Each rung of the ladder marks out her own 'climb to fame': distribution of bank accounts, spectacles, the creation of a National Women's Day,[67] and finally, her work with the Seva Vanitha Movement.[68]

Nevertheless, woman's progression up the ladder of political success was not without its pitfalls. Despite Chatterjee's assertion that bourgeois woman traverses the 'public' cloaked in the 'spirituality' of mother or goddess, I suggest that one also has to take into account the patriarchal gaze of the nation that constantly seeks to scrutinize the underbelly of respectability. Thus, in the patriarchal gaze of the nation, the 'public woman' simultaneously exists as a signifier of respectability ie., as wife, mother etc., but also of degradation and debasement. As feminists, it is time we shatter such a binary construction of identity and recognise the multiplicity of subject positions that are available to us. It is time we stood 'respectability' on its head and reconfigured our notions of national and sexual bodies.

Notes

*   My grateful thanks to Pradeep Jeganathan for his incisive comments, concern, and

above all, patience! Special thanks also to Qadri Ismail, Kumari Jayawardena and David Scott for their thoughtful suggestions and support.

1   Daily News, 5/8/93.

2   cf. Kumari Jayawardena, "Widow's Might in Sri Lanka," *Frontline*, (June 18, 1993), pp. 46-7.

3   Partha Chatterjee, "Colonialism, Nationalism, and Colonialized Women: the Contest in India," *American Ethnologist*, (Fall 1989), pp. 629.

4   ibid.

5   George L. Mosse, *Nationalism and Sexuality: Middle Class Morality and Sexual Norms in Modern Europe* (Madison: University of Wisconsin Press, 1985). pp.1

6   op. cit., p. 9.

7   For example, Mary Ryan, *Womanhood in America: From Colonial Times to the Present* (New York: New Viewpoints, 1975); Barbara Ehrenreich & Deidre English, *For Her Own Good: 150 Years of the Experts Advice to Women* (New York: Anchor/Doubleday, 1979); Leonore Davidoff & Catherine Hall, *Family Fortunes* (Chicago: Univ. of Chicago Press,1987).

8   Jean Comaroff & John Comaroff, "Home-made Hegemony: The Civilizing Mission and the Making of Domesticity in South Africa" (Ms), p. 2.

9   For example, Jean Comaroff, *Body of Power Spirit of Resistance* (Chicago: Univ. of Chicago Press, 1985); Ann Stoler, "Making Empire Respectable: The Politics of Race and Sexual Morality in 20th Century Colonial Cultures," *American Ethnologist*, (vol. 16 (4), 1989), pp. 634-660; Partha Chatterjee, "Colonialism, Nationalism, and Colonialized Women: the Contest in India," in *American Ethnologist*, (Fall 1989) & 'The Nationalist Resolution of the Women's Question," *Recasting Women.. Essays in Colonial History*. eds. Kumkum Sangari & Sudesh Vaid. (New Delhi: Kali for Women,1989); Nancy Hunt,"Le Bebe en Brousse: European Women, African Birth Spacing and Colonial Intervention in Breast Feeding in the Belgian Congo," *International Journal of African Historical Studies*, (vol. 21, 1988) & "Domesticity and Colonialism in Belgian Africa," *Signs*, (vol. 15 (31), 1990); Lata Mani, "Production of an Official Discourse on Sati in Early Nineteenth Century Bengal," *Economic and Political Weekly/Review of Women's Studies*, (April 1986) & "Contentious Traditions: The Debate on Sati in Colonial India," *Cultural Critique*, (vol.7, 1987), pp. 119-56.

10 Comaroff & Comaroff, p.4.

11 cf. Samita Sen, "Motherhood and Mothercraft: Gender and Nationalism in Bengal." *Gender and History* (vol. 5 (2), Summer 1993), pp. 231.

12 Many versions of this essay have been published upto date. It first appeared under the title "Colonialism, Nationalism, and Colonialized Women: the Contest in In-

dia," in the *American Ethnologist,* Fall 1989, while a longer version "The Nationalist Resolution of the Women's Question," appeared in *Recasting Women.. Essays in Colonial History,* that same year. A revised version, "The Nation and Its Women" has been published in Chatterjee's recent book, *The Nation and its Fragments: Colonial and Postcolonial Histories* (Delhi: Oxford University Press, 1994).

13   cf. Chatterjee, "Nationalist Resolution…" pp. 238-40.

14   Dipesh Chakrabarty, "The Difference-Deferral of a Colonial Modernity: Public Debates on Domesticity in British Bengal," in *Subaltern Studies VIII,* eds. D. Hardiman & D. Arnold. (Delhi: Oxford University Press, 1994), pp. 58.

15   While Sri Lanka is a multi-ethnic and multi-religious country, the focus of this paper is on a small group of people— middle class Sinhala Buddhists, who were/are nevertheless, an extremely powerful and hegemonic bloc within Ceylonese/Sri Lankan society.

16   Sen, op. cit., pp. 233-4.

17   Malathi de Alwis,"Towards a Feminist Historiography: Reading Gender in the Text of the Nation," *An Introduction to Social Theory.* eds. R. Coomaraswamy & N. Wickremasinghe. (Delhi: Konark Press, 1994).

18   Hilda Pieris, wife of a distinguished civil servant quoted in D.B. Denham Ceylon at the Census of 1911. (Colombo: Govt. Press, 1912), p. 426. See also Kumari Jayawardena, *Feminism and Nationalism in the Third World* (London: Zed Press, 1986), p. 121.

19   cf. Sen, op. cit., p. 232. This is not to deny the fact that there were many Sinhala Buddhist women whose educational qualifications extended beyond mere proficiency in 'home science' (cf. Denham 1912, Jayawardena 1986).

20   For example, see J.P. Jayasuriya, *Educational Policies and Progress During British Rule in Ceylon (Sri Lanka) 1796-1948* (Colombo: Associated Educational Publishers); Ranjit Ruberu, *Education in Colonial Ceylon* (Kandy: The Kandy Printers Ltd, 1962); K.H.M. Sumathipala, *History of Education in Ceylon -1796-1965* (Dehiwala: Tisara Prakasakayo, 1968) and Swarna Jayaweera, "European Women Educators Under the British Colonial Administration in Sri Lanka," *Women's Studies International Forum,* (vol. 13 (4), 1990), pp. 323-331.

21   cf. Swarna Jayaweera, "Women and Education," in *The UN Decade for Women: Progress and Achievements of Women in Sri Lanka* S. Jayaweera (ed.) (Colombo: Centre for Women's Research, 1989).

22   However, this greatly hindered the opportunities of minority groups like the Tamils, Muslims and Burghers whose first language was not Sinhala. Unfortunately, this aspect of state policy is beyond the scope of this paper and cannot be adequately discussed here.

23   Ernesto Laclau & Chantal Mouffe, *Hegemony and Socialist Strategy: Towards a Rad-*

ical Democratic Politics (London: Verso, 1985), p. 142.

24   Kumari Jayawardena & Swarna Jayaweera, *A Profile on Sri Lanka: The Integration of Women in Development Planning* (Colombo: Women's Education Centre, 1986) p. 3.

25   Ananda Guruge (ed.), *Return to Righteousness: A Collection of Speeches, Essays and Letters of the Anagarika Dharmapala* (Colombo: Govt. Press, 1965), p. 82.

26   cf.Catherine Hall, "The Early Formation of Victorian Domestic Ideology," *Fit Work for Women* Sandra Burman (ed.) (New York: St Martins, 1979).

27   Ann Summers, "A Home from Home: Women's Philanthropic Work in the Nineteenth Century," *Fit Work for Women.* ed. Sandra Burman (New York: St Martins, 1979), p. 59.

28   Peter Stallybrass & Allen White, *The Politics and Poetics of Transgression* (Ithaca: Cornell Univ. Press, 1986), p. 128.

29   Chatterjee, "Colonialism, Nationalism...;" p. 629.

30   Sirimavo Bandaranaike was first appointed Prime Minister of Ceylon in July 1960 when her party won a landslide victory after the assassination of her husband S.W.R.D. Bandaranaike, Prime Minister of Ceylon from April 1956 to September 1959. Mrs Bandaranaike has ruled the country from July 1960-March 1965 & May 1970-July 1977. At the age of 78, she continues to be the Leader of her party and the Leader of the Opposition. (Ms. Bandaranaike passed away on the 10th of Oct. 2000- eds.)

31   Quoted in Maureen Seneviratne, *Sirimavo Bandaranaike* (Colombo: Hansa Publishers, 1975), p. 151.

32   The Lanka Mahila Samiti had 1400 samities across the country and a membership of 150,000 in 1959 (Handbook of the Lanka Mahila Samiti 1983: 29). It continues to be the single largest women's social service organisation that is not affiliated to a political party, today.

33   Seneviratne, op. cit., p. 96.

34   "Letter to the Editor," Daily News 4/26/60.

35   Mahila = women and Samiti = association in Sanskrit and Sinhala. This name was inspired by the Bengali organization of the same name in India (Handbook of the Lanka Mahila Samiti, 1983), p. 9.

36   ibid., see also, Kumari Jayawardena, *Dr Mary Rurnam: A Canadian Pioneer for Women's Rights in Sri Lanka* (Colombo: Social Scientists' Association, 1993), pp. 27-8.

37   Seneviratne, op. cit., p.104 &102. Stalwarts of the social service movement such as Cissie Cooray and Lady Evelyn de Soysa also seem to have found this genteel vocation a useful stepping stone to a somewhat marginal yet nevertheless, political role

in the Ceylon Senate, which was abandoned in 1971. Cissie Cooray was appointed to the Senate on the advice of the Cabinet in 1947 and Lady Evelyn de Soysa in 1958. Sirimavo Bandaranaike too was appointed to the Senate in 1960 before she ran for Prime Minister later on that year (see Robert N. Kearney, "Women in Politics in Sri Lanka," in *Asian Survey*. vol. 21, No: 7, July 1981, p.740).

38   Seneviratne, op. cit., pp. 104-5.

39   Quoted in Yasmin Gooneratne, *Relative Merits: A Personal Memoir of the Bandaranaike Family of Sri Lanka* (New York: St Martins, 1986), pp. 160. Mrs Bandaranaike's reply to this constant taunt through the years was: "A woman's place is everywhere and anywhere duty requires her to be and also in her kitchen" (quoted in Maureen Seneviratne op. cit. : 204, emphasis in original).

40   With the abolishing of the parliamentary system of government in 1978, the leader of the country became the President and not the Prime Minister.

41   Seva =service and Vanita = women in Sanskrit and Sinhala.

42   Though Mrs Hema Premadasa invited women in the private sector to join the SVM during its 1986 Annual General Meeting, there were no takers.

43   However, the SVM was in quite a quandary when D.B. Wijetunga assumed office as President on May 2nd 1993 as his wife was unavailable to take on the Presidency of the SVM and the Prime Minister was a bachelor ! The compromise candidate was the wife of the Leader of the House who was next in seniority, within the government ranks.

44   On the rare occasion of a Cabinet Minister, Department Head etc., being a woman, she takes on the leadership of her respective ministry's, Department's SVM as well.

45   Carmini de Livera, "Seva Vanitha Movement" (Ms), 1990, pp. 3-5.

46   Personal communication, Carmini de Livera 8/10/92. Elena Jayawardene, 11/2/92.

47   *Ceylon Daily News*, 7/13/91.

48   Comment by an irate Trishaw driver in March '93.

49   Khema de Rosairo (pseud), "Gender Agenda," *Pravada* (vol. 1(4), March/ April 1992), pp. 10-11. In addition, Mrs Premadasa decided to Institute the celebration of a National Women's Day to co-incide with Uduvap Poya which commemmorates the arrival of Sanghamitta Theri to Lanka bearing the sacred Bo sapling. The fact that she decided to choose a specifically Buddhist event to co-incide with National Women's Day in a multi-ethnic and multi-religious country is the subject of another paper!

50   When I met her on March 13th 1992 she spoke very eloquently on the issue of unpaid labour within the home and was even suggesting that the government should have a scheme to recompense such silent labour.

51 Malathi de Alwis & Pradeep Jeganathan, "Talking About the Body in Rumours of Death," in *Matters of Violence*, Jayadeva Uyangoda & Janaka Biyanwila (ed.) (Colombo: SSA, 1997).

52 Michel Foucault, *The History of Sexuality*. vol. I. trans. Robert Hurley (Penguin Books, 1981), pp. 103.

53 'cf. T.D.S.A. Dissanayaka, *Dudley Senanayake of Sri Lanka* (Colombo: Swastika Press, 1975), pp. 65. I also take this opportunity to gratefully acknowledge all those who shared their memories of this period, with me.

54 Gooneratne, op. cit., p. 160.

55 Quoted in ibid, emphasis mine.

56 Quoted in Sunday Times 11/8/59.

57 Quoted in Neville Kanakaratne, "The World's First Woman Prime Minister," *Ceylon Today* (vol. 21(1-2), Jan-Feb. 1972), p. 17.

58 *Sirimavo Nohot Avicara Samaya*, Illustrated Pamphlet, 1977, p.2.

59 ibid.,p.6.

60 Kanakaratne, op. cit., p. 17.

61 Enter Sri Lanka's Imelda Marcos, Anonymous undated fax, 1993, p.2.

62 It was a well known fact that Mr. and Mrs. Premadasa had been occupying separate residences for several years while it was rumoured that the only reason Mr Premadasa did not divorce his wife was because she was the source of all his good fortune (cf. Bradman Weerakoon, *Premadasa of Sri Lanka: A Political Biography*, New Delhi: Vikas, 1992, p.25).

63 Names withheld for obvious reasons, emphasis in original statement. I am grateful to many friends, relatives and acquaintances who freely expressed their views to me during this time period.

64 Raymond Williams, *Marxism and Literature* (Oxford: Oxford University Press, 1977), p. 112.

65 Seneviratne. op. cit., p. 105.

66 *Sunday Island*, 5/30/93.

67 See foot note 49

68 *Yukthiya*, 5/16/93.

Gendering Tamil Nationalism: The Construction of 'Woman' in Projects of Protest and Control

Sitralega Maunaguru

Introduction

Nationalism, I argue in this essay, is a gendered project. A gendering that produces a construction of women which is subordinated to that of men. While the force of this argument is now gaining ground in analyses of nationalism,[1] it remains an argument that must be re-made, until it can be assumed.

If a nation is a simultaneously imagined community as Anderson would argue,[2] what remain unaddressed are the relations of gender and power in that imagined community. Put another way, the history of the constructions of women in this social field of nationalism needs to be written. This is not to read or posit a single construction of women in such a field, for that would be to equate gender with biology. My argument, rather, is that the construction of 'women' is in itself a product of the irreducible intersection of the relations of power and gender in a social field. As such, the construction of women in the field of nationalism will not be one but many, as dense points in that field are produced by the historical and social practices of its agents.

A central feature of the project of nationalism is the construction of feminized and masculinized practices and ideologies in the imagined community of the nation. I do not argue that these constructions are the preserve of men, as opposed to women. Both women and men are agents in the production of the construction: my point is that these constructions betray the logic of the intersection of the relations of power and gender. As such, the constructions of both men and women produce this gendered logic. While this remains the dominant logic of nationalism, it should not be maintained that this is its only logic. The body of my paper will show that other subordinate logics of gender resist and contest the dominant logic of the nationalist project. Cynthia Enloe echoes the concerns of the feminist project with the gendered nature of nationalism, "...nationalism typically has sprung from masculinized memory, masculinized humiliation and masculinized hope...."[3] It must also be maintained, however, that these very constructions are open to contest.

The production of gender in the discourses and practices of latter day Sri Lankan Tamil nationalism illustrates my argument. While the orthodox analytical narrative of Sri Lankan Tamil nationalism would trace its historical origins to the nineteenth century in general, and the sign of Arumuga Navalar in particular,[4] it does not locate gender in the center of that narrative. Scholars might refer in passing, for example, to Navalar's concern with female education,[5] but they surprisingly do not read his positioning of women in relations of power and gender:

> Women should be protected, during their childhood by their fathers, during their youth by their husbands and during old age by their sons. Hence women are never independent... A woman who likes to be on her own without father, husband and children will bring ill fame on to the family.[6]

My task in this essay, however, is not to re-write a gendered narrative of early Tamil nationalism, but merely to question it; what concerns me here are the militant nationalisms of the recent past and present and their immediate antecedents: the rise of armed resistance to the Sri Lankan state's repression of Tamil nationalism since the 1970s, the subsequent militarization of this conflict, and the agitation during the 1960s and the 1970s, for Tamil language rights through the organizational form of civil disobedience. Yet I will remain with Navalar's forgotten lines, throughout the rest of this essay. His pronouncements remain within the logic of a patriarchal discourse, the critique of which informs my analysis. For Navalar, women must be positioned in relation to men: father, husband or son. Not only is this patriarchal relationship stressed, the subordinated position of the women to these men is central. Simple as this construction is, it demonstrates in a stark, telling manner what I mean by the intersection of the relations of gender and power, and as I examine the variations of the intersections of these very relations, throughout the rest of the text, Navalar will never be very far away.

Gendered Spaces of Protest

(a) Within Patriarchy
• The Wife, the Mother and the Warrior

In the aftermath of discriminatory language legislation in 1956, after which Sinhala, and 'Sinhala Only' was legitimized as the official language of the land, the 1960s saw more efforts on the part of the state to further entrench these linguistic laws with the addition of other provisions, and simultaneous counter-efforts on the part of representative Tamil groups to resist these moves. During the early phase of agitation for Tamil language rights carried out by the Federal Party (the major Tamil political party of the sixties), women were among those participating in *satyagrahas* and protest marches. In political meetings, women were used as speakers and crowd pullers. During the *satyagrahas* of 1961 and 1963 in the North and East, women participated quite prominently. However, their role was perceived within patriarchal social constructions; first as wife and then as mother.

I now define the relationship between the analytical categories of 'wife' and 'mother' in these discourses: the relationship is an interconnected, intersecting one. As Malathi de Alwis[7] has argued recently:

> 'Motherhood' within the contemporary Sri Lankan context can be defined as not only incorporating the act of reproduction...but also the nursing, feeding, and looking after of babies, adolescents, the sick, the old and even grown women and men, *including one's husband.*

It is within these practices of 'nurturence,' then, that the relationship between 'wife' and 'mother' should be understood.

During the political period under discussion, many of the women who led other women in political activities of protest were the wives

of male politicians, and their role as nurturing wives was greatly emphasized in public. These women themselves perceived their role as supportive and nurturing. Take this text by Mangayarkarasi Amirthalingam,
President of the Women's Front of the TULF, and wife of a leading
member of the TULF. She articulates the concept of woman as 'wife'
which was popular at that time. While praising the "service" of some
women activists, Amirthalingam says:

> Gomathy[8] made her home itself as a political camp. She pro-
> vided political explanations as well as food for those who came
> to her house. She was a great help for her husband. Jothi from
> Trincomalee also had guided the women of her region…The
> women who were then leaders, now having lost their husbands,
> withdrew themselves from political activities.[9]

Mrs. Amirthalingam then confesses that she herself became involved in political activities in order to be with her husband.[10]

In order to glorify and emphasize the nurturing role of Tamil
women, some mythic characters from old legends and classics were reconstructed. The manipulation of womanhood was strongly reflected in
the way in which these characters were described. One character based
on the *Puranaanuru*, an anthology of Tamil heroic poems from the first
century A.D., idealizes mothers who had sent their sons to the battlefield
with pride in their heart. Another character was *Kannaki* the main character of the seventh century epic *Silapathikaram* who challenges a king
who wrongly ordered the killing of her husband. She proves her husband's innocence in the royal court and the king realizes the injustice he
had caused and dies of guilt immediately. *Kannaki* meanwhile burns the
city of Madurai where her husband was killed and thereafter joins him in
heaven. Her name is usually evoked when referring to the power of
chaste Tamil women.

Leaders of the early phase of Tamil cultural resistance referred to
these two characters as *Veerathayar* (Brave Mothers) and appealed to
women to follow these characters as their ideals. Photographic captions
of women's rallies, sit-ins and picketing which were published in the Federal Party weekly *Suthanthiran*, during the sixties , and subsequently in
their felicitation volumes and annual journals, interestingly reveal the

roles expected from women. The captions - for a photo of a women's procession to attend an annual conference of the Federal Party - read as follows:

> (1)"The march of brave Tamil women who created a new *Purananuru*"
> (2)"Tamil mothers of the past sent their sons to war against injustice; mothers of today have gathered their sons to wage a similar war"
> (3)"Mothers determined to end the grievances of their children"
> (4)"Kannaki of the past rebelled against the injustice of the *Pandya* king. Thousands of young women have rebelled against the injustice of the Sinhala state."[11]

It is not only 'motherhood at stake' in these captions; violence is also an issue: although the Federal Party claimed its method of protest as non-violent in the Gandhian sense, its rhetoric was filled with violent battle imagery. Women were constructed here either as victims of the Sinhala state or as those who would nurture valor in their sons, so that they would fight to regain the lost dignity and pride of the Tamil community.

Parallel developments took place in the South in the late eighties. With the growth of armed militancy among the Tamils, the state recruited large numbers of young Sinhala men into the army in an attempt to intensify its military activities. Appeals were made to Sinhala mothers to send their sons to war in order to protect the unity and sovereignty of Sri Lanka: the Sinhala Buddhist nation. The state, political, and religious organizations praised the military men as heroes, and their mothers as heroic women who sacrificed their children for the nation. The image of woman constructed here was an inseparable part of the growing militaristic culture - as Serena Tennekoon observes: "Male military heroes and their 'supporting' cast of mothers and admiring wives and lovers are invoked to condone the insanity of organized male violence...."[12]

✦Women Warriors

With the rapid growth of various Tamil militant organizations that sought the path of armed struggle to establish a separate Tamil state from the early eighties onward, women were also drawn into them.

When more fighters were needed to safeguard the "traditional homeland" from the occupation of the Sri Lankan military, women could not just remain at home after sending sons and brothers to war. These women themselves had to evolve as fighters. This was the time when almost all Tamil militant groups emphasized the participation of women in the national liberation struggles, citing examples from other similar situations. Many appeals were made to women to join the struggle:

> Women are half of our population and hence their participation in various levels of armed struggle is extremely necessary. Women are the internal revolutionary force in any national movement. The level of participation of women in the Eelam struggle including armed combats will prove the revolutionary potentialities of Tamil women.[13]

From the early eighties, women in militant, Tamil nationalist organizations became prominent, as these groups formed women's wings during this time. Although women were initially only involved in propaganda work, medical care and fund raising, soon they were trained to handle all modern weapons accessible to the militant organizations and were active in combat situations. The Liberation Tigers of Tamil Eelam (LTTE) was in the forefront of providing military training to women. The LTTE's overt concern with training women, however, owed more to its militarism than to an ideological allegiance to feminism. In this context, then, 'woman' was not only considered to be a reproducer of male heroes, but also as a fighter herself. This resulted in a categorical shift in the construction of 'woman' from 'brave mother' to that of 'woman warrior.'

The role of woman as the biological reproducer, however, was not abandoned. In fact, a currently dominant construction of the Tamil woman that has evolved, is one of a supernatural being performing two different but inter-connected duties for the ethnic group. The woman who holds an automatic rifle in one hand and a child in another has become a popular image of this supernatural Tamil woman. This is of course a cliched image used by other national liberation movements throughout the Third World during the '60s and '70s and also in other male-dominated revolutionary traditions. For example, the LTTE's publication, "Women and Revolution: The Role of Women in Tamil Eelam

National Liberation"[14] carries a prominent photograph of a Palestinian woman cadre holding a gun and a baby. The message was very clear. In addition, a poster campaign carried out in Jaffna by one of the militant groups, asked Tamil women not to be fooled by the state's family planning policy on the grounds that this policy was a conspiracy to control the demographic size of the Tamil population.

(b) Protesting Against Patriarchy
✦ The New Woman

All major Tamil nationalist groups addressed the woman question as part of their political agendas. This was framed in a conventional Leftist format, which aimed at first eliminating the barriers for women to participate in the national liberation struggle. In addition, it was argued that women would be equal in a society that would eventually emerge out of the conflict. Even though this is an ideological commonplace, which did not recognize the specific oppression of women within the movement for national liberation, the acceptance of the concept of women's liberation, even in this very limited form, provided an important space for issues relating to gender, power and oppression to be debated by feminists.

The women's fronts of militant organizations as well as other autonomous women's groups tried to use this opportunity to discuss the concepts relating to the subordination of women. Since this issue was personal as well as political for them, they had extended the discourse beyond the boundaries of ethnic repression. The literature that emerged during the eighties bears witness to the debates among and within women's groups on women's emancipation and the national liberation struggle. While the nationalist LTTE claimed that their vision of Eelam was a socialist state in which a "radical transformation of women's lives and social attitudes towards women"[15] would occur, the women's wing of the Eelam People's Revolutionary Liberation Front (EPRLF) expressed the view that the liberation of women could not be automatically achieved through national liberation. They saw the subordination of women as stemming from economic dependency that was linked with private ownership in society, and asserted that women should consciously and constantly struggle against patriarchy in order to attain their own liberation while participating, simultaneously in the common struggle.[16] Note, however, that this is a fairly orthodox materialist-feminist ideological position that argues that gender oppression is derived only from property and class relations: there were no debates on cultural traditions as reproductive sites for patriarchal relations within the women's front of the EPRLF.

Importantly it was from within this ideological space opened up by discussion on the 'woman question,' that a new image of women emerged which embodied all the qualities, rights and dignity that women were dreaming of. A new categorical formulation - *Puthumai Pen* - (New Woman) began to occupy the discourse on women. This construction which first emerged in Tamil nationalist poetry in the context of early twentieth century Indian nationalism, began to be quoted widely by the Sri Lankan Tamil women activists in the debates of the eighties. Feminist activists, operating with this new construction, challenged the celebrated 'traditional feminine,' qualities of passivity and submissiveness. One of the slogans used in a joint march by the various women's groups on the eve of the 1986 International Women's Day, aptly expressed this new mood. The slogan said:

> Let us forget the Four Virtues
> Let us own a fighting spirit[17]

An important feminist gain from this move was the contestation of patriarchal aspects of Tamil cultural ideology through a new understanding of sexual violence against women. This was in the context of a large military presence in the Tamil majority regions that had led to numerous incidents of rape and sexual harassment of women. Even though, of course, rape was committed in Tamil society during earlier times, it had not been a site of social debate; rather it was constructed as an isolated act that concerned only the individualized victim. In the context of hostile military presence that was ethnically 'other,' however, it became an important political issue for male-dominated nationalist militant groups. These groups, on the one hand, considered rape as an instance of the general 'racial' oppression faced by the Tamil community. On the other hand, the activist women's groups focussed on rape as a question linked to gender/power, also stressing, importantly, its relationship to the general level of violence directed against women.

Feminists consolidated their efforts to change the nature of the construction of rape in Tamil society by calling for fundamental semantic shifts in discourses about rape. To explain: they initiated discussions on the stigma attached to rape victims, the concept of chastity in Tamil culture, and the patriarchal interests underlying it. Women's groups consciously rejected the Tamil term *Katpalippu*, which was in common usage to refer to rape, because of its connotation of purity/impurity: the term literally meant "the abolition of chastity." They substituted other formulations, such as *Paladkaram* (act by force) and *Paliyalvanmurai* (sexual violence). They even extended the campaign against militaristic sexual violence to become a rallying point to explain patriarchy as a systemic oppression of women.[18] These contestations suggest how Tamil women used the new context created by militant nationalism to articulate their interests as women. It is also important to note the link the women's groups formed between the constructions of 'woman warrior' and 'new woman.' In this particular situation, they argued that it was both tactically and politically wrong to separate or alienate gender interests from national interests.

✦ The Social Mother

I now turn to another construction of 'woman' that emerged in the period of military repression by the Sri Lankan state in the '80s which resulted in young men being killed or arrested arbitrarily and held for long periods of detention without trial, while being subjected to torture. Civilian protests against these human rights abuses were difficult to organize due to the extraordinary power of the military presence and its ability to suppress dissent. In this context, women, positioning themselves as mothers, organized themselves in order to contest human rights abuses, since they thought it was their legitimate and moral responsibility to do so. As Malathi de Alwis argues in her work on the Southern Mothers' Front, which followed the example of the Northern one, the positioning of motherhood as a site of protest is complicated. On the one hand, "[b]y appealing for a return to the 'natural' order of family and 'motherhood' these women openly embrace the essentialized and homogenized cultural scripts of their society." On the other hand, "by accepting this responsibility to nurture and preserve life, which is valourized by the Sri Lankan state, they reveal the ultimate 'transgression' of the state as well: the state has denied women the opportunities for mothering through a refusal to acknowledge life" by resorting to violent repression.[19] It was this contradiction that the women in the North who organized themselves as mothers, forming groups such as the Mothers' Front, and the Association of Mothers of Missing Youth, operated to use their 'motherhood' as a political force.

It is also important to note the peaceful, non-violent tone that was embodied in the activities of these mothers. Furthermore, these groups tried to link themselves with women's organizations in the South, and in many instances called for a political settlement to the ethnic conflict. Initially, at least, during the heights of repression by the Sri Lankan or Indian (IPKF) armed forces, the military acted with restraint in dealing with the protesting mothers. Unfortunately, the possibilities of "motherhood" being mobilized in a peace movement were near impossible within the Tamil context which was, and continues to be, dominated by warmongering and violence. Two years after its inception, unfortunately, the Mothers' Front in the North disintegrated. Nevertheless, this construction of "motherhood" - appealing for peace - represents an important moment of protest which contradicted the image of the mother calling for war.

So far, I have tried to identify the different constructions of womanhood in the different moments of ethnic conflict. I have also attempted to show the different interests that have fueled the different constructions created by male nationalist leaders and women's groups respectively. While the nationalist ideology perceived women as objects that were to be controlled for their interests, women formulated constructions that expressed gender interests that attempted to empower women. Even though these attempts and visions failed to materialize into positive changes, they must not be forgotten. This narrative of relative failure, must be framed, in turn, by a concentrated glance at the operation of patriarchal relations within Tamil society in the current context. These patriarchal relations of power, and hence control - over the construction of the new categories of woman produced by projects of protests - are new formulations of Navalar's old injunction. It is to these tempts at control, and accompanying acts of resistance, that I now turn.

Constructions of Control: Body and Sexuality
(a) Controlling the Female Body

Tamils, like other ethnic groups, conventionally expected their women to be couriers of their cultural and ideological traditions and often required that they signify that identity with their bodies and behavior. Yet, the war situation and the recruitment of young women into armed groups resulted in a situation in which other women started to behave in a non-conventional manner. Women began to ride bicycles freely on the roads, for example, and to wear dresses that suited their physical movements. These moves challenged the conservative conventions of Tamil society. During the height of women's activism in 1985, an unsigned handbill appeared throughout Jaffna that put forward several troubling restrictions with respect to women's dress and behavior. All women's groups responded immediately by issuing counter-statements condemning the handbill as anti-social and anti-women. It is interesting to note, however, that while condemning the hand bill, the women's wing of the LTTE emphatically stated that Tamil women should keep their ethnic identity in their dress and make-up.

> It is important for women to take care in their dress, in their *pottu* and make-up. It doesn't mean that we are enslaved if we dress according to our tradition. Some married women say that it is expensive to wear saris. This is not acceptable. Women should dress simply, and they should not attract men by their way of dressing. Some women say that it is difficult to maintain long hair. These pretensions are wrong... We are engaged in a struggle for national liberation. But, the changes which have been taking place in our culture will only demean our society.[20]

This illustrates the link between women's dress and ethnic identity, expressed by the nationalist women's front itself. Although they dressed in camouflage battle uniforms whenever they appeared in public, the LTTE women, nevertheless, could not relate to Tamil identity without referring to the sari.

(b) Controlling Female Sexuality
✦ The Raped Woman

During times of race riots and war generally, the 'protection' of women's sexuality is usually foregrounded: women of the oppressed group became vulnerable targets for the males of the dominant group. The act of rape particularly marks the assertion of authority of one group over the other and in this way women's sexuality becomes an object through which the social control of women is rearticulated. Women's bodies become a staging site on which the re-performance of the drama of one group's dominance over the other group takes place. At another level of patriarchal ideology, women's sexuality is considered necessary to relieve the 'tension' and 'fatigue' in men caused by riots and war. After the 'October 1987' war in Jaffna, in which incidents of rape by Indian soldiers increased, a group of women complained about it to a high-ranking Indian military officer. When they confronted him with specific cases, he was unable to deny them as rumors (as he had done earlier); rather, he tried to pacify the angry women by saying: "I agree that rape is a heinous crime. But my dear, all wars have them. There are psychological reasons for them such as battle fatigue."[21]

Oppressed ethnic groups, however, believe that women should be protected during the time of crisis from the pollution caused by 'other' men. For them, a woman's honor is based on her sexuality, and masculine power is based on protecting this honor. Men feel humiliated and castrated when their women are violated by 'others.' In times of heightened ethnic conflict, speeches are often made to intensify ethnic sentiment by referring to the alleged rape of women - the violation of their honor. This was a recurrent emotive theme of speeches and writings whenever the crises of the conflict in Sri Lanka deepened. Women are also constructed as thirsting for revenge in return for the humiliation inflicted upon them. When Indian Prime Minister Rajiv Gandhi was assassinated in May 1991, the LTTE was widely blamed for the killing. The LTTE promptly denied this allegation, but suggested that the assassination might have been carried out for revenge by an IPKF rape victim. Little attention was paid to this statement in relation to the initial shock and confusion that was caused by the killing. I consider this an important text that reflects the multiple layers of meaning embodied in that mode of killing. The concept of revenge, the purification of oneself, and the courageous nature of the Tamil woman are all fused into one act: the highly symbolic act of killing an important political figure. Why did the LTTE suggest the assassin was a raped woman?

A raped woman is considered one who has lost her chastity: the 'super virtue' of a Tamil woman. She is not only violated but polluted. She cannot regain her purity by any means except by negating her polluted body. In addition, rape by a soldier of an enemy country is considered a political act. Hence, the Tamil woman has to perform two sacred tasks together. One action is to take revenge against those who violated her, and by that act violated her country and caused her to experience additional shame within her community. The other action is to purify herself. The woman killing her oppressor using her polluted body as a weapon symbolically performs the above two functions. In other words, by killing Rajiv Gandhi, she not only takes revenge against the enemy, but also performs an ancient purification ritual - the *agnipravesam* (immolation by fire).

✦The Loose Woman

Women who differ from a community's dominant ideological view point are often accused of moral looseness. Here, sexuality is seen as a dangerous sign of gender that needs to be controlled. With the recent resumption of the war in the north, the LTTE imposed restrictions on the movement of persons and goods between the North and the South. People have been expected to participate in the war effort by remaining in their 'traditional homeland.' However, links continue between the North and the South for many reasons.

In April 1991, the LTTE's official newspaper *Eelanatham* published an unsigned letter, which serves as an example of how women's sexuality could be used as a weapon to prevent them from forming links with others. The letter, entitled "The Degeneration of Tamil Women in Colombo," states:

> Young Tamil women who travel to Colombo come into contact
> with the military at various points. They are physically handled

by male soldiers on the pretext of checking. In Colombo, these women become friendly with policemen from Sinhala and Muslim communities and lose their morals. In addition, they pass on information on the struggle which is taking place in the North. Hence, a total ban should be imposed on young women travelling to the South. And women who return from Colombo should be considered anti-social elements and punished accordingly.[22]

The message is clear and frightening. A woman who merely travels to the South is constructed as 'sexually loose,' and therefore as a traitor to the cause: her sexuality is a site for the control of her movements.

Conclusion

In beginning this essay with examples of protest, my aim was to highlight the relations of power and gender in an unequal social field. Doubly oppressed in the Sri Lankan context —by state racism, and by patriarchy, the construction of the protesting positions of the Tamil 'woman' first took place within that patriarchy, in received positions that were inflected by the general context of Tamil nationalism. These positions of 'wife,' 'brave mother' and 'woman warrior' were, however, inherently limiting and difficult, and the category of the 'new woman' as a position of protest against patriarchy marked a new, liberatory moment in the struggle for gender equality. Importantly, the condition of possibility of this new emancipatory position was the space created by the struggles that went before: in particular, the debate over the 'woman question' which took place in the context of militant, left-leaning Tamil nationalism. In the face of further repression by the military operation of the Sri Lankan state, and the IPKF, yet another new construct, 'social motherhood,' emerged as a site of gendered struggle in the Tamil context. 'Social motherhood,' it is important to note was a different construct from that of 'Brave Mother' produced in an earlier phase of Tamil nationalism. Crucially, the position of social motherhood was also an attempt to construct a space for peace in the increasingly militarized context of Tamil politics.

If these attempts to fundamentally contest the existing patriarchal socio-cultural system are read as a failure, we must remember that this failure takes place within a heightened context of extreme, militarized nationalism. In the final section of this paper I sketched the contours of gendered control that operate in this new context. Two sites of control were highlighted: the body and sexuality. While the female body has often been an object of attempted control in many nationalist contexts, the rapid militarization of Tamil society led to new forms of dress, posture and movement emerging among Tamil women. These new directions then became objects of new patterns of patriarchal control. In the same vein, even as military rapes foregrounded the practice of rape in Tamil society and feminist groups attempted to forge new categories and constructs to highlight the violence of the act, patriarchal nationalist movements reconstituted the 'raped woman' through the violent negation of the suicide killer. While these efforts at control have taken as their objects new gendered sites that had recently created crises in patriarchal ideological practices, the last effort of control that I examined takes as its object the most mundane and ordinary of social practices, the movement of women from one province to another. Hence it is most troubling, but also not altogether surprising, for the construction of a 'dangerous sexuality' for women, is a patriarchal project of long standing.

Gender emerges, then, as a central category in the history of latter day Tamil nationalism, in both its peaceful and militant moments. It is not that 'women' must also be included as an 'add on' in this narrative; it is rather that relations of gender and power, central as they are in any historical narrative, produce the position of 'women' in their operation. These relations of power and gender are also relations of inequality; it is within and against this field of inequality that multiple positions of "women" are produced. The very multiplicity of these positions and the efforts of feminist struggle and patriarchal appropriation that produce them are central to the story of nationalism.

Notes

1   *Nationalisms and Sexualities*, Andrew Parker, Mary Russo, Doris Sommer and Patricia Yaeger (eds.) (New York: Routledge, 1991).

2   Benedict Anderson, *Imagined Communities* (London: Verso, 1983).

3   Cynthia Enloe, *Bananas, Beaches and Bases* (Berkeley: University of California Press, 1990), p. 44.

4   See, for example Dagmar Hellman-Rajanayagam, "The Politics of the Tamil Past," in *Sri Lanka: History and the Roots of the Conflict,* Jonathan Spencer (ed.) (London: Routledge, 1990) and Bryan Pfaffenburger, "The Political Construction of Defensive Nationalism," in *The Journal of Asian Studies.* vol. 49 No. 1 (1990).

5   Hellman-Rajanayagam, p. 238.

6   *Palapadam-Nankam Puthakam* vol. 4 (Madras: 1969), p. 80. (All translations from the Tamil are mine).

7   Malathi de Alwis, "Motherhood as a Space of Protest: Women's Political Participation in Contemporary Sri Lanka," in *Appropriating Gender: Women's Activism and the Politicization of Religion in South Asia,* (eds.) Amrita Basu & Patricia Jeffrey. (London: Routledge, 1997), p.186. de Alwis builds on the work of Joke Schrijvers, *Mothers for Life: Motherhood and Marginalization in the North Central Province of Sri Lanka* (Delft: Eburon, 1985), pp. 14- 15.

8   Gomathy and Jothi respectively were the spouses of Vanniasingham and Rajavarothiam; prominent politicians of the Federal Party.

9   *Federal Party Silver Jubilee Volume* (Jaffna: Federal Party, 1974), p. 76.

10   Amirthalingam, p.77.

11   *Federal Party…(1974).*

12   Serena Tennekoon, "Macho Sons and Man-Made Mothers," *Lanka Guardian,* Vol. 8 No. 15 (1986).

13   *Thalir,* Issue 21 (1984), p.31.

14   Adele Balasingham, *Women and Revolution: The Role of Women in Tamil Eelam National Liberation* (Madras: 1983), p. 30.

15   Adele Balasingham, p. 30.

16   *Senthalal* (Jaffna: EWLF, 1984), p. 13.

17   An ideal Tamil woman is expected according to traditional values to possess the Four Virtues of modesty, charm, coyness and fear.

18   *Thalir,* Issue 30 (1985), p. 31.

19   de Alwis, p. 15.

20   *Mukamoodikal Kilihinrana* (Jaffna: Suthanthirap Paravaikal, 1986).

21   Rajan Hoole, Daya Somasunderam, K. Sritharan and Rajani Thiranagama, *The Broken Palmyra: The Tamil Crisis in Sri Lanka - An inside Account* (Claremont, California: SLSI, 1990).

22   *Eelanatham,* 1.4.1991

The Efficacy of 'Combat Mode': Organisation, Political Violence, Affect and Cognition in the Case of the Liberation Tigers of Tamil Eelam[1]

P. L. de Silva

Introduction

This paper discusses the phenomena of affect (emotion) and cognition and their impact on forms of organisation and political violence in the context of the contemporary conflict in Sri Lanka; it focuses on the Liberation Tigers of Tamil Eelam (LTTE). The analytical categories of affect and of cognition have been employed (as binary opposites) in social psychology, and anthropology and the anthropology of emotion from the mid—1970s.[2] However, the use of constructed binary oppositions by social scientists has generally failed to throw new light on the subject matter being analysed. The weakness of this rather conventional mode of thought is that social, cultural and other realities are much more complex than can be understood from a binary perspective.

Despite my misgivings about this mode of analysis, the importance of the affect—cognition debate within social psychology, psychological anthropology and the anthropology of emotions obliges me to look at this particular debate at greater length. In this process, I will also attempt to bring out some of the heterogeneity of violent representations in Sri Lanka, which will not be adequately highlighted through a discussion primarily in relation to these two categories.

First of all, by phenomena of cognition, I refer to all those conceptions, values, categories, distinctions, frameworks of ideas and systems of belief through which human beings construe their world and render it *orderly and meaningful*. It thus covers a whole range of mental phenomena, including philosophies and theologies, as well as traditional cosmologies and 'plain common sense.' These 'mentalities' or ways of thinking are, in turn, closely linked to ways of feeling and sensibilities.[3]

With regard to the LTTE, I argue that *socially constructed* sensibilities[4] and mentalities[5] have had a significant impact on the specificities of their organisational form, and concomitant acts of political violence. The LTTE has achieved international notoriety and a reputation for being one of the most efficient and ruthless paramilitary organisations currently in operation. In this paper, I examine the veracity of their reputation for efficiency. Here, organisation is an important category which needs to be examined, for it is the cornerstone upon which the LTTE has achieved its international reputation. The international media and various institutions of power (international, regional and local) have a great deal of admiration (sometimes grudging) for *efficient organisations*, especially in the context of warfare and political violence. Therefore, an analysis of the reputedly efficient and well organised LTTE could shed some light and reveal other aspects of organisational 'success' which are not heralded or championed. However, prior to a descriptive representation and analysis of the organisational phenomenon of the LTTE, it is necessary to survey the theoretical landscape with regard to such issues as organisation, political violence, and phenomena of emotion and of cognition.

Theoretical Landscape

Gareth Morgan[6] writes about *metaphors* of organisation and presents the case for organisation as a way of thinking. However, on the level of practical application, Morgan's theoretical observations are rather inadequate. In this paper I use the metaphor of organisation as *psychic prisons* somewhat differently. That is, I deviate from the largely management oriented perspective of Morgan, discussing the entrapment of the LTTE within their organisational methods and societal constructions. Henry Mintzberg[7] on the other hand, has a more practical approach, viewing organisation as consisting of processes of ordering, integrated efforts of systemization, and processes of stmcturation. He also looks at the loss of these processes due to ineffectiveness brought about by over–efficiency.

In the context of the contemporary civil war in Sri Lanka, if organisation is interpreted as a process of ordering, we find that ordering is constructed from different and opposing sides, where it is simultaneously imposed and counter–imposed. In other words, the Sri Lankan state and its military attempt to impose a process of ordering upon the minority Tamil community. Likewise, political groups from within the Tamil ethnic community counter–impose their notions of ordering. Both these heterogenous blocs perceive and/or allege that their actions are carried out in the best interests of the community they represent. These notions of ordering within and without the majority and minority communities have led to conflicts of interests, and to inter– and intr–acommunal violence along heterogenous political lines.

Political violence can be defined as *a process where force is deliberately used, or threatened, with an intention to cause death, and/or injury, and/or destruction of person(s), property and interests, by organised groups or members of such entities, to their perceived political enemies.*[8] With the above definition as a starting point, I would like to agree with Allen Feldman that violent practice has the ability to develop into an ideological formation and an institution in itself, possessing "its own symbolic and performative autonomy."[9] This is evident in politically charged and polarised contexts in deeply divided societies, for example, such as those in Northern Ireland (as demonstrated by Feldman) and Sri Lanka.

My definition of political violence is designed to cover *politically motivated violent acts carried out by members of judicially accountable (i.e. regular armed forces) and extra – judicial (i.e. death squads and irregulars) state forces, private armies and anti–state paramilitary groups.* Political violence, therefore, is always to the *detriment* and *coercion* of perceived enemies and is a continuation of political affairs by means other than dialogue, debate, discussion, accommodation and compromise.[10] In this paper, the relationship between organisation and political violence deals with the manner in which political organisations or groups within and without the majoritarian - minoritarian divide in Sri Lanka impose and counter-impose their notions of 'order', and thereby engage in the chaos[11] and carnage of political violence.

In social psychology, the manner in which the phenomena of emotion and of cognition interact to influence social understanding, viewpoints, and notions of self and of others, has long been the source of controversy. While Zajonc[12] argues that affective responses occur with virtually no-higher level cognitive processing of stimulus content, Lazarus[13] argues that extensive cognitive processing of stimulus invariably precedes affective responding. More recent work suggests that the affect-cognition relationship is not as simple as presented by either Zajonc or Lazarus. Robert Bornstein, for instance, argues that, "The interaction of affective and cognitive processes is complex, subtle, difficult to study empirically and differs across situation and circumstance."[14] I agree, but find that the generally accepted definitions of affect and cognition in the field of social-psychology as presented by him to be rather narrow and unsuitable as an analytical tool in the discussion of the category of *political violence* in relation to the concept of *organisation*.[15] The weakness of social psychological approaches as presented by Bornstein, is that affect is limited to simply being a 'quality-assigned to a stimulus,' which omits a broader formulation of the linkages between symbol systems and affect (e.g. symbol systems as emotional shields).[16] Similarly, the definition of cognition is limited to the internal processes of the self and thereby omits the broader impact of systems of ideology, culture and societal processes.

A.L. Epstein[17] adds a new dimension to the study of emotion, from an anthropological perspective. He presents, combining elements from neurology, psychology, phenomenology and linguistics, a novel approach that avoids a simplistic and dichotomous view of the relations of mind/body and reason/emotion. There are, however, other elements that can be worked into this approach to further broaden its scope. For instance, the impact of cultural and symbolic systems is marginally presented in the approach advocated by Epstein. This is a reflection of his anti–cultural relativistic bias. From my experience in the combat zones in Sri Lanka, cultural images, symbols and rhetoric play an important role in the orientation of emotional responses in crisis situations. To highlight this point—that emotion is not registered mechanically— let us imagine a person incarcerated in a cell with no windows or light. After some time this person becomes disoriented due to a lack of familiar (i.e. social and cultural) reference points. This disorientation is heightened in the context of solitary confinement. Such disorientation enables interrogators (in this hypothetical instance) to intimidate and break down the resistance of the person concerned. In other words, the human person, who constitutes the contested space in our example, is subjected to a myriad of emotions which involve shock, disorientation, fear, terror, subjugation, and finally control. Interrogators use this method to deny the prisoner any right to have a sense of who he/she is, and thereby relegate this person to a sub–human realm of existence.

My point in this illustration is to argue that, while neurophysiology plays a role, people need social and cultural reference points in order to express/respond emotionally and to have a sense of being.[18] This sense of need is exacerbated in the case of the prisoner (especially in a conflict situation) who is denied all human rights. That is, even within a single social, cultural and linguistic context, there are a myriad of meanings and expressions to each emotion term such as sadness, anger, shock, fear or terror. Further, these emotions do not occur in isolation, but in a continuous process or cascade. At present, research has not developed sufficiently in order to analyse such complexities. The divisions deployed in analysis function to highlight differences, which in actuality do not exist as singular events. An awareness of the limitations and difficulties facing research, however, is a first step towards further progress. Thus, the approach that Epstein advocates has in fact encouraged and challenged new approaches that must continuously strive to expand their boundaries. While this is not the aim of this particular paper, I hope I have made clear some of the limits of binary thinking, as well as the present boundaries of more complex and necessarily multidisciplinary approaches. I move now to a discussion of the LTTE and some of the heterogeneity of violent representations in Sri Lanka which escape the ambit of emotive and cognitive issues.

The LTTE

I have presented a broader interpretation of cognition that incorporates all conceptions and values, categories and distinctions, frameworks of ideas and systems of belief which human beings use to construe their world and render it orderly and meaningful. Being orderly and meaningful, therefore, is assumed to be of extreme importance. This is very true in the case of paramilitary organisations. In the current civil war in Sri Lanka, the most successful paramilitary organisation is the LTTE and the key to its success is efficient organisation. Therefore, while acknowledging that the interaction of affective and cognitive processes is complex, subtle and differs across situation and circumstance it is of interest to scholars in the fields of ethnic/ national conflicts and South Asian studies to look more closely at the organisational success of the LTTE[19] and its impact on the broader issue of political violence in the Sri Lankan embroglio.

I hypothesize that in the process of construing their world orderly and meaningful, the 'Tigers' manipulate or attempt to manipulate phenomena of cognition and of emotion to their advantage. Ironically in this process (where they themselves become entrapped by their own constructions of reality) they create more chaos, carnage and disorder around them. This process involves the representation and reconstruction of internal relations within the organisation (i.e. between the leadership and the cadres) and without, where images, symbols and language are used as hiding places and a way of interpreting or mapping the world (e.g. the organisation as the womb). While this process has enabled the LTTE to incur heavy casualties on the battlefield and still continue purposefully, the organisation is unable to transcend the cognitive maps of the world and of reality. The latter, themselves constructed, turn the very symbols, which act as emotional shields and provide sustenance, into barriers through time. In other words, the closure of the mind or thinking within the organisation precludes the possibility of the organisation being caught up in its own web of cognitions, which obstructs the organisation from adapting to different situations. Here, the balance between order as imposed from inside and ordering incentives from outside (e.g. public moral outrage) is disturbed. Therefore the outside then becomes a mirror image of inside ordering, where agency is denied to the outside world. In such a scenario, the step to violence becomes less burdensome. The same applies to opposing organisations/groups (e.g. the Sri Lankan armed forces and other Tamil paramilitary groups) who engage the LTTE in combat.

In this process, where representations and reconstructions of internal relations within the organisation take place, communication becomes a 'battle' and not a smooth flowing exchange. The high internal control of order, communication and practically every other aspect of human action within the LTTE and similar organisations leads to symbolic systems becoming increasingly closed. *In my opinion, the LTTE is trapped within the 'combat mode' and are uncomfortable, therefore unsuccessful, when operating in other scenarios, such as in negotiated political settlements, mainstream parliamentary politics, or in a pluralistic democratic climate.* The internal struggle within the LTTE from the end of 1993 to the beginning of 1994 and the triumph of its supremo Velupillai Prabhakaran's point of view, illustrates this point vividly.

The 'combat mode' within which the 'Tigers' operate precludes the application of emotional shields. The application of emotional shields are made operative through commemorations and celebrations of the dead (i.e. martyred) LTTE paramilitaries. Death and mourning are stage managed by LTTE cadre and celebrated in the imagery and language of ritual and symbols. For example, coffins of the dead are ceremonially draped with the LTTE flag and local school bands are press–ganged into conducting march–pasts at the head of mourning processions. At the grave–site, salvos of small arms fire form part of the burial ritual.[20] This process also involves the narration and propagation of a martyrology of the LTTE.[21] Commemorative bill boards depicting fallen 'Tiger' heroes and heroines in larger than life colour paintings, 'Tiger' insignia and monuments to the dead, notice boards in the centre of Jaffna announcing the latest casualties in battle, poems and songs played out loud in public squares, official LTTE photograph albums dedicated to the martyrs, newspaper and magazine articles, etc., all play a cumulative role in this complex process.

In the case of the LTTE, much of reality is shaped by meanings and order. Those, in turn, are constructed and shaped by images, symbols and language, which represent a one dimensional world view. Such an orderly and meaningful world view in fact functions as a 'psychic prison'[22] where members and sympathizers are presented with one universal and monolithic truth, beyond the confines of space and time. In other words the successful operation of a single consciousness is in fact the triumph of militarism and fanaticism in the name of 'liberation.' The cadres of the LTTE construct their identity in opposition to the other (i.e. enemy stereotype), in accordance with the truth and reality of the master narrative constructed by the organisation's hierarchy (as they have no access to any other). However, there are instances where even the hierarchy of the LTTE cannot control or manipulate reality and truth and instead become subject to them. A good example of this is the sense of security the LTTE's hierarchy derives from 'combat mode,' which in fact dictates a large part of their organisational actions.

When operating in a 'combat mode' there is no room for dialogue and dissent within or without. There are enemies everywhere and the only protection is the organisation (i.e. organisation as the womb). A vivid instance of this can be seen in the story narrated to me by an ex-LTTE field commander. He told me, pointing to his throat, "the knife is here," and said, "I could walk out (of the window) at any time" (I have nothing to live for). The reason for this, he explained, was his feeling of bereavement and loss after leaving the organisation. He said that for him the leader of the 'Tigers,' Velupillai Prabhakaran, was a big brother whom he had looked up to, and the organisation was literally everything to him - father, mother, brother and sister.

Such constructions of reality bounded by emotional shields enable the LTTE to function, in its opinion, efficiently. However, from another point of view, it appears that the order imposed by the LTTE upon the civilian population in the north and east of Sri Lanka has created more chaos, carnage and disorder than anything else. It is apparent that the fanaticism and militaristic world view of the LTTE has enabled it to commit atrocities and gross human rights violations, which have become all too common in Sri Lanka.

Before I conclude, I want to touch upon certain perspectives of violent representations which were omitted above as they did not fall within the ambit of a discussion on emotive and cognitive issues. For example, a more heterogenous approach would be to include gender- and historical-perspectives. I have not done extensive research into the gender perspective but I have come across examples in interviews with a group of ex-LTTE prisoners. The young men with whom I spoke said that they were absolutely terrified of the women cadres of the LTTE. The physical maltreatment meted out by the male cadres was a pale shadow to what the female cadres did. One, rather common, explanation of this phenomenon is that female cadres have to be more tough, ruthless and less-sympathetic — in a word, more macho — in order to compete for status and recognition in a traditionally patriarchal context. Another group of interviewees said that women were stronger in coping with the vagaries and extremely adverse conditions of war (i.e. in many instances being the economic, moral and emotional mainstays of their families).

Similarly, history too represents an important part of violent representations. Through a series of well planned military strikes carried out from 1985 on, the LTTE was able to 'clear the field' of other competing Tamil paramilitary groups. The history of this internecine warfare clearly illustrates the undemocratic and authoritarian character of the LTTE as an organisation. This also reflects on the internal killings within the organisation, of ex–LTTE cadres being held prisoner in secret locations.

Conclusion

The LTTE and its networks of sympathisers and admirers have, over a long period of time, attempted to maintain a continuum vis–a–vis the emotional bonds that enable large sections of the Tamil people (both at the national and transnational[23] levels) to empathise with the 'Tamil Liberation Struggle' and the activities of the LTTE. In the representations of the LTTE both phenomena are mutually inclusive.

The principle problem with this stratagem is the fact that the 'Tamil people' are *not* a homogenous entity. Despite the linkages which occur through the usage of a common language and cultural heritage, there are a myriad differences and oppositions, at regional, local, politico–ideological and cultural levels to identify but a few. In the long term, this variety of interests disables the LTTE project of maintaining an emotional continuum between their organisation and 'the Tamil people.' Therefore, they have been obliged to adopt the strategy of short–term actions at the level of the *spectacular*.[24] Through such short–term measures attempts are made to rekindle the 'emotional continuum,' whenever it is in low ebb. Another reason which calls for such spectacular situations and response specific actions is the inconstant nature of populist, emotion based support. Of course, spectacular action is not the only important strategy adopted by the LTTE. It has, for instance, succeeded in presenting itself as the only obstacle to the total defeat and destruction of 'the Tamil people' by the Sinhala state and its armed forces. Given the bloody history of the Tamil national liberation struggle, such apocalyptic visions generate a degree of appeal even among those who are either politically or morally opposed to the unpalatable and unsavoury practices[25] of the LTTE.[26]

In effect, the 'Tigers' have so far been able to hold the civilian population in large sections of the north and east to ransom through a combination of coercive and symbolic strategies. These strategies involve an important ingredient, feelings (emotions), which "have the power to move people to action."[27] In my opinion, the LTTE is efficient only in a limited and short term sense, confined to the narrow boundaries of the 'combat mode.' Similar to other monolithic enterprises, the integrated efforts of the LTTE to systematize a heterogenous Tamil community towards conformity with their dictates are doomed to failure in the long term. This is because the 'combat mode' offers only limited space and options to manoeuvre with. In the long term such an inward looking outlook involves continuous military actions and/or propaganda in order to give meaning to the notions of an efficient organisation and 'community' at war. The LTTE agenda here is 'efficient' internal ordering *versus* outside impositions, which in their perception become 'chaotic.' And, in striving to control and order reality in accordance with their own agenda, the LTTE has become trapped in a vicious circle, where more control and more order brings about more disorder and chaos. Order and high internal control lead to 'imprisonment' within the confines of a constructed reality and more chaos and carnage. In other words, the organisational efficiency of the 'Tigers' that is much heralded, brings about disorder and chaos in its wake. On this basis it is evident that commonly held notions of 'good organisation' vis—a—vis warfare and political violence are in fact limited in perspective and scope. Moreover, what is good and efficient for the pundits and the leaders of organisations and institutions engaged in conflict is not the case for the civilian population in such situations. In situations of warfare, low intensity conflict and political violence, the majority of casualties belong to the non—combatant civilian population. Apart from the dead and the injured, there is large scale deprivation of basic human needs (i.e. housing, health, education, work and most importantly the right to live in peace and security) and infrastructural damage. The hardships that the civilian population in the

LTTE controlled areas of northern Sri Lanka have to endure is an example of this.

An alternative to such disorder and chaos would be to foreground hitherto silent forces. A first step towards this can be through the dissemination of knowledge; for example, that the master narrative and reality as described by the 'Tigers' is constructed. The success of such a process of 'deconstruction' would enable new narratives and realities to be constructed. Such new representations would have the ability to present alternatives to the 'combat mode' world view and the operation of emotional shields. Being conscious that reality is constructed enables people to understand that there is no one universal truth beyond space and time. It also enhances the ability to negotiate, to have multiple identities and to be able to move between them, in other words to be able to 'feel through realities.' The space for manoeuvre[28] that alternative perspectives create will help accommodate *plural* narratives, realities and political practices in Tamil society. Another important facet in this process would be the endorsement of dialogue and negotiation as constructive measures for opponents to voice each others' standpoints and to accept multiple authenticities.

The Tamil intelligentsia[29] has embarked on the first attempts to break the silence, in the face of the master narrative of the LTTE. This is illustrated through the proliferation of Tamil language journals, magazines, pamphlets and news sheets which are being published transnationally in accordance with the spread of the Tamil diaspora. The 'Tigers' in turn attempt to coerce such anti–LTTE' enterprises with violence (e.g. petrol–bombing of outlets for such publications in Canada, the murder of the human rights activist Dr. Rajini Thiranagama[30] in Jaffna, to name a few). People who have experienced the tragedies of the Sri Lankan embroglio know that making war is easier than making peace. However the success of those who are struggling to create more democratic space for manoeuvre, and for the replacement of the single consciousness of the master narratives[31] with multiple realities and identities, will result in the triumph of dialogue, emancipation and freedom over militarism, despotism, and fanaticism.

Notes

1   This paper was first presented at the Department of Cultural Anthropology and the Sociology of Development, Free University Amsterdam in January 1993. A revised version was presented at the 4th Sri Lanka Studies Conference (held in Colombo, Sri Lanka, from the 10—13th August 1993). Special thanks are due to members of the 'Culture Club' study group in Amsterdam (in particular — Toine van Teeffelen, Jan Nederveen Pieterse, Michael Chai, Guus Meijer, Azza Karam and Judith Richter), as well as to Quarles van Ufford and Peter Kloos of the Free University Amsterdam, for their helpful comments and stimulating discussions.

2   See Catherine A. Lutz and Geoffrey M. White, "The Anthropology of Emotions," in *Annual Review of Anthropology* (Vol. 15, 1986), pp.405—436; A.L. Epstein, *In the Midst of Life: Affect and Ideation in the World of the Tolai* (Berkeley: University of California Press, 1992); Philip K. Bock, *Rethinking Psychological Anthropology: Continuity and Change in the Study of Human Action* (New York: W.H. Freeman and Company, 1988).

3   I have borrowed extensively from David Garland who uses the same formulation of the categories of cognition and of emotion to define the concept of culture. See David Garland, *Punishment and Modern Society: A Study in Social Theory* (Oxford: Clarendon Press, 1990[1991]).

4   Also referred to in the literature as phenomena of affect or of emotion.

5   Also referred to in the literature as phenomena of cognition.

6   Gareth Morgan, *Images of Organization* (London: Sage, 1986).

7   Henry Mintzberg, *Mintzberg on Management Inside Our Strange World of Organizations* (New York: The Free Press, and London: Collier Macmillan Publishers, 1992).

8   The term 'injury' refers both to physical 'damage' as well as to psychological 'trauma.'

9   Allen Feldman, *Formations of Violence: The Narrative of the Body and Political Terror in Northern Ireland* (Chicago: The University of Chicago Press, 1991), p.21.

10 It should be noted that phenomena such as domestic violence or individual aggression could also fall within the ambit of the impact of political violence (e.g. political violence experienced at the societal level is also felt within households and vice versa). But addressing those questions is beyond the focus of this paper.

11 On chaos theory, see for instance Henry Mintzberg, *Minrzberg on Management* ...

12 R.B. Zajonc, "Feeling and Thinking: Preferences Need No Inferences," in *American Psychologist* (Volume 35, 1980), pp.151—175; "A One—Factor Mind About

Mind and Emotion," in *American Psychologist* (Volume 36, 1981), pp.102—103; "On Primacy and Affect," in *American Psychologist* (Volume 39, 1984), pp.117—123.

13 R.S.Lazarus, "A Cognitivist's Reply to Zajonc on Emotion and Cognition," in *American Psychologist* (Volume 36, 1981), pp.222—223; "Thoughts on the Relations Between Emotion and Cognition," in *American Psychologist* (Volume 37, 1982), pp.1019—1024; "On the Primacy of Cognition," in *American Psychologist* (Volume 39, 1984), pp.124—129.

14 Robert F. Bornstein. "Inhibitory Effects of Awareness on Affective Responding: Implications for the Affect–Cognition Relationship," in *Emotions*, Margaret S. Clark (ed.) (London: Sage. 1992), p.236.

15 Robert Bornstein (see "Inhibitory Effects..." p.236) illustrates the general framework used by many researchers in social psychology vis–a–vis affect and cognition. He introduces a twofold definition of affect—"affect may be viewed as a quality — valence — assigned to a stimulus...affect may also be viewed as a feeling state that people experience, such as happiness or sadness (A. M. Isen and G.A. Diamond, "Affect and Automaticity," in *Unintended Thought* eds. J.S. Uleman and J.A. Bargh (New York: Guilford, 1989), p.125, and a single definition of cognition as — "a series of internal processes involved in acquiring, storing, transforming and retrieving information" (N.R. Branscombe, "Conscious and Unconscious Processing of Affective and Cognitive Information," in *Affect, Cognition and Social Behaviour* eds. K. Fiedler and J. Forgas (Toronto: Hogrefe.198S). p.3.

16 Peter L. Berger for instance, argues that symbol systems provide a "shield against terror." See Peter L. Berger, *The Sacred Canopy: Elements of a Sociological Theory of Religion* (New York: Doubleday, 1967), p.22. David I. Kertzer adds weight to this argument by declaring that in order to understand political processes, it is necessary to understand how the symbolic enters politics, how politics is then expressed through symbolism, how political actors consciously and unconsciously manipulate symbols, and how this symbolic dimension relates to the material bases of political power. See David I. Kertzer, *Ritual, Politics, and Power* (New Haven: Yale University Press, 1988), pp.2—3.

17 A.L. Epstein, *In the Midst of Life...*

18 I tend to agree with many of the positions of the social constructionists. However, I also take into serious consideration their limitations, as well as the other elements (i.e. neurophysiology, etc.,) that must be taken into account, as highlighted by Epstein.

19 That is, the manner in which the LTTE construes its world to be orderly and meaningful.

20 This burial ritual is somewhat similar to that performed in Northern Ireland by

the IRA for their fallen (e.g. flag, black beret and gloves).

21 Peter Schalk. "The Concepts of Martyrdom of the Liberation Tigers of Tamil Eelam (LTTE)" — Unpublished Paper presented at the Third Sri Lanka Studies Conference (Free University Amsterdam, April 2—5, 1991).

22 Gareth Morgan, *Images of...* pp.199-231.

23 By transnational I refer to the Tamil diaspora of Sri Lankan origin, that is spread across the globe. In this categorisation I also include 'Tamilians' sympathetic to the Eelam national liberation struggle. These are Tamils who live in the southern Indian state of Tamil Nadu and who share a sense of community with their counterparts in Sri Lanka through linguistic, cultural, and religious affinities.

24 Such spectacular actions are always within the ambit of the 'combat mode'.

25 These practices include —summary executions, prolonged periods of incarceration and semi—starvation in communal pits dug into the ground for political prisoners, frequent use of torture, the use of 'soft' civilian targets (similar to the much publicised 'ethnic cleansing'), etc.

26 Ramanujan Manikkalingam, "The 'Tigers': A Weak Defence," in *Sudasien* (Number 8, 1992), pp.m—p.

27 A.L. Epstein, *In the Midst of Life*, p.249.

28 It must be noted that spatial control of mobility indicates an undemocratic and unfree environment. However, mobility alone does not mean freedom and democracy.

29 I use this term in a Gramscian sense, where intellectuals include all those who have "an organisational function in the wide sense." See Antonio Gramsci, *Selections from the Prison Notebooks* (eds.) Quintin Hoare and Geoffrey Nowell Smith (London: Lawrence and Wishart & New York: International Publishers, 1971), p.97.

30 Dr. Thiranagama was shot five times in the head by two LTTE gunmen, who had later even attended her funeral. She was killed, in my opinion, for opposing the LTTE's master narrative.

31 I use the plural in order to point out that there are two competing master narratives in Sri Lanka. That which represents the 'Tigers' and the other which represents the Sri Lankan state. The scope of this paper does not cover a discussion of the master narrative of the Sri Lankan state which, if I may add, is not homogenous.

Narratives of Victimhood as Ethnic Identity Among the Veddas of the East Coast

Yuvi Thangarajah

Introduction

In studies of Sri Lankan nationalism, Tamil and Sinhala identities have been conventionally approached as if they were monolithic entities. Such a perspective has been enhanced both by the the state-run media particularly, and increasingly other sectors of the mainstream press, who tend to portray a united, victimized Sinhala nation. The state terror inflicted on the Tamil population tends to be rationalised from this point of view. The case is similar with the Tamil community. Tamil nationalism in general has attempted to present a unified defense of Tamils and Tamilness as a homogeneous and monolithic entity. This has been so particularly since it has been thought that in order to win the rights of the Tamil people any attempt to highlight internal differences would be detrimental to the 'Tamil cause.' The intolerance of dissent within Tamil nationalism symbolizes this thinking. Writings on Tamil nationalism, therefore, have paid only scant attention if any, to the internal structural and cultural cleavages within the so-called Tamil community.

The inter and intra—militant group conflict is constituted by this difference. It is the outcome of what each group sees as *the* problems of Tamil people; education and employment in the North and a threat to the land through largely a state-sponsored land colonization in the North-Central and Eastern sectors. The communities in different parts of the so-called Tamil areas having specific political, socio-economic, and cultural conditions, and living in specific ecological zones as they do, are bound to have different ways of life. The impact of colonial intervention has also been diverse in different parts of the perceived Tamil nation in quality and character. Despite all this, there are very few instances of explicit reference to these differences in writings on Tamil nationalism.

If this is the case with the Tamil community, there are other distinct minorities who live among the Tamil community who have been marginalised by mainstream Tamil nationalism. They have been granted citizenship in the Tamil nation by the denial of their distinctness. The attempted introduction of the phrase 'Tamil-speaking people' into the ideology of the Tamil nation reflects this phenomenon. The experience of inter–militant conflict and Tamil–Muslim violence, however, amply illustrates the failure of this ideology. The usage of the phrase 'Tamil speaking' clearly failed to integrate the minorities, the Muslims specifically, living in such places as the Eastern province, within the patronizing hold of Tamil nationalism. Overall, this ideology, however, also held other politically marginalised groups within its embrace. In the East, the Burghers and the Veddas for instance.

The idea of the Veddas being seen as anything other than Tamil in identity may come as a shock to those Tamils in the North-East of Sri Lanka who have 'naturally' begun to consider the Veddas, living in the Eastern province, as Tamils. In addition, the state response to Tamil nationalism, in the form of brutal repression of those in the North-East has also failed to recognize the internal differences within the Tamil community. The attitude of the armed forces involved in the counter-insurgency program, particularly the Special Task Force (STF) in the mid and late eighties has been to respond with greater terror on the Burghers and Sinhalese settled among Tamils regarding them as 'traitors' and 'bastards.' The Sinhalese and Burghers of Batticaloa, for example, in the eyes of the STF, do not belong to a clear and easily distinguishable category from that of Tamils, as do the Sinhalese people in the exclusive Sinhala settlements organized by the state. The Sinhalese who have been operating with ease among the Tamils have been transcending and negotiating their ethnic identity within the overall space of Tamil nationalism. The STF, therefore, perceives these 'non–Tamils' as indirect participants in the conflict and a hindrance to the blanket repression of Tamils. But the state armed forces are not alone in this view. Within certain sectors of Tamil nationalism the response has been to treat the Sinhalese who have been living for generations in the so-called Tamil nation as 'aliens' and 'invaders' in the Tamil nationalist effort to construct and legitimize a homogeneous Tamil nation.

It is in the context of this effort that the case of the Veddas as a distinct community living in the East coast has to be placed. The question of Vedda identity and how they have maintained that identity has a bearing on issues of ethnicity and nation building within the context of Tamil nationalism.

The People and the Place

This paper is a preliminary ethnographic document on the indigenous people of Sri Lanka living in the East – the East Coast Veddas. The villages in this study are situated in the Vaharai Secretarial Division in the Northern part of the Batticaloa district. The paper attempts to chronicle the transformation of ethnic identity of the East coast Veddas over time vis– a– vis Tamils. It is informed theoretically by arguments of ethnicity and ethnic consciousness. The specific issue of a Vedda identity, however, is based on what I call an ideology of 'victimhood' that is characteristic of one particular village. The question that the paper poses in the form of an internal critique of the taken–for–grantedness of the Tamil nation is, how the East Coast Veddas have managed to maintain their ethnic consciousness as Veddas despite tremendous pressure to integrate. We all remember the Seligmans' concern in 1911 that the Veddas were a fast disappearing group.[1] In 1994, the Veddas of Vaharai are still proudly claiming to be Veddas.

Theories of Ethnicity

There are several trends that can be identified in the theories of ethnicity. Peoples and nations have fought for what they consider their essential and intrinsic qualities and claim thousands of years of culture. People have located the colonial intervention as the process which constructed and enhanced racial identities. This, in turn, formed the foundations of ethnic identities retrospectively, as in the case of Sikhs and Gurkhas in India.[2] A similar case in Uganda is noted by Mazrui.[3] Smith, meanwhile, argues that unequal economic development and economic insecurity of the elite might be the cause of a revival of ethnic consciousness,[4] and this economic argument is sometimes advanced for Sri Lanka.[5] From the perspective of understanding violence within nationalism, Kapferer also views Sinhala nationalism as a cultural phenomenon. He subsumes the 'cultural' within the concept of 'ontology'.[6] This ontology, in his formulation, is a particular subjective condition of the Sinhalese predicated on an 'essential' Sinhala tradition of two thousand years or more, real or imagined.

Yet others have advanced a Foucauldian approach to ethnic identity – as contingent and performative. This view posits that ethnicity is not a prior condition but a phenomenon that is constructed in and through the very acts which give rise to and define the conflict in the first place, and determines the subsequent form of ethnic identity.[7] Ethnicity is defined and constructed within the dynamic of the action that takes place in the name of ethnicity.

I will also attempt to show that ethnicity is not essential or inherent, a prior condition, but historical and contingent. I view ethnicity as dynamic; it is contingent on the historical condition at different points in time, and constructed accordingly, deriving its meaning in that social construction. As we will see in the case of the Veddas, their willingness to integrate with the Tamil community in the recent past is to be seen as a sign of the contingency of ethnic identity; so are their current efforts to retain their identity as Veddas. In summary the history of Vedda identity in the Eastern province is this: first an attempt to renounce Vedda identity as part of a larger 'civilizing process' of modern nation–building. This leads to disappointing consequences for the Veddas. This disappointment has made them return to the refuge of a prior form of identity and consciousness which they articulate in terms of a nostalgia for the past, represented in a distinct way of life, fast disappearing and even deliberately denied. The terms in which they articulate this consciousness is what I call an ideology of 'victimhood.' That is, the images of the past as prosperous and glorious are viewed in the present with nostalgia; concurrently the narratives of the transformation of their identity, and the present condition are couched in terms of discrimination, misery, and suffering.

In my formulation, there are three phases of movement as perceived by the Veddas themselves. I will distinguish and historically trace these phases in terms of the transformation that was imposed on the

Veddas and their consequences for Vedda identity. Then I will briefly discuss the present and formulate my conclusions.

Vedda Identity

As for the question of Vedda identity itself, Dart in research conducted among the Veddas of the East coast has argued for an ethnic identity of the Veddas based on a concept of 'marginality.'[8] In his view the Veddas are distinguished by a relative marginality, both structural and cultural. He posits this marginality as a means of defining their identity. In an earlier study conducted among the Veddas of Anuradhapura, Brow had advanced a theory of self identity. Brow accepts anyone who acknowledges him/herself to be a Vedda, as such, rather than purely positing an externally imposed criterion.[9] According to this argument the definition is a relative one with reference to other groups with whom they coexist.[10] Dart's definition, as interesting as it may be, has one major flaw. It is the perception of his own observations and interpretation, that of the objective and privileged researcher who knows it all. In this regard Brow's approach is relatively closer to the 'native's point of view.' I employ the approach adopted by Brow.

In describing Vedda identity, Brow discusses the various categories defining that identity on the basis of language or lineage. The primary unit of identity among the Veddas is called *waruge/warige*.[11] Brow makes a distinction between the urban middle-class perception of the Veddas and the self–perception by the Veddas themselves. He states that what defined the Veddas in the urban perception was the opposition of wild and cultured, hunting and paddy cultivating, and the fact that the Veddas formerly spoke a distinct language:

> The Veddas are here thought of as a remnant group of primitive hunters, racially distinct from the Sinhalese and formerly speaking a separate language, who until recently preserved their ancient way of life in the Eastern jungles of Veddarata... [T]his reduction of the Veddas to a "numerically small population verging on extinction" (Seligman and Seligman 1911:xii) stems from the inability of the 19th century investigators to separate matters of race and culture.[12]

In contrast, Brow's approach is as revolutionary as it is practical. He states: "I am prepared to consider as Vedda all those who identify themselves as such who are so described by their neighbors regardless of their actual racial origins."[13]

On Power and Representation

Having made an observation on identity, I also want to make a brief note on the mode of representation in this paper. To a large extent I have used first person narratives to give immediacy to the events related, whether it is ancient past, recent past, or present. This does not mean, however, that I have eliminated by this process a power relationship albeit a subtle one, between me and my informants.

All my conversations with my Vedda informants were carried out in Tamil. There is no denying that my relationship to the informants was embedded in a power relationship however subtle it may be; that of an educated *mahan* (son) to poor *padippilladha* (illiterate) villagers. In the many hours of conversation I had with these people, I was continuously referred to as *mahan*. This acceptance was after they came to know that my mother is from a village with which they identify closely. In fact, in almost all the villages I identified people who were from my mother's native village, who even claimed a certain relationship and familiarity.

Some of them had even been my playmates and were now married into Vedda families. All these I hope, would have helped level some of the imbalances created by the country/town, researcher/ informant.dichotomy and the power relationship inherent in it.

I also feel that in the spirit of 'new ethnography' one must see that the speaker's voice is given its due place.[14] The illusion of the anthropologist being able to objectively state, let alone interpret, the informants' 'rumblings' is not valid anymore. This is especially so in the case of the 'UN Decade of Indigenous People;' allowing them to speak directly is but only a small recognition of their own voices.

The Three Phase Movement

The Veddas clearly identify three stages in the transformation of their identity. The first phase was when they were brought 'out of the jungle life' and were settled along the tanks; the second phase began when they had to move further towards the coast as wage-laborers; the third and final phase was when they began to be profoundly affected by the decade-old ethnic conflict and were denied even the basic relief package. The three stages, they argue, have progressively contributed towards the decimation of Veddas as an ethnically distinct community.

Phase I: The 'Civilizing' Process and Settlement along the Tanks
The Transforming Reach of the Colonial State

The first phase of the process was initiated with colonial intervention to bring the Veddas into the folds of 'civilization.' The colonial approach was defined by the effort to transform the jungle dwelling, 'traditional' hunter–gathering groups – 'savages,' into replicas of 'civilized beings.' This process continued with successive colonial powers, first the Portuguese, then the Dutch, and later the British. It was the British colonial government in the second half of the 19th century that entrusted the civilizing process in earnest to the mission stations. This process profoundly affected the Veddas. In the East this civilizational project was carried out by the Wesleyan and Jesuit missions.

The colonial state, methodical as it was, first laid claims to the land as the primary source of revenue. This fundamentally altered the relationship of a people to the land which until then was everything to them. Since the entire country 'belonged' to the state, anyone making use of the land could only do so with the express permission of the Crown. By these means state authority was imposed by alien rulers. *Chena* cultivation, hunting, and other activities integral to the mode of life of the Veddas had to be restricted, and recategorized with a view to extracting maximum tax revenue. The way of life of the people had to be uniform in the best economic interest of the colonial state which had an eye on surplus for the commercial market; any activity therefore could proceed only as defined and approved by the state.

Independence and the Post-Colonial Elite

The post-colonial elite who followed in the footsteps of their colonial masters in 1948 were fired by a vision of 'national development.' To the East coast Veddas, development came in the form of a - not entirely forced, but certainly not voluntary - relocation along the irrigation tanks. The Veddas had always cultivated some marginal lands along bodies of water in the jungles. This was integral to the slash and burn system that they practiced which allowed greater mobility. It was never a cash crop-oriented life with a view to surplus production. It was not a question of merely providing the facilities. Earlier, the colonial regime wanted the natives to pay for the infrastructure and irrigation facilities after having provided them with funds from state coffers in the initial stage. As Dart notes, in the perception of the colonial state it was a program of "unproductive and sparsely populated areas...[being transformed] to programs of economic development."[15]

This formed the first systematic movement away from the jungle habitat and an introduction to an entirely new way of life. Hitherto they could oscillate between a semi–settled and nomadic life. But the new settlement process prevented movement back to the jungle and a way of life in the jungle as and when they wanted. The post–colonial state was also armed with the necessary regulations to control and regulate their life–cycle.

Of course when confronted with a life associated with sustained paddy cultivation, the Veddas could not cope. They did not know about fertilizer application or pesticides, let alone bank loans. As a Vedda lamented in early 1994:

> We did not have the money. Nobody told us what to do. We were given three acres of land; they called it highland and highland it was; the water would not flow from the tank because the water level was lower than the land. We were doomed from the beginning.

Yet they were more alert than the representatives of the newly-independent state. They continued chena cultivation unofficially to supplement the doomed enterprise of paddy farming:

> We cultivated chenas in small plots; it was something. But it was not like the old days. When we were living in the jungle without all these restrictions, we would hunt wild animals. We ate maize, *kurrakan, kavalai* yams, *kattula* yams, wild boar and

many other wild animals. We used to cook monitor flesh with wood apple. *Thambi*, have you eaten that? It is not merely delicious but gives strength and long life too. Look at me; I am 85 years old. Despite starving for the last two decades I am still alive and healthy. It is only because of the food that I ate then.

While the attempt at transformation brought a sense of national(ist) pride for the post-colonial state, for the indigenous people it brought only a rich "harvest of hunger."[16]

Disciplined vs. Docile Bodies

It was with renewed vigor that the rulers of the new nation-state attempted to impose the regulations drawn by their colonial masters. The net result was: no hunting; no clearing of jungles; permits had to be obtained to cultivate small plots. The arm of the state was long and methodical in its reach. Not being sufficiently 'civilized' to understand the functioning of the modern state, the Veddas were criminalized and penalized for breaking numerous laws against hunting and not obtaining permits for clearing the jungles, now categorized as state land.

It was a new order of discipline and as good citizens they had to accept the authority of the state. It was through the discipline of submitting to state authority that the citizens were defined even if they lived in the interior of the jungles, outside the direct gaze of the state. In *Discipline and Punish* Foucault shows that the goal of this disciplinary power is to produce a human being with a 'docile body.' Though docile, it has to be productive.[17] While the discipline of weaning away from the jungle was designed to produce this docile body, the encouragement of paddy farming was the attempt to form a productive body, to contribute to the national wealth: "[d]isciplining control and the creation of docile bodies is unquestioningly connected to the rise of capitalism."[18]

The precise nature of this relationship between the state and the agents of civilization and the Veddas was defined by the disciplining of the Veddas and the careful control of the productive resources which formed the very basis of existence of the Veddas:

"Kattamuttu .... you did not obtain the permit. Don't you know it is illegal?.... You can be put in prison for this; you will have to pay heavy fines. You must not destroy the jungle Kattamuttu. It is your jungle."

"Ilayan.... do not hunt animals; it is against the law. Deer are a protected species. Don't you think our animals should be saved."

"Vandan, why not cultivate your paddy land. You can sell the produce and use the money to buy all you want. You can improve your life...You can educate your children... Don't you think your children have to live better, brick houses, good jobs and all...."

So it went on, a reprimand here, a warning there, a gentle pat here, a subtle threat there, the voices of modernity and 'civilization' extolling a materially and spiritually higher form of life. But the Veddas were great survivors; there were loopholes too in mediating the state intervention and the situation was not entirely hopeless. The village headman was fond of wild-boar meat. A bottle of wild bees honey was much treasured by the 'civilized' people and agents of the state. Hence there was another realm of Vedda life that was sustained by this demand. As Dart notes:

> [T]he government has tried for many years to restrict this practice (of abandoning slash and burn cultivation) and induced the Veddas to adopt other occupations.... In populated areas near the coast there is now a tendency to cultivate the same fields year after year since it is difficult to get permits to clear new fields and the people who had chenas are not supposed to extend them.[19]

They were not good, disciplined citizens. Time and again they were reprimanded. But there were "good" officers too. These officers ignored the 'illegal' chena cultivation:

> We used to laugh at these *kattupadu* (restrictions). We have been doing chena cultivation for generations. Suddenly, to cultivate your own food was illegal. They tell us that we must take care of the jungle without destroying it. Look at all these firewood being taken away (indicating loads of firewood taken in tractors for limestone kilns). Are we the ones who destroy the jungle?

Hunting for food was against the law. Even our gods were po-
werless. Their power comes from the respect we give them. But
they understood us. The gods are good ones too. For they never
settled in one place. They moved along with us whenever we
shifted. They did not need elaborate buildings or expensive rituals. A stone worshipped with reverence ensured their presence. Our gods blessed us and sure enough when we made
mistakes they punished us.

When wild boar destroyed our chena we knew immediately
that the gods were displeased. Some wrong had been done. We
immediately took steps to propitiate the gods.

Integration into a Wage Labor Economy

The civilizing process wanted the Veddas to transform and
adopt 'decent' behavior, settle down, become good paddy farmers, and integrate into the capitalist market economy. Yet, this was not to be. Even
when distribution of land took place among the Tamil landless peasants,
it eventually led to a few powerful land owners known as *podiyars* gaining
control of much of the land, particularly the better land. If the fate of the
Tamil farmers was such, one can imagine the plight of the Veddas not so
well versed in the art of large scale paddy farming, dealing with the state,
the land department, and eventually the notary. They lost the best
acreage around the water resources. No wonder then, that the water did
not flow to their allotments.

The general consequences of paddy farming were twofold: the
rise of petty landowners who were Tamils; and the rise of a lower pea-
santry who were to swell the labor gangs and emerge as a class of proleta-
riat peasants. This was clearly a far cry from the promises and
expectations of a civilizing state. The Veddas joined the multitude of *vi-
vasaya coolies* (seasonal laborers) who seek employment in the paddy
fields at the beginning of the monsoon, and during harvest time, moving
from area to area. Leaving home for long periods in search of employment was not part of their life–style. The closely knit character of the
Veddas discouraged long absences from home. This caused the more disciplined and enterprising Tamils to look at the Veddas as 'lazy' and 'reluctant' to sell their strong bodies even when they found employment at
their doorstep as in the *fishingwadis*.

Phase—II: Sustained cycle of wage laboring in paddy farming and fishing industry

This phase is characterized by the impact of settled paddy farming reflecting a movement towards the sea and further integration of the Veddas into the wage labor economy as perceived by the Veddas. Migrant fishermen from the South who are Sinhalese with a fluency in Tamil, arrive on the East coast during the South–West monsoon from January to May. They erect temporary huts during the period of their stay which are an established norm year after year. These fishermen who work under a *mudalali* practice deep sea fishing in mechanized boats, and beach seine fishing. They come with only a few skilled hands, equipment and capital, but they also need a large number of hired workers for numerous tasks such as pulling in the beach seine nets, helping repair nets, and working generally in the *fishwadis*. They are known as *karai valai coolie*, beach seine fishing laborers. During the fishing season there is opportunity for sustained employment. Money is readily available since most of the fish is sent to Colombo for an enhanced price.

The Veddas having been introduced to wage labor finally had found a lucrative avenue for employment. In the new activity they could earn some money in their own villages. It was better than migrating long distances to work in the paddy fields. Perhaps in cultural terms this activity is closer to hunting and gathering, where the catch is immediately available. Cultivation needs a longer period of gestation:

> Well it was never as good as it used to be when we were in the jungle, but it was better than doing paddy cultivation. There was money at the end of the day. We could come home after a day's work with something to cook. That was not possible when you have to travel distances and keep away from home when working on somebody else's paddy land. Some days the catch is good. Then we get more money because a portion of the catch is divided among us. There are bad days too; some days there is no fish. On these days we borrow money from the *mudalali* to be repaid on a good day. We also get 'kariku meen' (literally, fish for curry) which is given as part payment.

Here again the transformation in terms of a capitalistic wage economy is evident and its repercussions in turn, affected the social structure. In the old system of chena cultivation men from families of siblings would get together and clear a set of interconnected blocks in the jungle. They put up a common fence around the outer perimeter made of poles and sticks from the cleared jungles neatly planted close to each other.

> We had to be united in order to cultivate the jungles. If the 'kaval' (watch - meaning both safe fencing and guarding by the gods) is slack, wild animals would destroy the crops. So everyone has to be united not only in maintaining their section of the fence but also in leading an 'acceptable' way of life so as to not to offend the gods. Wild animals are sent in to destroy the crops when the gods are angry. All of us had to be concerned and were responsible for everyone else. But all this changed with the new found employment in the fishing sector.

Consequence of Fishing Labor Economy

While the fishing industry provided sustained employment for a brief period every year, it also fragmented the Vedda community. There were different *mudalalis* who had separate groups. Towards the singular objective of obtaining maximum profit they were all united; but underneath there were subtle differences among them. This had its impact on the Veddas who worked with different *mudalalis*. Loyalty brought internal divisions. Competition for employment seems to have nurtured jealousy. Access to money and the availability of liquor in copious quantities for the fishing community also took its divisive toll among the Veddas. Not that they were new to alcohol; this type of drinking was, however, different. It was more frequent and sustained as compared to the infrequency of alcohol consumption of the wandering life of harvesters or the seasonal celebration of annual festivals.

During this phase the close residential pattern characteristic of Vedda life changed and families scattered. The basic residential and kinship structure of a Vedda community is exogamous and closely knit as typical for South Asia and as noted by Wijesekere.[20] Ego marries mother's brother's daughter or father's sister's daughter (cross cousins). Families live together in closely situated settlements. Parents and children live close to each other. Even today villages like Madurankerny consist of exclusive clans. In the jungle, it is impossible for more than four families to be together for there is not enough land at a stretch to be cleared for chenas. Thus the unity of the families was maintained in closely knit groups. Even during the brief period of paddy cultivation this close residential pattern was possible. This close knit pattern seems to have been fragmented during the fishing employment season:

> There used to be frequent quarrels. There were a lot of problems of drinking. Young people had money and they could not be controlled by the elders. There was conflict all the time. Those who had the money would not listen to the others. There was much in–fighting.

Clearly, the move towards the coast and exposure to money has also brought about a radical change in life style, food habits and values. For the first time they sold their labor to buy food in a sustained manner throughout a good part of the year. The food was rice and curry. The introduction of wheat based products such as bread and *rotti*, seem to have taken place around this time. The hitherto sustained availability of meat, tubers and other jungle products was not possible in terms of the new lifestyle. This, they complained, has affected their lifestyle and health.

> We have never been healthy since then. What strength is there in some rice and a few curries? We gave up on the cultivation of food. The land given was bad. In any case you cannot cultivate one little piece of land over and over again; the land must rest. How can you tax the land so cruelly? You need rest don't you son, after talking to me? You go home and lie down for a while. Well that's how it is. But here the land could not produce constantly, that also only paddy. What about other things like meat, maize and all the wild fruits, roots, and tubers. We could not even keep our dogs healthy. We used to have dogs to help with hunting. Later there may have been just one or two dogs in a village. They were only symbolic. They lost their *pirayosanam* (They became useless).
> Do you still use dogs for hunting?

Hunt.... ha!..ha!...*no aiya*, we don't go to the jungles any more unless you want to get shot. Look, we don't eat even one meal a day. How can we find food for the dogs?

When the seasonal fishermen headed back to the Southern coast when the sea turned turbulent during the North-East monsoon, the Veddas began to look for employment in the paddy fields of the more prosperous Tamil paddy farmers. They worked with Tamil labor gangs. Here again there does not seem to have been exclusive groups of Vedda laborers. It may be surmised that prejudice against the Veddas and a distrust of their reliability and discipline may have been the reason. This state of affairs continued until the fishermen returned. The dynamic of capitalist wage labor has completely absorbed the Veddas into the cycle of the wage labor economy.

Problems of Integration

During both phase I and II, the Veddas seem to have had problems of integration. In the initial stages of settled paddy farming it was the intention of the state to settle the Vedda community along with the Tamil community. In fact, the land allotment in some villages were for new settlers, both Vedda and Tamil. But this attempt to integrate seem to have failed with almost all the Veddas becoming wage laborers. During the British colonial period, the colonialists relied on the native population for many aspects of local administration. Thus much power was conceded to the dominant local groups i.e. the Tamils. The Veddas continued to be a group to be relocated and civilized. The Veddas, however, were "the last to listen to the invitations or to avail themselves of the assistance of Government" as Tennent lamented.[21]

Some villages were claimed as traditional (*poorviha*) Vedda villages both by the Veddas themselves and the *Grama-Sevaka*.[22] What was meant by 'traditional' was clearly a life with a mixture of hunting, honey-gathering, paddy cultivation, a closely knit kin and residential pattern, and a significant absence of paddy laborers. A few Tamil families settled in these villages only during the last few decades.

Some Veddas working in the shipping sector in the southern, colonial port of Kalkudah, were encouraged to take up farming and move closer to the tanks in the north (first to Pannichankerny and later to

Madurankulam, Karadikkulam, Kattumurivu etc.), after World War II and the decline of maritime activities. Though this movement seems to have been away from the coast, it was not quite towards the jungle either. These Veddas' position seems to be sort of a half way one.

"The Veddas Are Not Clean"

An important component in Vedda life is the mission station. The mission schools have been functioning since the 1840s. The colonial governments encouraged the missionaries for two reasons: to proselytize but also to 'civilize the savages'. The Tamil teachers who later worked in these areas having internalized similar core values, were also similarly 'concerned' with improving the lot of the Veddas. According to some older members of the teaching staff, until the 1960s "the Veddas did not even know the use of soap or comb," these being perhaps the two artifacts of middle-classness representing as it did, 'good looks' and 'cleanliness.'

"Even today they do not bathe often. They just wrap their dress around and take off," said a GS while talking to this researcher and watching some of the indigenous people walking along the road, implying that they need to be civilized more. The economic backwardness and the problems of integration are attributed by the teachers and the GS to a lack of motivation to change. The Veddas, however, are convinced that no matter how much they try, they will remain marginal and second-class citizens. They argue compellingly that they are discriminated against by the state and the majority community i.e. the Tamils.

It is against this background that the rise of Tamil nationalism had its added impact on the Vedda community. That is when the sympathy of the GS found a unique avenue. The race cage in a birth certificate is usually filled in as Veddas for the Veddas. But some enthusiastic GSs 'elevated' the Veddas by registering them as Tamils. The Veddas also thought that this process would ensure their integration and upliftment. They thought that such a denial of identity was part of the process, of modernization. In the numerous discussions the researcher had with the GSs they insisted that the Vedda community must be improved to be like themselves. Since most of them depended on the state and the Tamil community that they were brought to live along with, they were made to 'officially' renounce their ethnic identity. However, to renounce one's identity on paper is one thing and to retain it in consciousness is another.

"Yes, we are Veddas!": The native's point of view

After all such pressures, manipulations and mediation, today in almost all the Vedda villages in the East coast, the elders emphatically claim that they are Veddas:

> "Why should one hide ones birth?" said one elder of 78 years. "I was horn a Vedda and am proud to be so. I don't see any reason to hide it."
> *"How are you identified on your birth certificate ?"*
> "Vedda of course. Even my children are recorded as such. There was a tendency to transform us into Tamils. The GS would encourage us to record ourselves as Tamils. In fact, two of my daughters are married to men from Valaichenai. But we have integrated them into our community. They are happy too."

That optimism may however be somewhat belated. The state machinery represented by the GS and largely indifferent Assistant Government Agents have been increasingly converting the Veddas into Tamils in terms of their racial category. For many of the Veddas the questions of official identity are not as important as survival:

> What else son? Whether Ram rules or Ravana rules or the monkey which came along rules, what does it matter to us? Only if we cultivate a few blocks of paddy land can we eat. Or if we hunt an iguana, deer, or something then we get meat. How many times did we run from this place in fear of the army. What relief did we get?

While this conversation was being carried on with the elder of the group, his son who just returned from the jungle was heard to say in a loud voice: "Yes, yes, we are Veddas indeed! Hey you, bring the bow and arrow. We are Veddas with loincloth. Yes we are Veddas! But now we look a bit different that's all."

I asked him that night when he was more relaxed, whether he resented my having come to look for Veddas. He related a story of misery and frustration. They had been forced to run away from the village more than four times. Their village had been shelled, fired upon from helicopter gunships, and shot at. At one point they were in a refugee camp for more than five months:

> After living in the refugee camps we realized what it would mean if we had to continue living there. I am not ashamed to tell you; I was ready to sell even the sari that my wife wore in order to exist. So we decided to return. The army wanted us to leave. But we stayed put and informed the International Red Cross team which visited us of our wish. Then we were allowed to stay. Now we are able to exist reasonably. The jungle takes care of us. Otherwise...what will be our plight now?

This man is himself married to a woman from Valaichenai, the daughter of a driver for the 'peoplised' bus service. Said the mother:

> He used to go to Valaichenai to sell the fish and buy provisions etc. He met her there and became friendly with her. So we got her people to come and organized the marriage. They live quite happily.

These people were able to inhabit an exclusively Vedda village and maintain that exclusiveness because of the remoteness of the village. The Tamils were less willing to come and settle in such interior areas. But in the case of the other areas along the roads and with better access, the story was different. There seems to be some movement of Muslim landless peasants in these areas who have settled gladly and gradually acquired lands owned by the Veddas. This was possible because of their familiarity with the bureaucracy, their better organization vis–a–vis the state machinery, and greater access to capital.

In the settlements along the tanks, the Veddas lived mostly in a collection of huts a little away from the Tamil community. Even though the state records gave them equality, spatially and spiritually, they lived in the margins. Because, according to the dominant belief among the Tamils, Veddas are distinctive in physical features, behavior, and according to some Tamils, even in body odor. Having failed in the process of integrating with the Tamils another avenue was found. Some Vedda children found their way into the households of some state bureaucrats in Batticaloa town as domestic servants. The Veddas do not cite poverty as a reason for sending away their children; rather they insist that they sent their children for a better life, and to get an education while helping with household chores. Both formal and informal integration seems to have been achieved in this manner within a 'master–slave' relationship. Another powerful and overwhelming influence of domination was the realm of the religious. Since the overall aim of the Tamil nation was a unified cultural and religious agenda it also was to be a 'civilizing' one. This aspect of the religious transformation and its impact, then, is my next focus.

The Transformation and the Reformation of the Vedda Religion
The Influence of Sanskritization

The improvements envisaged for the Veddas are ones that come through formal education and values such as 'cleanliness,' familiarity with a capitalist economy, and associated life style. The movement towards modernization entails for such 'noble savages' the continued transformation through the local guardians: the post colonial elite and their agents. Within Tamil society this larger project of civilization was to be the 'cultured' form of local religion symbolic of a modern society. Consequently, there has been a tendency to do away with what is considered to be 'ancient' (read:pagan) rituals. This tendency is generally referred to as sanskritization, a concept introduced by M.N. Srinivas.[23] What this means is that the more 'regional' and 'local' (read: low) forms of worship are being replaced by a form influenced by the 'Brahminic' (read:high) tradition. This tendency has already been noted in the East by Obeyesekere.[24]

The entire East coast has traditionally been dotted with temples of territorial gods and goddesses such as *Kannaki, Peichi* and *Kali* and other minor deities such as *Veera Pattiran* and *Vairavar*. Other forms of worship include the worship of the snake goddess *Nahakanni*. These mother goddess cults have very elaborate and theatrical rituals. The temples usually conduct a festival once a year called *saddanku* beginning around May–June. In these *saddankus* there are elaborate possession ceremonies. Dart observes:

> The Hinduism practiced by the Veddas is different from that practiced by the higher-caste Tamils. *It includes less prestigious and less orthodox forms of worship*…[T]here is considerable al-

lowance for variation in belief and practice among groups; and there is little emphasis on hierarchy and rank.[25]

Civilizing the Local Deities

But today the process of civilization has overtaken such folk religious forms. Elements of South Indian agamic temple traditions are fast influencing these religious forms propelled by a unified Tamil nationalist agenda and a coterminous Tamil culture. Traditional village priests are increasingly being replaced with Brahminic priests. Offerings of meat, arrack, ganja and other wild produce are being shunned as sacrilegious in a sacred area. In some temples there are only remnants of these ceremonies conducted outside the main shrines. Today the annual *sadangus* of the Vedda temples in Mankerni and Palchenai have been enhanced with the conduct of weekly Friday poojas. In the past traditional ceremonies such as "the capture of the wild buffalo" took place during the annual festival. These performances are now almost extinct. The weekly *pooja* represents the pressure of a "civilizing" process while the annual festival represents the old tradition. In Mankerni which is claimed to be a totally Vedda village, there is a Murugan temple built by a Tamil landowner from Jaffna, and officiated by a Brahmin priest who commutes every week from Valaichenai. The Veddas themselves admit that these kinds of rituals and elaborate permanent structures are not typical of their religion:

> It does not matter any more. After the emergence of violence and the proliferation of guns the gods are never present in any of these temples. Their powerful presence takes place only once a year during the annual rituals. Other days they are always in the background guarding us. But today the ritual grounds are polluted by people carrying guns. The gods never enter the grounds where unholy metal is found.

This last statement was made while looking at the tense soldiers walking with guns at the ready. The army had moved into the village only a few weeks before. But the informant was clearly not referring to the military alone. Until recently it was under the control of the 'boys' (Tamil militant groups). Clearly the religious domain from which the community has derived its strength has also been weakened in the perception of the Veddas. Religion has also deserted them. On the contrary, they are moving towards a more systemic, *agamic*, more sanskritized form of worship. The only person who sang old Vedda incantations during the worship had died two years ago and had not been replaced. Some Veddas claimed that this is the end of that particular ritual. That observation brings the narrative to the present and to the sustained impact of the ethnic conflict.

Phase III:
The Impact of Ethnic Conflict

The 'ethnic' conflict and the related security considerations have had a tremendous impact on the Vedda villages of the East coast. The jungle around these villages have been places of confrontation between the armed forces and the militants. In this conflict the Veddas have suffered immensely. Retaliatory attacks and detention by the army have been common among the Veddas. The control of these areas has oscillated between the armed forces and the militants and taken its toll every time the balance of power changed. *An important point is that the military does not treat the Veddas as different from Tamils. For them what matters is that the area is full of militant activity and needs to be sanitized.* Eking out even a meager living has become suicidal.

The conflict during the past decade has periodically caused a proliferation of refugees. Further, it has become impossible for seasonal laborers to operate far away from their villages because of restrictions in movement imposed by the army. A general ban on paddy cultivation has minimized any opportunity for employment that may have been available. In other areas people who were affected by the violence have been assisted at various stages by governmental and non–governmental organizations. Even this benefit that was available to almost all the others in the East was not within the reach of the East coast Veddas. For the Veddas this would have been a final chance of deriving some economic compensation for their other losses. But this has been denied them. How were the Veddas denied this right as persons qualified for assistance for loss of livelihood?

The Implications of Cleared and Uncleared Areas &
the Delegitimation of the Refugees

In the East there is a division (as defined by the army), between the 'cleared' and 'uncleared' areas. The cleared areas are where the army is reportedly in control, state activity can go on, and the inhabitants, are provided with 'development assistance.' These areas are portrayed as normal. What this means is that any anomaly in this normality which may be contestory must be denied. Uncleared areas are those where militant activity is thought to persist and the army is not in control. As the army declares an uncleared area a cleared area after moving in, those displaced due to army operations are defined as victims of 'terorist' violence and are acknowledged as refugees. Refugees are entitled to dry rations. In the East, there are a large number of refugees who are entitled to such relief measures.

Since early 1993, there have been attempts to reduce the number of refugees and consequently even those who were entitled to a relief package, were denied them. This has been done to indicate that normalcy has returned. Clearly, if an area is 'normal' it is incongruous to have refugees in it. This has resulted in hasty resettlement programs. The army moved into the areas inhabited by the Veddas at the last stage of 'clearing' operations. This being the time the government was attempting to resettle the refugees, there was a general unwillingness to recognise the Veddas as refugees and consequently to extend assistance to them. Within this context of delegitimized refugee claims, the Veddas' claims as refugees came at the tail end.

As a consequence, even though the Veddas have been denied their usual occupation and been forced to live in the village in close proximity to the military camp, they are not recognized as being eligible for assistance. In addition, there have been instances of 'excesses,' an occupational hazard of forced co–habitation with the army. There are cases of disappearance and killings by 'unidentified people,' usually an euphemism for the army. Under these circumstances, the Veddas feel totally vulnerable and utterly defenseless.

There is an overwhelming feeling of betrayal. While every single village in the East was entitled to relief assistance, they have not been given any form of assistance despite being confined to the surroundings of the camp. As one old Vedda aged eighty-five said:

> We asked the government to increase the amount of welfare as-
> sistance extended to old people. But we were told that our vil-
> lage is entitled to only a specific number of such payments. So
> they told us that if another person has to get assistance, it is
> possible only after the death of one already receiving assistance.
> So you see, in order for one to live another must die. That is the
> *niyayam* (justice) of the government.

Conclusion

The problem of ethnic identity, I have posited, is due to the love–hate relationship between the Sri Lankan state (in whatever form or representation), the Tamil community, and the Veddas. In some Vedda villages where there had been a strong Vedda identity it has been completely integrated into a dominant Tamil one. In yet others there has been a willingness to integrate which has failed due to discrimination both intentional and accidental. But integration must be viewed as an outcome also of the Tamil nationalist agenda of projecting a unified and homogeneous Tamil nation.

Nevertheless, Vedda identity is qualitatively different from the hegemonic and integrating Tamil consciousness. The Vedda attitude vis-a–vis the Tamils who have intermarried among them is to allow them complete freedom regarding the choice of their identity. This is in sharp contrast to the hegemonic pressures of Tamil nationalism that the Veddas are subjected to.

In some Vedda villages, this latter feeling has been predominant. In today's perception of the Veddas what is to be noted is the consistent pattern of the feeling of being victims at different historical junctures. It is in the historical continuity of the narratives of victimization that I rest my case. This feeling of having become first the victims of the process of civilization, and also the victims of the project of integration with Tamil nationalism, explains the re–assertion of Vedda identity. Having at-tempted and failed in the process of integration, the Veddas have begun to take refuge in an ideology of 'victimhood.' This feeling is attributed to them being Veddas and this has helped, in a circular way, to reassert that identity.

Today the demand from at least a section of the Vedda community is that they be left alone to enjoy their traditional pattern of life without interference from the state or other communities. It is the move away from the jungle that they see as the cause of the destruction of not only their health and habitat, but also of their deities and way of life. They also complain about malnutrition and other maladies such as deformed births among themselves. Entire families live in miserable conditions in huts that can hardly accommodate two people, after having been forcibly relocated.

This bitterness has created in the Veddas a nostalgia about the past, and hence they have asked that they be allowed to return to the jungle. But surrounded by the military, any request to go back to the jungles is bound to be viewed with suspicion. One Vedda informant in his late seventies said:

> May be you could help us. We have been destroyed by the move to 'improve' us; our life has been destroyed; our youth have been killed and burnt; our children don't have any food and they are born with all kinds of deformities. If they (the state) give us some poison mixed in the free rice given to us, then we can all eat that and die peacefully in our sleep. It will bring a peaceful solution to all of us. How long can we beg for our existence?

Perhaps the various contenders of the imagined Tamil nation could prevent the final requiem for the Veddas.

Notes

1   Charles C. Seligman and Brenda Seligman, *The Veddas* (Cambridge: Cambridge University Press, 1911).

2   Richard Fox, *The Lions of the Punjab: Culture in the Making* (Berkeley: University of California Press, 1985).

3   Ali Mazrui, "Ethnic Stratification and the Military Agrarian Complex: the Ugandan Case," in *Ethnicity: Theory and Experience* (eds.) Glazer and Moynihan, (Cambridge: Cambridge University Press, 1975).

4   Anthony Smith, *The Ethnic Revival* (Cambridge: Cambridge University Press, 1981).

5   A.Sivanandan, "Sri Lanka: Racism and the Political Underdevelopment," in *Race and Class*, Vol. 26, No. 1, (1984), pp. 1-37.

6   Bruce Kapferer, *Legends of People, Myths of State* (Washington D.C.: The Smithsonian Institution Press, 1988).

7   Allen Feldman, *Formations of Violence: The Narrative of the Body and Political Terror in Northern Ireland* (Chicago: The University of Chicago Press, 1990).

8   Anderson Dart, *Ethnic Identity and Marginality Among the Coast Veddas of Sri Lanka*. Unpublished Ph. D dissertation, (San Diego: University of California, 1985).

9   James Brow, *Vedda Villages of Anuradhapura District: The Historical Anthropology of a Community in Sri Lanka* (Seattle: University of Washington Press, 1978).

10   Brow, p. 31.

11   See "Introduction," Brow, for an excellent discussion of *waruge* as a category of race and caste.

12   Brow, *Vedda Villages...* p. 27.

13   Ibid.

14   James Clifford and George Marcus, *Writing Culture* (Berkeley: University of California Press, 1986).

15   Dart, *Ethnic Identity...* pp. 26-27.

16   John Comaroff and Jean Comaroff, "The Colonization of Consciousness" in *Ethnography and the Historical Imagination* (Boulder CO: Westview Press, 1992).

17   Michel Foucault, *Discipline and Punish: The Birth of the Prison*, Allen Sheridan (trans.) (New York: Vintage, 1979), ch. 7.

18   H.L. Dreyfus and Paul Rabinow, *Michel Foucault: Beyond Structuralism and Hermeneutics* (Chicago: The University of Chicago Press, 1985), p. 135.

19   Dart, *Ethnic Identity...*, p. 44.

20   Nandadeva Wijesekere, *Veddas in Transition* (Colombo: M. D. Gunasena Ltd, 1964).

21   Tennent quoted by Dart, *Ethnic Identities...*, p. 28.

22   Hereafter referred to as GS.

23   M. N. Srinivas, "The Cohesive Role of Sanskritization" in *The Cohesive Role of Sanskritization and Other Essays* (Bombay: Oxford University Press, 1989).

24   Gananath Obeyesekere, *The Cult of the Goddess Pattini* (Chicago: University of Chicago Press, 1984).

25   Dart, *Ethnic Identity...*, p.15, emphasis mine.

Notes on Contributors

Malathi de Alwis teaches Women's Studies at the Faculty of Graduate Studies, University of Colombo. She is co-author with Kumari Jayawardena of *Casting Pearls* (2000), co-editor of *Embodying Violence* (1995), & *Feminists Under Fire* (2002) and author of a large number of articles on feminist politics, humanitarianism and grief.

P. L. de Silva served as a UN consultant on terrorism for several years. He has written widely on the question of violence and is co-editor of *Postmodern Insurgencies: Political Violence, Identity Formation and Peacemaking in Comparative Perspective* (2000).

Qadri Ismail is Associate Professor of English at the University of Minnesota, Minneapolis. He is the author of *Abiding by Sri Lanka* (2005), and has been published in *Social Text, Interventions, Postcolonial Studies, Subaltern Studies* & *Cultural Critique*.

Pradeep Jeganathan is a Senior Consultant Social Anthropologist at the Consortium of Humanitarian Agencies, Colombo. He is co-editor with Partha Chatterjee, of *Subaltern Studies X1* (2001), founding editor of *Domains*, and author of *At the Water's Edge* (2004) and *Living with Death* (2007).

Sitralega Maunaguru is Professor of Languages at the Eastern University, Chenkaladi. She advises several national and international institutions on questions of gender.

David Scott is Professor of Anthropology at Columbia University. He is the author of *Formations of Ritual* (1995), *Refashioning Futures* (2000) & *Conscripts of Modernity* (2005), and editor of *Small Axe*.

Yuvi Thangarajah was acting Vice Chancellor of the Eastern University, Chenkaladi, and then affiliated with the University Grants Commission, Sri Lanka. He is co-editor with Markus Mayer and Darini Rajasingham of *Building Local Capacities for Peace* (2003).

Jonathan Walters is Associate Professor of Religion at Whitman College, Walla Walla, Washington. He is author of *The History of Kelaniya* (1996) and co-author with Ronald Inden and Daud Ali of *Querying the Medieval* (2000).

Index